THE
POLITICS
OF
AMERICAN
RELIGIOUS
IDENTITY

THE POLITICS OF AMERICAN RELIGIOUS IDENTITY

THE SEATING OF SENATOR REED SMOOT, MORMON APOSTLE

KATHLEEN FLAKE

The
University of
North Carolina
Press
Chapel Hill
& London

Manufactured in the United States of America
Set in Sabon and Publicity Gothic types
by Tseng Information Systems, Inc.

The paper in this book meets the guidelines for
permanence and durability of the Committee on
Production Guidelines for Book Longevity of the
Council on Library Resources.

Library of Congress Cataloging-in-Publication Data
Flake, Kathleen.
The politics of American religious identity : the seating of Senator Reed
Smoot, Mormon apostle / Kathleen Flake.
　　p. cm.
Includes bibliographical references (p.) and index.
ISBN 978-0-8078-2831-1—ISBN 978-0-8078-5501-0 (pbk.)
1. Smoot, Reed, 1862–1941. 2. Mormon Church—Apostles—History—
20th century. 3. Legislators—United States—History—20th century.
4. United States. Congress. Senate—History—20th century. 5. Christianity
and politics—United States—History—20th century. 6. Polygamy—
Religious aspects—Mormon Church—History of doctrines—20th century.
I. Title.
BX8695.S74 F57　2004
328.73′092—dc22

2003014536

TO JAN SHIPPS

CONTENTS

ILLUSTRATIONS

ACKNOWLEDGMENTS

This book began as a dissertation, but before that it was simply a very good research topic suggested by Greg Prince. Given my initial resistance, he deserves to be acknowledged first and to hear me say that he "told me so." The intervening years between his suggestion and this publication have left me in debt to many. It is a pleasure to acknowledge my teacher and dissertation adviser, Clark Gilpin, for his wise counsel and generous support during all stages of my education at the University of Chicago. Similarly, I thank Martin Marty, David Tracy, and Richard Bushman for their constructive criticism of and enthusiastic support for this project. It was truly a gift to receive their attention to my student work. In addition to my dissertation committee, many other scholars have graciously shared their ideas and expertise with me. I thank especially Thomas G. Alexander, James B. Allen, James P. Byrd Jr., Jill Mulvay Derr, Ronald K. Esplin, Sarah Barringer Gordon, Harvard S. Heath, James Hudnut-Beumler, Joan Smyth Iversen, Scott G. Kenney, Patricia Lynn Scott, Jan Shipps, Steven R. Sorensen, Ferenc Szasz, Ronald W. Walker, and David J. Whittaker. While I alone am responsible for the use I made of it, their insightful criticism has improved this project materially, as well as given me encouragement to proceed.

I thank the sponsors of the several fellowship programs that financially supported my research and writing at significant stages in the development of this book. The 1996 Sawyer Seminar in Religion, Law, and the Construction of Identity, sponsored by Mellon and under the direction of Frank Reynolds, provided not only the means but the occasion for discovering the significance of the Smoot hearing. A 1997 summer fellowship at the Joseph Fielding Smith Institute for Latter-day Saint History at Brigham Young University gave me access to extraordinarily rich primary source material in Mormon history as well as to the finest minds who study it. A Lilly Fellowship for Future Theological Educators in 1998 and subsequent participation on the board of the Martin Marty Center at the University of Chicago disciplined me to consider the public implications of my work, and for that I am deeply grateful not only to the Lilly Endowment and the Marty Center but to Clark Gilpin and Stephanie Paulsell. A 1999 Pew Dissertation Fellowship enabled me to devote myself full time to the completion of the dissertation draft of this project and introduced me to many in the academy whose own work constructively challenged and, hence, bettered my own. Most recently, a 2002 BYU Visiting Scholar Fellowship with the Smith Institute gave me the intellectual conversation and material resources necessary to turn my dissertation into a publishable manuscript. Finally, I thank the American Academy of Religion, the Mormon History Association, and the Western History Association for providing forums in which I could present and develop various ideas contained in this book. A generous grant from the Vanderbilt Divinity School supported the publication of the book. Portions of chapters 2 and 5 are published with the permission of *Religion and Culture: A Journal of Interpretation*.

Of course, histories can be no better than their sources. Therefore, I owe much to the many archivists and library lending staffs who patiently guided me through their own collections and, where necessary, obtained materials from far-off places. Because of their number, I can only recognize these professionals here by their institutional affiliations, but I am no less personally indebted. I thank especially the archivists and staff of the Divinity Library of Vanderbilt University, the Giovale Library at Westminster College, the Harold B. Lee Library at Brigham Young University, the J. Willard Marriott Library at the University of Utah, the L.D.S. Family and Church History Library of The Church of Jesus Christ of Latter-day Saints, the National Archives and Records Administration, the Regenstein Library at the University of Chicago, the U.S. Library of Congress, the U.S. Senate Historian's Office, and the Utah State Historical Society. I recognize also that books can be no better than their editors. I thank Sarah Barringer Gordon and Jed Woodworth for their editorial comments on the original manuscript and Jennifer Reeder for filling in so many blanks. Finally, I am indebted to Charles Grench and all those at the University of North Carolina Press who brought it together in print.

Most personal and impossible to express is the degree of my indebtedness to individuals who sustained me in a variety of ways during the preparation of this manuscript. They listened patiently as I tried repeatedly to speak my way through the tangles of this project, and they gently steered me in more productive directions. By reading early drafts, they made this book more readable for others. In addition, each in his or her own way made it possible for me to do my work and live my life. For sharing their bright minds and good hearts, as well as their homes and cars at times, I thank Elouise M. Bell, Cass Butler, Monica Cawvey, Melissa and Darin

Clay, Aileen and Hal Clyde, Brook and Jill Derr, Liz Dulany, Christine and George Durham, Judith and Joe Friedman, Brent Hall, Brian and Ann Johnson, Elbert Peck, Tony and Jan Shipps, and Wendy and Dave Ulrich.

THE
POLITICS
OF
AMERICAN
RELIGIOUS
IDENTITY

INTRODUCTION

Two questions frame the story told in this book. The first is an enduring one for religious studies: How do religious communities change over time and retain a sense of sameness with their originating vision? The other question has to do with the First Amendment as an agent of religious change. What are the political terms by which diverse religions are brought within America's constitutional order? Specifically, given the historically Protestant shape of that order, how do non-Protestant religions obtain the benefits of it, namely, religious freedom? The investigative hearing catalyzed by the election of Mormon apostle Reed Smoot to the U.S. Senate in 1903 serves here as case study for both questions. The crisis his election created for both church and state illuminates the broader phenomena of religious adaptation and religious liberty in pluralistic societies. Moreover, the U.S. Senate's resolution of the crisis articulated the political terms by which increasingly diverse religions would be recognized and accommodated in America for the remainder of the century.

This book attempts also to fill a gap in American religious studies and history. Defined by polygamous family structure, utopian communal economy, and rebellious theocratic government, nineteenth-century Mormonism seems to have little relation, except by contrast, to the twenty-first-century Church of Jesus Christ of Latter-day Saints (L.D.S. Church). Indeed, the church's present reputation, for good or ill, appears to be based on a reverse set of identity markers: idealization of the nuclear family, unapologetic capitalism, and patriotic republicanism. It is as if there were two Latter-day Saint churches, not one. Making sense of this anomaly is fundamental to answering the theoretical questions raised above. What happened in both the nation and the church to permit political acceptance of Mormonism after so many years of mutual antipathy, even religious violence? This book argues that the Smoot hearing casts in high relief a number of changes to Protestantism, Mormonism, and the U.S. Senate that made settlement possible and paradoxically reveal the continuity of nineteenth- and twentieth-century Mormonism.

Between 1903 and 1907, a broad coalition of American Protestant churches, acting directly through their ministers and indirectly through various reform agencies, sought to expel Utah's new senator on the grounds that his ecclesiastical position made him a conspirator in the L.D.S. Church's continuing violation of the nation's antipolygamy laws. In the Smoot hearing, as in every other Mormon conflict of the previous century, the Protestants were the chief combatants. As Jan Shipps has documented in her statistical analysis of publications about Mormonism between 1860 and 1960, "If the author could definitely be identified as Protestant, whether religious leader or not, the article was seven times more likely to be negative."[1] Though they no doubt objected to polygamy, Catholics and Jews seldom participated in the Smoot protest as identifiable religious groups, appearing in only a very few instances as signatories on citizen petitions. Their dilemma was summarized by Senator Isidor Rayner of Maryland, who explained to Smoot's personal secretary that "the reason he voted against the Senator was that he is a Jew, and he felt that the Christian people of his State would have felt that he took advantage of his position to slap the Christian religion if he had voted for the Senator's retention."[2] The Smoot protest was essentially a Protestant endeavor. Fittingly, then, those who formulated the protest against Smoot were referred to as "protestants" (lower cased) in the hearing record. Because "protestants" accurately reflects the nature of the religious interests at stake, as well as the record itself, the term will be used here, too.

The protestors of Smoot's election represented all the varieties of American Protestantism, some of whom would have considered themselves marginalized by the five historic denominations (Episcopalian, Presbyterian, Congregationalist, Baptist, and Methodist) that constituted the so-called Protestant Establishment. This book does not do justice to that diversity, largely because Protestant differences were elided by common concerns about Mormonism. I agree with Laurence Moore's observation that American religious history, at least in the eighteenth and nineteenth cen-

Reed Smoot. This picture was taken shortly after the barely forty-one-year-old apostle Smoot arrived in Washington to take his seat in the Senate. Courtesy of L. Tom Perry Special Collections, Harold B. Lee Library, Brigham Young University, Provo, Utah.

turies, is best explained in terms of innovations upon traditional Christianity, or what the frustrated colonial Anglican Richard Woodmason called "schism shops."[3] With respect to the history of American church and state, however, a generalized Protestant ethic has had an undeniably unique importance. This is so, in part, because certain issues rallied Protestant schismatics to join with their more traditional neighbors, forgetting confessional differences in support of a common project to build a "Christian America."[4]

Mormons did not, nor were they invited to, participate in the effort to reform American social institutions. Indeed, they were at best the objects of reform and at worst deemed incapable of reform. For nineteenth-century Americans, including church history scholar Phillip Schaff, there was an "'irreconcilable antagonism of the American nationality with the pseudo-Christian, polygamists, deceitful, rapacious, and rebellious Mormonism.'"[5] Though rightly stripped of its normative indictment, Schaff's finding in historic Mormonism an extraordinary degree of otherness remains the scholarly consensus. "The Mormons attracted attention as a useful counterimage," according to one modern analysis, "a glaring example of what America was not and should not be."[6] Because of this, the term "Mormon" is heavily freighted with both historical and theological baggage. Signaling as it does the antebellum biblical culture's reaction against the young sect's canonization of the Book of Mormon, the term was a negative epithet. During the period discussed here, "Mormon" retained its extremely pejorative connotation. "Mormonism," said the *New York American* in 1904, "is a repulsive anachronism, a dangerous plague spot, a gross offense to the nation's moral sense."[7] Today, the L.D.S. Church objects to the use of "Mormon" as a denominator, preferring that its entire name be used in order to avoid any inference that the church is not Christian.[8] With due respect to these concerns, this historical study uses the term to convey the historic animus at play in the Senate hearing, not to comment on the theological claims of either group. Therefore, as with the protesting Protestants, the use of "Mormon" here is meant to reflect as nearly as possible the attitudes and speech habits of both the protagonists and the antagonists of the Smoot hearing.

Several factors contributed to the L.D.S. Church's bad reputation, and they are discussed in the chapters that follow. For now, the observation must suffice that aside from the fear they inspired by successfully dominating the mountain West as a political domain, the Latter-day Saints attracted the hostility that belongs to the foil, that dramatic persona whose very likeness exaggerates opposition to its difference. Organized in 1830 and rooted in New England restorationism and frontier utopianism, Mormonism had early and always attracted the negative attention of its fellow citizens, but no more so than when it claimed the right to restore Old Testament polygamy. Rumors of it contributed to the mob violence that chased Mormons from the Western Reserve to the banks of the Mississippi and, finally, to the isolated Great Basin on the far side of the Rockies. By the middle of the nineteenth century, Americans were so aggravated by Latter-day Saint beliefs and practices that a sixth of the antebellum U.S. Army was stationed in the foothills overlooking Salt Lake City to police the Mormon kingdom. After the Civil War, a series of antipolygamy statutes criminalized the church's marital practices and sent more than a thousand of its members to federal prisons, as well as disincorporating their church and confiscating its property. After several failed attempts, statehood was granted the Utah territory in 1896, largely based on the church's 1890 promise to abandon its unique marital practice.[9] When the Smoot hearing showed that the Mormons had continued to practice polygamy, the national debate on Mormonism was reinvigorated and performed on the public stage of the U.S. Senate.

The four-year Senate proceeding created a 3,500-page record of testimony by 100 witnesses on every peculiarity of Mormonism, especially its polygamous family structure, ritual worship practices, "secret oaths," open canon, economic communalism, and theocratic politics.[10] The public participated actively in the proceedings. In the Capitol, spectators lined the halls, waiting for limited seats in the committee room, and filled the galleries to hear floor debates. For those who could not see for themselves, journalists and cartoonists depicted each day's admission and outrage. At the height of the hearing some senators were receiving a thousand letters a day from angry constituents. What remains of these public petitions fills eleven feet of shelf space, the largest such collection in the National Archives.

Notwithstanding the news coverage dedicated to the trial, there was nothing new to report. Or more accurately, the only news was that the Mormons had not changed. After following the hearing for a year and a half, Illinois senator Shelby Cullom concluded, "Mormonism is the same menace to this country as it was from the beginning."[11] Indeed, the basic facts of the case were so familiar that over the years they had been reduced to the label, "the Mormon Problem."[12] Only in hindsight is the real news of the Smoot hearing appreciable: politics had succeeded where war and criminal penalties had failed. The Senate solved the nation's Mormon Problem and in doing so settled for a century the conflict of laws—

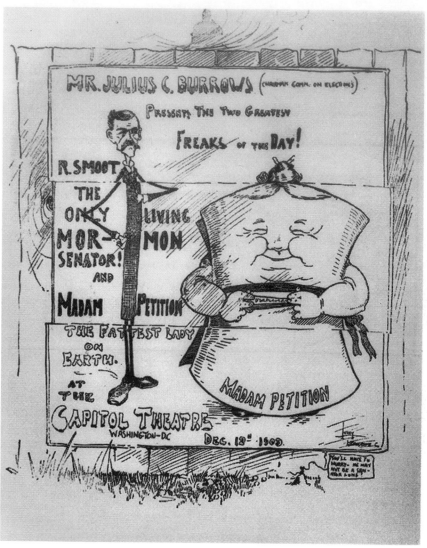

"Freaks of the Day." In this 1903 Alan J. Lovey cartoon, both Reed Smoot and his antagonists are lampooned as "freaks" in the circuslike spectacle of the nationwide protest against seating the new senator from Utah. Used by permission, Utah State Historical Society, all rights reserved.

religious and secular—implicit in the religion clauses of the First Amendment.[13]

America's problem with the Latter-day Saints was not simply or even primarily a matter of unlawful action, but of conflicting authority. The Latter-day Saints appealed to the law of their god, given through modern prophets, to justify their resistance to the law of the land. When Latter-day Saint morality, effected by a priestly order, confronted American morality, effected by a Protestant legal establishment, the philosophical underpinnings of the First Amendment were made explicit, and conflict arose between the nation with the soul of a church and the church with the soul of a nation. The Mormon Problem made it obvious that, by not establishing any religion, the Constitution had subordinated every religion's authority over believers to the state's authority over citizens.

By the early twentieth century, the limits imposed by the American constitutional order upon all churches, not merely the iconoclastic ones, had yet to be felt by the religious majority. More specifically, because Protestants had always enjoyed the liberty that comes from writing the law, they were confident that no difference existed between one's duty to church and to state. This confidence would falter at the end of the twentieth century and be replaced by protest that religious morality had become marginalized and organized religion suppressed by a secular and hostile government.[14] During the first decades of the twentieth century, however, Protestants were conscious only of the problem posed by nonconformists to America's dominant moral order.

The Progressive Era is universally described as a time of extraordinary change, though rarely is religion admitted to this political and cultural assessment. The few histories that consider Progressive Era religion generally limit their analysis to Protestantism. Such studies agree that during the first decade of the twentieth century, the theological concerns of the late nineteenth century—evolution, historical criticism, and comparative religious studies—were just beginning to break out of the seminary and enter popular pulpit and culture. Liberal and conservative labels would soon measure institutionwide breeches, but not quite yet. It was a period when Protestant denominations were, as William Hutchison says, challenged but not threatened.[15] The challenges are axiomatic to historians: science, immigration, urbanization, industrialization, and the new national market with its oligarchical impulses. My intention is not to minimize these developments in the narrative of American religious history, but to add to them the challenge of the religious margins. Mormonism was only one of several non-Protestant and marginalized Protestant communities that sought and obtained some measure of legitimacy, if not respectability, during the twentieth century. Such new legitimacy was, I argue, the result of the Progressive Era's broader political understanding of religious liberty and narrower reading of permissible establishment.

Most simply stated, I argue that the U.S. Senate's solution to the nation's Mormon Problem was a compromise that required the Mormons to conform their kingdom to that most Protestant form of religion, the denomination, with its definitive values of obedience to law, loyalty to the nation, and creedal tolerance. In return, the Senate gave the Latter-day Saints the benefit they sought by sending a representative to the Senate, namely, that form of religious citizenship that provided them protection, at home and abroad, for the propagation of their faith. Each of the ways in which the Mormons satisfied the criteria of First Amendment "citizenship" is enumerated in chapters that follow. The short version of the story is that, first, Mormon abandonment—in deed in 1906, not merely word in 1890—of polygamy vouchsafed the church's subordination to the state. Second, the church demonstrated by both benevolent actions and military enlistment that it created loyal citizens who could contribute to the nation's common good. The third criterion of tolerance—or the privatizing of its truth claims in deference to those of others—was limited to the political arena. The Senate was satisfied by the implementation of a more democratic process in Utah government and, on the eve of the Smoot hearing, the announcement by the church that it was not a political institution with political objectives. More confident in its capacity to regulate rather than eradicate concentrations of power, the Progressive Era Senate would not ask for more. Thus, the Senate's solution required the protestants to abandon their demand that Mormonism be excluded from First Amendment guarantees and to settle for federal enforcement of monogamous marriage.

Why the Senate succeeded where the army and criminal statute failed had as much to do with Progressive Era changes in the nature of Protestant and Senate power as it did with Mormon obedience, loyalty, and tolerance. In the first decade of the twentieth century, Protestants had less power to leverage the instruments of state in support of their religious goals. Thus, the demands placed on the Mormons by the state could be less absolute and less overtly religious than in previous battles. As for the Senate, the Progressive Era ushered in a dynamic that would characterize government for the remainder of the twentieth century: the exercise of federal regulatory power to ensure procedural fairness, not substantive morality. By the time Smoot arrived to take a seat in the Senate, the U.S. government had new confidence in its ability to manage formal concentrations of power by means other than military might. The prime example of this is, of course, antitrust legislation and related court cases beginning in 1890. These were the years when the role of government began to change from enforcing a particular moral order to ensuring that competition was fair among the various concentrations of power, whether they be political parties, economic enterprises, or religious communities.[16]

The Latter-day Saints benefited from these developments, but not unreservedly so. The changes required of the church in return for state protection created a crisis within the church, even as they solved the church's external problems with the state. Polygamy or "plural marriage," as the Latter-day Saints originally denominated their marriage practice, was considered divine revelation, not personal proclivity; it was primarily a sacramental, not romantic, attachment. Moreover, the Latter-day Saints' experience of fighting for the right to practice their belief had further identified plural marriage as central to the church's biblical restorationism. Any change in the practice had to be balanced by measures to shore up the confidence of the faithful in their church's authority to mediate eternal truth. Hence, the religious studies question that frames this study: How did church leaders make such radical changes in doctrine and practice without losing their members' confidence in the church's continuity with its originating vision?

It is axiomatic that religious communities are not exempt from the human condition; they must adapt to their circumstances or die. Change over time is, however, a particular crisis for those who seek to transcend time. Indeed, it is doubtful that religious identity can survive the awareness of certain kinds of change. Formed in response to a sense of immediate divine call, which aggrandized the expectation of imperviousness to time, and yet originating in a literate era, which inevitably documented their changes over time, the Latter-day Saints were especially susceptible to an awareness of the conflict between time and eternity, history and faith. And at no time had they felt the conflict more keenly than during the Smoot hearing, when their divine law of plural marriage was subordinated to the antipolygamist law of the land.

Thus, like most explanations of Mormonism's entry into modern American culture, mine, too, finds the Latter-day Saints' abandonment of polygamy to be pivotal. Unlike others, I place the pivot after 1890 and, consequently, do not explain twentieth-century Mormonism solely in terms of capitulation to the force of antipolygamy law. Rather, this book argues that politics, not law, finally solved the nation's problem with Mormon polygamy and did so in 1907 as part of a negotiation of interests, not a one-sided capitulation. The Senate would arbitrate Protestant-Mormon differences in a very public political trial. Consequently, the solution would be found in a forum that—unlike warfare or criminal indictment—by its very nature assumed complexity and sought to preserve the deepest interests of the greatest number of parties. The truism is true: politics is the art of compromise. None of the Smoot hearing combatants were completely victorious. Federal lawmakers did not eradicate Mormon political and economic power; the Protestant establishment had to modify its design for a Christian America; and the Latter-day Saints subordinated themselves to the state.

Thus, this study concludes by asking whether the antagonists got the benefit of their bargain. The short answer is a qualified yes. The Senate both solved its Mormon Problem and articulated, for the foreseeable future, the means by which new and diverse religious communities would be constitutionally ordered and free. As for the Protestant reformers, they achieved their primary goal of imposing monogamy upon the Mormons. Ironically, the Protestants spent the rest of the century edging toward accepting a wider variety of consensual relationships among adults, while the Mormons moved in the opposite direction to become aggressive defenders of the traditional family structure. The benefit of the bargain to the Latter-day Saints was longer lasting. Reed Smoot's intervention on behalf of the L.D.S. Church during his thirty-year senatorial career enabled the church to thrive domestically and follow the American flag abroad, making it, in the early twenty-first century, America's fifth largest denomination and an international church of several million members.

Thirty years after the hearing, an observer could marvel that "the Church which was the great scandal of all right-thinking men, is now one of the bulwarks of righteousness, being simply a more romantic version of American evangelical religion."[17] Today, a century after the hearing, Mormon Americanness is such a given to both its critics and advocates that its nineteenth-century scandalousness is largely forgotten, as is the Smoot hearing itself. It is even ignored by the Latter-day Saints, for whom it brought new forms of political power and a measure of social acceptance.[18] Such forgetting and selective representation is a measure of the change that the hearings catalyzed, not only for the Mormons, but also for the Protestant establishment that had opposed them for decades and for the federal government that had long regarded them as a hostile foreign power in the West. The purge of these differences by political trial required an evolution of American and Mormon identity, the accomplishment of which obscures what was and why it is no longer. Ultimately, the Smoot hearing was the forge in which the Latter-day Saints, the Protestants, and their senators hammered out a twentieth-century model for church-state relations, shaping for a new generation of Americans what it meant to be free and religious. Mormonism's transition during the Smoot hearings from un-American to American, from dangerous infidel to peculiar church, is not its story alone, but the story of the changing relation of churches to the state in the early twentieth century.

Mormonism must first show that it satisfies

the American idea of a church, and a system of

religious faith, before it can demand of the nation

the protection due to religion.

—*Rev. A. S. Bailey*, Christian Progress in Utah

(1888)

1

THE AMERICAN IDEA OF A CHURCH

On 20 January 1903, Utah's predominantly Mormon legislature elected Reed Smoot to the U.S. Senate.[1] A longtime leader in the local Republican Party, Smoot had hoped to run in 1900 but withdrew from the race on the advice of the presidents of his nation and church, leaving victory to wealthy miner and Catholic Thomas Kearns. By tacit agreement, Utah's seats in Congress were shared equally by Mormon and non-Mormon citizens, and it was now the Mormons' turn. Smoot convinced his church president to support his candidacy, though some of Smoot's brethren were wary of the unwanted attention his election would invite to Utah's already too-scrutinized politics. Smoot was, after all, not merely a prominent Republican; he was a very prominent Mormon, even an "apostle," one of only fifteen men with plenary authority over the L.D.S. Church and in direct succession to its presidency.[2] The prospect of a Mormon hierarch in the Senate was troubling to the new Republican administration, too. Senator Kearns carried the message home for the president. "'This afternoon,' he told the local press, 'President Roosevelt requested me to state . . . that he desired to be placed on record as kindly but firmly advising against the election of any apostle to the United States Senatorship.'"[3]

The concerns of both church and state leaders were validated when, six days after the election, the Salt Lake Ministerial Association petitioned the president and Congress to reject Smoot's credentials. They protested that Smoot was part of an ecclesiastical conspiracy that impermissibly ruled Utah's citizens and used its power to violate federal antipolygamy law, making Smoot a lawbreaker by association. The protest was drafted by the Reverend W. M. Paden, Princeton graduate and pastor of the First Presbyterian Church of Salt Lake City, with the editorial assistance of local attorney E. B. Critchow, law partner of the unsuccessful incumbent Joseph L. Rawlins. Already vulnerable as a lapsed Mormon and Democrat in an increasingly Republican state, Senator Rawlins had sealed his electoral fate by announcing on the Senate floor that Republican Kearns had earned his seat in a deal with the L.D.S. Church for "favors on the polygamy question."[4] Kearns responded by purchasing the *Salt Lake Tribune*, which had first made the charge against him. Later, when Kearns himself was deposed, he employed the paper to harass Smoot with the same allegation. Such conflation of Utah politics and commerce with religious creed was evidenced by other signers of the protest against Smoot's election. The local Congregational pastor, the superintendent of Methodist missions, and the Episcopal bishop were joined by several mining superintendents, officers of various railroad companies, the former *Tribune* editor, and a federal chancery judge. Even the mayor of Salt Lake City added his name, though doing so indicated that the Latter-day Saints were not as much in control of Utah as even they would have liked to believe. In all, eighteen prominent clergy, business leaders, and public officials signed the petition against the new senator from Utah and called upon their co-religionists to support their cause.

Support was not long in coming. Petitions in opposition to Smoot poured into the Senate quickly. Some came from individuals; others, from orchestrated gatherings of concerned citizens. All were encouraged by Protestant para-church organizations and moral reform agencies. Neither did the churches themselves hesitate to act directly through their governing bodies. Within three months of Smoot's election, salvos from two of America's largest Protestant denominations were fired from opposite ends of the country. The General Assembly of the Presbyterian Church, meeting in Los Angeles, and the Baptist Home Mission Society, assembled in Buffalo, New York, passed resolutions in opposition to Smoot. The Presbyterians received their charge from assembly secretary Rev. Charles L.

"Possible Future President of the Mormon Church," *Chicago Tribune*, 23 November 1902. Smoot's senatorial contest was national news. The *Chicago Tribune*'s coverage in this issue was typical in its stimulation of public fear of Mormon theocracy. Courtesy of L. Tom Perry Special Collections, Harold B. Lee Library, Brigham Young University, Provo, Utah.

Thompson: "It [Mormonism] is not to be educated, not to be civilized, not to be reformed—it must be crushed." Warning that "relentlessly it fastens its victims in its loathsome glue," Thompson exhorted, "Beware the Octopus. There is one moment in which to seize it, says Victor Hugo. It is when it thrusts forth its head. It has done it. Its high priest claims a senator's chair in Washington. Now is the time to strike. Perhaps to miss it now is to be lost."[5] In response to the furor, Smoot asked that it be remembered, "I was a Republican before I was an apostle."[6] But for Americans, such things were so hopelessly mixed in Utah that the only cure seemed to be to eradicate the source of the confusion, the Mormon church.

Smoot was merely the opportune subject, not the true object, of the protestors' campaign. In briefs filed with the Senate, the protestors took care to stipulate, "We accuse him of no offense cognizable by law." Rather, they argued, Smoot's ineligibility for office was based on his participation in a religious cabal that violated the law, corrupted the home, and controlled Utah's government and economy at the expense of the nation. The senator-elect was, they said, "one of a self-perpetuating body of fifteen men who, constituting the ruling authorities of the Church of Jesus Christ of Latter-Day Saints, or 'Mormon,' claim . . . the right to . . . shape the belief and control the conduct of those under them in all matters whatsoever, civil and religious, temporal and spiritual, . . . encourage a belief in polygamy and polygamous cohabitation . . . [and] protect and honor those who with themselves violate the laws of the land and are guilty of practices destructive of the family and the home."[7] The protestors' interests ran deeper than the rejection of Smoot from federal office, however. They hoped, in the words of one commentator, that "the Smoot case will abolish Mormonism without war. The scandalous blemish will be wiped out by the irresistible abrasion of the public intelligence, judgement, conscience and indignation."[8] Such overt intolerance, shocking to today's sensibilities, was consistent with the times. Indeed, the adoption of means other than warfare to manage religious difference was an advance worthy of a Progressive Era.

Religious liberty did not come naturally to Americans. Rather, necessity mothered its invention and has directed its growth ever since. Freedom of conscience began as a "lively experiment" in the Puritans' New World, but with strict limits, as the exiled Roger Williams and executed Mary Dyer could attest. Only gradually did the failure of any one church to dominate convert all churches to the principle of tolerance. Uniformity was simply impossible. As historian Sidney Mead observed, America's colonial churches "seem to have placed their feet unwittingly on the road to religious freedom . . . not as the kind of cheerful givers their Lord is said to love, but grudgingly and of necessity."[9] For a century and a half after the Revolution, constitutional guarantees of religious freedom limited only the powers of the federal government.[10] States were free to establish religion with state support, and they did so to varying degrees and over several decades. Not surprisingly, the descendants of the Puritans made Massachusetts the last to abandon formally the right to religious establishment.

THE REAL OBJECTION TO SMOOT.

"The Real Objection to Smoot," *Puck*, 27 April 1904. As depicted in *Puck* magazine during the first year of the hearing, the L.D.S. Church's priestly leadership and its assumed power over the new senator constituted the "real objection" to Smoot being received into the national legislature. The various charges against the church are labeled on the puppet master's cloak. Courtesy of L. Tom Perry Special Collections, Harold B. Lee Library, Brigham Young University, Provo, Utah.

Even so, the staunchest *religious* defenders of religious liberty were not libertarians. The independent-minded Baptists, for example, agreed with the Congregationalists that non-Protestants should not be allowed full rights of citizenship. Thomas Curry's indictment that both sects "adhered to Church-State arrangements that were co-extensive with their own theological, religious, and societal views" could apply to virtually all Americans in the early nineteenth century.[11]

The extension of religious freedom to non-Protestants was early and often subject to the arbitrariness of majoritarian politics. Minorities who felt stifled or abused were encouraged to vote with their feet, as had the Mormons. Of course, indigenous religions, too, were expelled to the western frontier. Protestant homogeneity and hegemony were maintained by sending dangerous iconoclasts or other unwanted peoples out into the apparently limitless American frontier. By the late nineteenth century, however, it was no longer possible to believe that America was religiously homogeneous or able to safely consign its barbarians to the wilderness. Scientific advances in communications and transportation left everyone feeling the "centripetal tendency of the times" and the sense, if not the actuality, that "the frontier has gone." It appeared that the nation's interior was settled and its continental limits set, erasing the geographical buffer zones between religious antagonisms. Cities were filling the frontier, especially in the public's imagination, and the cities themselves were being filled by increasingly diverse immigration and religious innovation.[12]

Moreover, by the turn of the twentieth century, no Protestant church could claim numerical dominance. America's Catholic population had doubled, making it twice the size of the largest Protestant denomination. During the same period, America's Jewish population quadrupled. The profile of the Protestant center had changed also. Methodists and Baptists outnumbered Presbyterians, Congregationalists, Episcopalians, and Lutherans. All Protestants were feeling the strains that would lead to the crisis over fundamentals in the 1920s. Meanwhile, the margins—comprised most obviously of Christian Scientists, Adventists, Mormons, and Holiness adherents—had not been evangelized into conformity, as traditional Protestants had hoped. Instead, new religious movements were growing through their own proselytizing efforts. Though mainstream churches still dominated the cultural center, they were losing their exclusive hold, and the margins were pressing noticeably toward the middle.[13] This was nowhere more apparent than in Utah, where the homogeneous Latter-day Saints had turned the tables and ruled at the expense of a Protestant minority.

Senator Smoot represented not only Utah but Mormon rule brought to the national legislature. His arrival in Washington was a very public signal that freedom to be religious could no longer mean freedom to be one of the varieties of Protestantism. The public response to his election invited, even necessitated, reconsideration of the meaning of religious liberty in an America that could no longer be considered a Protestant nation demographically or expect to rid itself of religious iconoclasts through westward movement. Only hindsight allows one to say this with confidence, however. For those engaged in the Smoot hearing, it was a call-to-arms in defense of Christian America. As the Reverend Mr. Thompson warned the Presbyterian leadership, "Now is the time to strike. Perhaps to miss it now is to be lost."

The Smoot hearing represented the last of several failed efforts to rid the nation of the Mormon Problem. From the church's earliest beginnings, mobs had catalyzed its movement from New York to Ohio and then to Missouri. There, too, religious antagonism and fears of Mormon control over land and politics led to violence. The governor of Missouri considered the Mormons such a threat that he issued an extermination order against them in 1838 and drove them from the state with his militia. Subsequently, Illinois officials took actions that precipitated the murder of church founder Joseph Smith in 1844 and the expulsion of his followers, once again by local mobs. Illinois had its side of the story, however. In 1860, U.S. Representative John Alexander McClernand explained that the Mormons were expelled from his state "because they were unwilling to submit to the laws; because, in an attempt to trample the authority of the State under foot, they were overcome. Their maxim then was, and still is, rule or ruin."[14]

Whatever his prejudices might have been, the congressman was not paranoid. The Mormons were radically separatist and triumphalist. They believed that God had rejected all other churches and had called Joseph Smith to institute a new dispensation of the Christian gospel, even "the fullness of times," when all knowledge and every power that had ever been revealed would be restored in their day, the last days preceding Christ's return. Thus they named themselves "The Church of Jesus Christ of Latter-day Saints." Capitalization of "the" was intentional and meant to be instructive. Though they had their beginnings in the evangelically "burned over" region of New York, the people who arrived in the Rockies in 1847 had parted philosophical company with seekers of primitive Christianity.[15] Smith taught his Saints that they were called to "[lay] the foundation of a work . . . that God and angels have contemplated with delight for generations past; that fired the souls of the ancient patriarchs and prophets; a work that is destined to bring about the destruction of the powers of darkness, the renovation of the earth, the glory of God, and the salvation of the human family."[16] This rhetoric of Old and New Testament types was accompanied by a zeal for concrete application that would ever after characterize the Mormons. Their church was an instrumentality for building Zion, a here-and-now kingdom governed by the moral, political, and economic laws of God revealed to Smith and his successors, who each presided as prophet, priest, and king over the kingdom of God on the earth.

The Mormons believed themselves commissioned to prepare the world for a millennial reign when the heavenly and earthly kingdoms of God would be joined. Until then, the two kingdoms would work in concert to accomplish this goal. Mormons generally preferred the metaphor of kingdom to that of *ecclesia*. It conveyed the scope of their project to live in a place, not just within an assembly, governed by the law of God and possessing the power or "keys" to "bind" or give efficacy to their earthly works and associations in the heavenly kingdom as well. Not unlike the traditional Catholic notion of the "communion of Saints," the Latter-day Saints believed that the earthly church participated in both eternal and temporal worlds. Three principles were derived from this fusion of the ideal and the real. First, there was properly no distinction between temporal and spiritual government. Second, temporal property and labor were to be dedicated to spiritual purposes, including the good of the collective body of the church and the building up of the kingdom of God on the earth. Third, covenants made between individuals and consecrated by church ordinance were not temporal but eternal. Based on these premises, Mormons constructed political, economic, and familial structures that governed their everyday lives and that were anathema to the rest of the republic. For example, when the Mormons made their first attempt at statehood in 1849, their petition proposed a government comprised exclusively of the ranking ecclesiastical officers of their church.[17]

In 1857 the federal government joined the fray by dispatching an army to subdue the Mormon kingdom. The so-called Utah War caused much trauma and expense but little immediate change. Brigham Young was deposed as Utah's official governor, but the Mormons continued to build their kingdom of God in the West under his direction, while North and South fought a real war. Between 1862 and 1896 the nation turned to the instrumentalities of law to enforce its version of Christianity upon the Mormons, jailing polygamists, revoking franchise, denying citizenship, disinheriting children, and confiscating property in an attempt to force change on the church. The church's promise, in 1890, to abandon polygamy made possible Utah's admission to the union of states in 1896. But a few years later, to the nation's chagrin, the Smoot hearing demonstrated that the church's economic, political, and familial orders, including polygamy, remained in place. Idaho senator Fred T. Dubois cannot be faulted for asking his colleagues at the end of the hearing, "Does it not occur to the Mormons themselves, or to you, perhaps, that there is something inherently wrong in their organization or else this conflict would not be perpetual?"[18]

There were, indeed, two organizational (as opposed to creedal) reasons for the stubborn antagonism between the Latter-day Saints and the rest of America. First, the Latter-day Saints preferred theocracy to democracy and, hence, did not accept the major premise upon which Protestantism had crafted religious liberty in America. They did not subordinate their church to the nation-state, and they conflated their local state with their church. Second, their theology dictated their morality. This, too, was a reversal of the American Protestant denominational form that based its religious commitments on morality—or "the nature of Christian life"—instead of theological creed.[19] The moral commitments of American Protestantism gave its churches common cause, notwithstanding creedal differences. Indeed, this shared sense of right religion undergirded the condemnation of Mormonism as not a religion but an "immoral and quasi-criminal conspiracy."[20]

The Mormon understanding of church resembled, though denied any inheritance from, those radical European reformers who retained, albeit in Protestant fashion, the Catholic notion of a visible church, comprised of the sanctified and governed by divine law in matters both spiritual and temporal. The contrary position of the magisterial reformers was stated in contemporary terms by the Reverend Meade Williams in the *Princeton Theological Review* of 1905. Protestantism's "pride is in that sixteenth-century movement which broke the spell of external union, and whose primordial principle is the freedom before God of the individual conscience," he wrote. In fact, "to press the necessity of visible oneness is the very essence of popery." Williams then listed the elements of "visible oneness." "It involves," he said, "a conception of ecclesiasticism, and of the externality of the kingdom of God, and of what is meant by oneness in Christ, and of the nature of Church ordinances, and of the nature and validity of ministerial function which is utterly foreign to that on which our Christendom has been built."[21]

Fulfilling all the criteria for "visible oneness," the Mormons' church was "utterly foreign" to Protestant Christendom. Instead of salvation through grace expressed in biblical word and acts of individual conscience, Mormonism taught that saving grace was mediated by the sacramental authority of the church. Through administration of ordinances performed by an ordained ministry of believers, the church constituted a tightly organized "external union." Moreover, Mormonism's sacramental order went beyond ordinances of individual salvation, such as baptism, to include temple ordinances that bound individuals into extended families, both temporal and eternal. The church, too, was believed to be constituted of sacramental family structures, especially by means of "plural marriage."[22] In this fashion, the L.D.S. Church was an externalized kingdom of God and proudly denominated as such by its members. To Protestants, equally proud of their contrary system, Mormonism was "popery" and the basis for one senator's warning his colleagues to beware of "the fine Italian hand of the Mormon apostles."[23]

The second "something inherently wrong" with Mormonism was derived from the first. The Mormons did not fit the mold of denominationalism, that new form of church and "the shape of Protestantism in America" created by the way in which Americans chose their churches.[24] The denomination was, in Mead's terms, a "voluntary association" defined primarily by its purposive, not its confessional, commitments. Freed by their political system, offered a variety of religious options, and informed by the principles of individual conscience derived from Reformation theology and Enlightenment philosophy, Americans were politically able and intellectually inclined to choose their churches for other than theological reasons. It was "the nature of the Christian life," not creedal belief, that drew Americans to their churches.[25] This religious privileging of a way of acting toward the world, over a way of thinking about God, resulted in an "interdenominational or superdenominational consciousness and cooperation which has been such an outstanding aspect of the American religious life."[26]

Agreement on the primacy of moral principles over theological precept was intended to and did ensure domestic tranquillity for the majority in a religiously diverse nation. But it authorized also a particularly uniform notion of what was genuine religious expression.[27] William McLoughlin summarized the point best: "Temporal and spiritual power were fused even while Americans proclaimed to the world that they were the first nation on the earth truly to understand that religious freedom means the separation of church and state. . . . By 1830 'religious liberty opened the highway to greater uniformity than the Church of Rome ever contemplated.'"[28] In the nineteenth and early twentieth centuries, this uniformity was promoted as a "Christian America" but was in actuality a Protestant Christian project.[29] Organized in 1830, the Church of Jesus Christ of Latter-day Saints did not fit either the denominational form of American religion or its interdenominational goals.

The Latter-day Saints believed their truths to be absolute and their church to be solely authorized to save, not civilize, the nation. Moreover, they did not hold these truths privately but acted publicly on the expectation that the nations of the earth would enter the order of the Mormon kingdom, not vice versa. This understanding of their church as "visible," not denominational, convinced other Americans that there was indeed, as Dubois had observed, "something inherently wrong in their organization."[30] In 1888, Congregationalist Rev. A. S. Bailey spoke for many when he said, "Mormonism must first show that it satisfies the American idea of a church, and a system of religious faith, before it can demand of the nation the protection due to religion. This it cannot do, for it is not a church; it is not religion according to the American idea and the United States constitution."[31] In other words, Mormonism could not receive the benefit of "free exercise" until it disestablished itself both structurally from the offices of the state and theologically from its doctrines that conflated temporal and spiritual purposes. Only then would it "satisf[y] the American idea of a church, and a system of religious faith."[32]

For the vast majority of Americans, the election of a Mormon apostle to the U.S. Senate was a step in the wrong direction. It was a rebellion against the constitutional compact by which all religion had been subordinated to the state. It demonstrated that, while the Latter-day Saints wanted the federal protection that disestablishment offered its minority status, they wanted also to exercise their majority rights to establish their religion in the entire mountain West and protect that establishment by placing an apostle in the Senate.

Public indignation over Smoot's election was deeply felt and broadly expressed.[33] The geographical and social range of the dismay was manifested in petitions from the Women's Republican Club of Delmonico's, New York City, to the Women's Synodical Society of Missions of the Oklahoma and Indian Territories—and every jurisdiction in between. As for diversity, the petitions from Ohio alone demonstrate the broad appeal of the campaign against Smoot. They include protests from the Coterie of Fremont; the Evangelical Alliance of Cincinnati; the Twentieth Century Club of Wellsville; the Reformed Presbyterian Church of Jonathan Creek; Dayton's Friday Afternoon Club; the Kingsville Ministerial Union; both

West Elkton's Ladies Aid Society of the United Brethren Church and its Missionary Society of the Friends Church; the seventy-five members of the Christian Church of Defiance, Defiance County; the Woman's Christian Temperance Union of Mt. Gilead; and Norwalk's Congregationalist Christian Endeavor Society. Some voters made their appeals in one-sentence telegrams. Others sent multipage letters attached to reams of signatures organized by religious affiliation. The town of Southeast, New York, tallied its numbers for the Senate's benefit: 250 Presbyterians, 250 Methodists, 200 Baptists, and 500 Catholics.[34] Quakers, too, participated, writing, "I hope thy voice will be against the retention of Reed Smoot."[35]

Promising heavenly rewards or, in the alternative, electoral damnation to the addressee, some petitions were explicitly threatening. One warned in red ink, "N.B. the last signature is the name of one of the strongest men politically in the State of Illinois."[36] On the eve of the Senate vote, Mrs. H. K. Schoff, chair of the National League of Women's Organizations, also warned that "there may be a greater danger to the Republican party" if it failed to oust Smoot, adding, "No permanent success is ever possible when the public opinion is outraged."[37] Pastor Berger of the Susquehanna Presbyterian Church promised that those who supported Smoot "will be buried under the avalanche of righteous indignation at the coming election."[38] Another citizen from Germantown, Pennsylvania, reminded Senate committee member Philander Knox that God was his ultimate judge in the matter of the Utah senator's seat: "As you . . . stand in the sight of God above, to whom you must some day render your account, I beg of you to do all in your power to check this insidious form of evil in our midst *NOW*, before it shall have grown too strong to be overcome without the shedding of blood."[39] Numbers added force to the threats. Pennsylvania senator George R. Patterson was notified that 1,000 of his constituents, led by Swarthmore president Josiah Swain, had gathered in Philadelphia's Horticultural Hall to protest Smoot's admission. In the end, however, regardless of their source, all of the petitions and personal letters combined religious sentiment with patriotism: "As our forefathers so zealously guarded our country against future evils, . . . we urge a speedy investigation of the [Smoot controversy], believing that now is the time to deal a death blow upon the hydra-headed monster of evil."[40]

The extreme anti-Mormon sentiment of the petitioners' rhetoric tempts today's reader to dismiss them as religious chauvinists. Yet, notwithstanding its often hysterical expression, the petitioners' understanding of Mormonism was not without rational basis. The L.D.S. Church raised the political specter of religious establishment by creating an organization of priestly believers in living prophets, who did not limit themselves to spiritual guidance but sought political office. In 1844 Joseph Smith had been a candidate for the U.S. presidency. Brigham Young was territorial governor of Utah until 1857. Now Apostle Smoot, a possible successor to the church's presidency, was in the U.S. Senate. Moreover, the Mormons seemed to violate free market principles in both their economic clout and clannish practice. Of course, the loudest objection was that the Mormons posed a menace to the moral underpinnings of the state by sanctioning multiple female marriage partners and constructing extended family relationships more akin to tribes than to families. Not surprisingly, then, in 1856 the Republican Party in which Smoot later rose to leadership had called on the federal government to eradicate "those twin relics of barbarism—Polygamy and Slavery." In 1904, no doubt inspired by testimony in the Smoot hearing, the Democratic Party platform followed suit, demanding "the extermination of polygamy within the jurisdiction of the United States, and the complete separation of Church and State in Political affairs."[41]

Eventually, to make peace with Protestant America in the twentieth century, the Latter-day Saints would have to come to terms with their deviations from the American Protestant idea of a church. To date, the terms had been absolutist and, therefore, even when delivered by the sword of the state, had only resulted in martyrdom and civil disobedience. At the dawn of the twentieth century, however, the terms were softening, if only because the Protestant influence on public opinion and governmental machinery was on the wane. Protestantism was heading for what Robert Handy has called "the second disestablishment." John Wilson elaborates by calling these years "a period of 'disestablishment'—not of state-recognized churches but of a Protestant religious consensus."[42]

There were many reasons for the loss of consensus among and the related loss of political power by the Protestant mainstream. As mentioned, Catholic and Jewish immigration was radically reducing Protestantism's numerical dominance and electoral influence. Urbanization was eroding Protestantism's traditional base of political organization. Higher education and industrialization were challenging the churches' cultural authority and moral values. The sciences, both human and physical, were causing conflicts within congregations. Each of these developments had theological and ecclesiastical consequences. During this period the social worker replaced the circuit preacher as the model of American religious activism. Even the home mission movement, which had been dedicated to evangelizing the frontier, began devoting itself to American cities and "the social question."[43] Financing was likewise redirected, leading to the removal of ministers and money from the frontier. Faced with their own higher-critical, nascent-fundamentalist differences and feeling the burden of saving the cities, Protestant leadership in the East began to lose interest in the threat of barbarism on the western frontier.

Utah was an especially unpopular mission field. Protestant evangelists had arrived in the territory a day late and a dollar short. Like most non-Mormons, they trickled into the territory beginning in 1869, only after the completion of the transcontinental railroad and in support of those who followed eastern business and governmental interests west. An 1870 census showed that 98 percent of Utah's 86,750 residents were Mormon. Though the next twenty years saw their numerical dominance decrease to 56 percent of the territory's population of 210,779, the L.D.S. Church was deeply entrenched economically and politically. Protestant powerlessness was aggravated by the fact that those non-Mormons hardy enough to exploit commercial opportunities in Utah did not tend to be churchgoing folk. Even after their families joined them, this small group of Protestants could not afford to support clergy, build churches and schools, and proselytize unbelievers. Consequently, Utah's ministers were highly dependent on the financial support of their sponsoring institutions in the East. As late as 1905, only five of Utah's fifty-two Presbyterian churches were self-supporting.[44] Thus, Utah's Protestant home missionaries both wanted and needed to keep their national organizations mindful of Mormonism.

In response to the shortage of funds and to avoid self-defeating competitiveness among the several denominations, state federations formed as early as 1900 to support the evangelizing of the West. The Salt Lake Ministerial Association was one such federation whose shared evangelical purpose was cemented by antipolygamy sentiment. Focusing on antipolygamy was also the Utah missionaries' means of competing for national financial support. Missionary work among the Mormons was, they argued, "wholly unique . . . a seed sowing duty, owed to Christ for the sake of Christianity, Society and the State."[45] Still, the poor ratio of dollars spent to converts made was a major source of concern to Protestants. In 1899, when the Ministerial Association calculated "the results of evangelization among the Mormons," it found that only 514, or 16 percent, of its total membership of 3,220 had come from Mormon sources.[46] Some doubted even these numbers. A Methodist minister confessed to his board that "during the last twenty-five years two millions of dollars have been put into Utah by the Christian Churches of the East. . . . But, so far as converting the Mormons is concerned, this has been largely wasted. If two hundred real Mormons have been changed and made into earnest evangelical Christians during that time we have not been able to discover them."[47] The Presbyterian Home Mission Board concluded that, in Utah, "our work has been met by granite resistance, and for this there is not dynamite."[48] Faced with pressing social problems closer to home and the possibility of doing more good among non-Christians abroad, eastern evangelicals increasingly withdrew their resources from Utah and the West. As has been said of the Presbyterians, so also it was true that all Utah Protestants were "in a state of crisis as the nineteenth century ended."[49]

The Smoot investigation gave the Utah Protestants new hope. At the hearing's halfway point, the Utah Presbyterian Synod announced its gratitude "that the country has at last been led to see that our words and warnings, which have been so long discounted and disregarded are true . . . [such] that we are no longer left alone in this protest against iniquity in high places. The people of our country have learned something, and while this Smoot case has accentuated the difference between the Saints and the Gentiles and we are more than ever watched, let us give thanks to God for what has been done."[50] By accentuating their differences from the Mormons and obtaining the cooperation of Protestant institutions, social reformers, and women's groups, members of the Salt Lake Ministerial Association had every reason to expect that they could convince the Senate to reject Smoot. As recently as January 1900, this same coalition of Protestant activists had successfully blocked the admission of Utah's congressional representative and Mormon official, B. H. Roberts, by using the identical charges and strategies. It was a quick rout, lasting only six weeks.[51] Unseating Smoot would prove to be a much more difficult challenge, however. Unlike Roberts, who was a polygamist, albeit one with a presidential pardon, Smoot had only one wife. In addition, unlike the House of Representatives, the Senate had greater concern for state constitutional prerogatives and seated Smoot before trying him on his qualifications. This shifted the burden to the protestors to prove why Smoot should not keep his seat, rather than to him to prove why he should obtain it. The import of these factors paled, however, in comparison with the L.D.S. Church's new willingness to negotiate a way out of its version of the "Mormon Problem."

In the fall of 1901, a year before Smoot's election, the L.D.S. Church got a new president with a new agenda. Sixty-two-year-old Joseph F. Smith was the nephew of founding prophet Joseph Smith and the first president from among the church's second generation. The new president stood at the end of a very tough experiential lesson: statehood had not brought the Latter-day Saints autonomy, but democracy and pluralism. The church's loss of absolute control over Utah and its increasingly necessary relation to the United States had removed any possibility of rebuilding Brigham Young's political version of a kingdom of God. Recognizing this and desiring a better forum for the church's message, Joseph F. Smith was committed to doing what was necessary to heal the breach between his people and the rest of America. He wanted to end Mormonism's Rocky Mountain isolation.

In the late 1840s, the Latter-day Saints went to the Rocky Mountains, outside the territorial boundaries of the United States, because the extremity of their religious differences made coexistence with their neighbors impossible. Apostle Orson Pratt spoke for many in his church when he said, "It is with the greatest joy that I forsake this republic. . . . If our heavenly father will deliver us out of the hands of the bloodthirsty Christians of these United States and not suffer any more of us to be martyred to gratify their holy piety, I for one shall be very thankful. Perhaps we may have to suffer much in the land of exile, but . . . Liberty in a solitary place, and in a desert, is far more preferable than martyrdom in these pious states."[52] The feeling was mutual, of course. Objections to overt violence against the Mormons were few, of no practical effect, and muted by agreement with its ends. The Presbyterian *New York Observer*, for example, denounced Missouri's anti-Mormon mobs as "wholly at war with the genius of our institutions" but concluded that "perhaps, however, it was the only method which could have been effectively put in practice to get this odious description of population out of the way."[53]

The church, too, wanted to be "out of the way" and embraced the isolation offered by the Great Salt Lake Basin. Buffered from the East by the Rocky Mountains and from the Pacific West by the vast deserts of Nevada, the Latter-day Saints found their "liberty in a solitary place." By the 1860s, thanks to geography and the nation's neglect, they had constructed political, economic, and familial structures that effected their highest theology and governed their everyday lives. If proto-sociologist Alexis de Tocqueville had lived to see the Mormon kingdom, he probably would have been amused that the nation with the soul of a church had given birth to a church with the soul of a nation. But the conflict inherent in the situation was serious. As discussed, the church and the nation were soon at war with each other. Having solved the first barbarism in the slaveholding South, the republic turned its attention west to eradicate the other barbaric twin: polygamy.

In 1862, the year Reed Smoot was born, Congress enacted the first antipolygamy statute, and for the next twenty-eight years, Smoot's people would be in open violation of American law. Beginning with the Morrill Act, which equated plural marriage with bigamy, moral outrage was coupled with federal legislative might to impose criminal penalties on individuals and political sanctions on the Utah Territory in order to bring the Latter-day Saints into conformity with the moral philosophy and social institutions of the rest of the country. Congress eventually enacted three more statutes regarding Latter-day Saint marriage practices. In 1874 the Poland Act placed Utah's territorial courts under federal jurisdiction in order to enforce the Morrill Act. Eight years later the Edmunds Act imposed civil penalties such as disfranchisement and simplified proof for polygamy convictions. Finally, the Edmunds-Tucker Act of 1887 dissolved the corporate status of the L.D.S. Church and provided for confiscation of its property.[54]

In addition to being criminalized, the Latter-day Saints were universal objects of ridicule and scorn. Burlesque treatments in plays and romantic novels made the Mormon man a symbol of unrestrained and predatory sexuality; Mormon woman, a dupe and sexual toy of a Rocky Mountain harem; and Mormon children, the abused and deformed offspring of monstrous parents. Gender stereotypes and racial slurs were freely applied.[55] As late as 1906, Idaho senator and Smoot panelist Fred T. Dubois, speaking at a Methodist antipolygamy rally, "commenced by comparing the Mormons to the negro, and asserted that, as the South will not be 'dominated' by the negro, so the loyal American citizenship of the Rocky Mountains will not be dominated by the Mormon."[56] Even where they were not damned in such good company, the Mormons were considered sexual and social curiosities. Mark Twain captured the less venomous spirit when he wrote satirically of his trip to Salt Lake City, "There was fascination in surreptitiously staring at every creature we took to be a Mormon. This was a fairyland to us . . . a land of enchantment, and goblins, and awful mystery. We felt a fascination to ask every child how many mothers it had, and if it could tell them apart; and we experienced a great thrill every time a dwelling house door opened . . . for we so longed to have a good satisfying look at a Mormon family in all its comprehensive ampleness."[57] An entire generation of Latter-day Saints, including Reed Smoot, matured in this climate of antagonism and shame. Understanding the testimony of the Smoot hearing witnesses for either side requires remembering the complexity and intensity of feelings engendered during this period of social ridicule and insult as well as armed conflict.

By the time Smoot was in his late twenties, more than a thousand Latter-

Polygamist prisoners. Seated in a doorway of Utah's federal prison, a member of the church's presidency, George Q. Cannon, is shown here with his co-religionists while incarcerated in 1886 for violation of antipolygamy law. Carefully posed, the photograph memorialized the prisoners' sacrifice for the sake of religious conviction. In a business suit and seated on the steps is Apostle Francis M. Lyman, a polygamist himself, who later played a major role in ending the church's practice of plural marriage during the Smoot hearing. Used by permission, Utah State Historical Society, all rights reserved.

day Saints had been sentenced to federal penitentiaries around the nation.[58] Since these men constituted the local leadership of Latter-day Saint communities and since the chief leaders of the church, who had yet to be arraigned, were in hiding, the church was under tremendous organizational strain. In addition, heavy fines for those convicted, loss of family support from those in prison, and confiscation of church property by federal agents impoverished the church and its members. Meanwhile, as indicated, completion of the transcontinental railroad and consequent growth of mining and mercantile concerns attracted a large number of non-Mormons to Utah. In 1890 the church's political control was so undermined by determined opposition that an anti-Mormon party had won the Salt Lake City elections.[59]

For the church, 1890 was also a terrible year in court. In February the Supreme Court upheld an Idaho statute disfranchising and barring from public office those who believed in polygamy, whether they practiced it or not. Refusing to make any distinction between bigamy and the Latter-day Saint practice of "plural marriage," the Court observed that "bigamy and polygamy are crimes by the laws of all civilized and Christian countries. . . . To call their advocacy a tenet of religion is to offend the common sense of mankind. If they are crimes, then to teach, advise and counsel their practice is to aid in their commission, and such teaching and counseling are themselves criminal and proper subjects of punishment, as aiding and abetting crime are in all other cases." This effectively removed several rights of citizenship for all Idaho Mormons and later served as the model for a proposed antipolygamy amendment to the federal Constitution. In another case, ominously titled *Late Corporation of the Church of Jesus Christ of Latter-day Saints v. United States*, the Supreme Court upheld statutory seizure of the church's property. "The organization of a community for the spread and practice of polygamy is, in a measure, a return to barbarism," the Court reasoned. "It is contrary to the spirit of Christianity and of the civilization which Christianity had produced in the Western world."[60] Promptly thereafter, church president Wilford Woodruff was notified by the federal marshal of his intention to seize the church's temples.[61] The limits of the church's resistance had been reached. It appears the Latter-day Saints could give up their property, their liberty, and even their rights of citizenship, but they could not part with their temples. On 24 September 1890, Woodruff issued a statement that would become known simply as "the Manifesto" and whose meaning would preoccupy the Smoot hearing panel. It read, "Inasmuch as laws have been enacted by Congress forbidding plural marriages, which laws have been pronounced constitutional by the court of last resort, I hereby declare my intentions to submit to those laws, and to use my influence with the members of the Church over which I preside to have them do likewise."[62]

Most historical analyses of the Mormon Problem and even general histories of the L.D.S. Church end here. The Manifesto was, however, just the beginning of the end of the Mormon Problem. The declaration's terms were ambiguous and, hence, encouraged an ambivalent response both inside and outside the church. Although the Latter-day Saints agreed by their law of common consent to accept Woodruff's declaration as the "will of the Lord" and, thus, binding on the church, it had been a "weak vote."[63] Many Latter-day Saints thought the Manifesto was a political expediency designed to save the church and continued to practice polygamy. All of the

"Gentiles" were convinced it was a ruse and continued to use every opportunity to state their case. The Senate hearing provided them with their most effective forum to date. But they were not the only ones who saw opportunity in Smoot's election. Opposed to Smoot's initial candidacy in 1900, Joseph F. Smith later became Smoot's chief advocate, adamantly rejecting arguments from other apostles that Smoot should resign to protect the church from the hearing's backlash. Access to Smith's papers is limited, and his reasons for changing his mind must be inferred from his public statements.[64] Between the date of his objection to Smoot's candidacy and 1902, when Smoot was elected, Smith became president of the church. In his inaugural sermon, Smith addressed concerns that may explain why he later insisted God wanted Apostle Smoot in the Senate.[65]

Smith introduced his main point by stating the obvious. "We have been looked upon as interlopers, as fanatics, as believers in a false religion; we have been regarded with contempt, and treated despicably; we have been driven from our homes, maligned and spoken evil of everywhere," he said. Indeed, the church's reputation was so bad that "the people of the world have come to believe that we are the off-scourings of the earth and scarcely fit to live." Smith's purpose was not to commiserate with his own people or to berate their critics. Rather, he was concerned, he said, about the "thousands and thousands of innocent people in the world whose minds have become so darkened by the slanderous reports . . . that they would feel they were doing God's service to deprive a member of this Church of life, or of liberty, or the pursuit of happiness, if they could do it."[66] For Smith, the problem with the church's reputation was not the threat of injury to its members. Rather, it was that no one was listening to its message.

To its members, the L.D.S. Church existed for the purpose of announcing the restoration of divine truth and saving authority. The primary function of the Book of Mormon, too, was as an "ensign to the nations" or harbinger of the millennial reign.[67] Thus, people's unwillingness to hear the church's message was for the Latter-day Saints an ontological crisis, not merely a problem of religious persecution. Evidence of the crisis was everywhere. In the preceding two decades, violence against Latter-day Saints was common in the United States, resulting in extreme cases in the burning of meetinghouses, the whipping and tar-and-feathering of missionaries, and the murdering of several missionaries and church members in unrelated incidents. As late as 1902, one missionary caught organizing a Sunday school in Arkansas was tied to a tree and given thirty lashes with promise of worse if he returned. Physical attacks were reported in the church's international missions as well.[68] In addition, both domestic and

Across the Frontier.

"Across the Frontier," ca. 1904. This unidentified cartoon from Smoot's newspaper clipping file parodies the condition of the church's missions. Depicted in tattered clothing, Joseph F. Smith is shown as helpless against the evicting hand of the state of Prussia. Courtesy of L. Tom Perry Special Collections, Harold B. Lee Library, Brigham Young University, Provo, Utah.

foreign governments had imposed legal restraints on the church, denying or terminating missionary visas, refusing to license the organization of
congregations, and proscribing convert emigration.[69] In 1903 the church's
First Presidency reported that "Mayor Low of New York has . . . with-
drawn all permits from our Elders to preach in the streets of that city. The
banishment of our brethren from Germany is another phase of this same
widespread effort; while at home and abroad scurrilous, lying tracts and
pamphlets are being distributed far and wide in the effort to create a public opinion actively hostile to the Church and its teachings."[70] The 1890
Manifesto had not changed the world's opinion of Mormonism, and as a
result, the church's missions were in trouble. This meant the church itself
was in trouble to a unique degree. If it could not make itself heard, the
church had no reason for being.

   Thus, when Smith took office, it was obvious that defensive capitulation was an insufficient response to the church's reputational and legal
problems. This may explain why Smith concluded his inaugural address
with a promise that constituted a demand. "The Lord," the new prophet
and president decreed to his church, "designs to change this condition
of things and to make us known to the world in our true light—as true
worshipers of God."[71] The Saints' god demanded a more positive engagement with the world. As we shall see, Smith used his considerable power
within the church to press for engagement and even change the church
"according to the American idea and the United States Constitution."[72]
But while Smith had both the family pedigree and ecclesiastical power to
effect change within the church, changing the "condition of things" required more influence than Smith possessed. Frustrated by national and
international government sanctions, Smith needed an apostle in the Senate.

If Mr. Smoot wants to wholly differentiate

himself from his church and his people and the

doctrine and life and living of those people, then

that is for him to determine; but I do assert, and

that is the heart of this thing, that he must do

that or else declare himself subject to this church

of which he is member.

— *Attorney Robert Tayler,* Proceedings *(1904)*

THE MAN WHO SERVED TWO MASTERS

Reed Smoot arrived in Washington, D.C., on 21 February 1903. *Harper's Weekly* welcomed him by opining, "Perhaps it may be for the best, in the long-run, that the Mormons should send an apostle to Washington. It calls attention to them and stimulates the public disgust with their intuitions. They have thriven on ignorance, obscurity, and sensuality. Attention—the irritated attention—of decent and enlightened people is the last thing that will profit them." Indeed, the senator-elect did not lack for "irritated attention." The Senate had already received the Ministerial Association's sixty-two-page protest. The powerful Woman's Christian Temperance Union and the National Reform Association were daily delivering protests from citizens throughout the states and territories. This massive grassroots campaign took advantage of lessons already learned in the ouster of B. H. Roberts and eventually gathered an estimated 3 million signatures in support of the proposition "that he is and ever must be unfitted to make laws who shows himself unalterably opposed to that which underlies all law." [1]

As Smoot expected, however, the Senate granted him his seat on

5 March based on the "orderly and constitutional method of procedure" of recognizing state certificates of election. To do otherwise could result in a third of the Senate being held in limbo and an indefinite delay in "a change in the political power of this Government which the people desired to accomplish."[2] Thus, studiously avoiding any argument on the merits of the allegations against Smoot and deferring to state electoral powers, the Senate accepted Smoot's credentials. Two days later, however, it referred the mountain of protests to the Committee on Privileges and Elections for investigation and recommendation on whether Smoot should keep his seat. Not surprisingly, the committee determined a public hearing was necessary. Not until February of the following year would it begin, however.

Smoot used the intervening months to introduce himself to his colleagues and court a more favorable view of his people in the press. By the fall of 1903 he could report good news to his church president about the Senate leadership: "I called on President Roosevelt this morning and met a great many Senators there, among them Senators [Redfield] Proctor and [Marcus] Hanna and they both assured me that they took no stock whatever in the charges filed against me." Smoot also called on Senator Nelson W. Aldrich, "though it was Sunday," and was reassured that not only petitions but also "a great many letters from ministers demanding that he define his position . . . had all gone into the waste paper basket."[3] The Senate's acceptance of Smoot and its initial calm, throughout 1903 and in the midst of intense antipolygamy lobbying, was in no small part due to the fact that Smoot himself was not a polygamist and even resembled in his demeanor the men whose company he wished to keep. The forty-one-year-old Reed Smoot was to all appearances very much a man of his time, not his place. He showed no hint of his native state's frontier ruggedness or its reputation for religious fanaticism and sexual license. Rather, he seemed to be "a retiring, unobtrusive, and friendly man."[4] In photographs from the period, his gaze was direct but not intense; he appeared serious but not stern. His suit was impeccably fitted to his slender, tall frame. "There is nothing of the apostle about Smoot," said one member of the press. "He looks like the village doctor or the man who has the milk route. He has a smile and a warm hand-clasp for everybody."[5]

Born in Salt Lake City to Abraham O. Smoot and Anne Kirstine Morrison, Reed Owen was the third child of a Norwegian convert to Mormonism who immigrated for her faith and became the fourth plural wife of a Kentuckian who made the exodus to the Rocky Mountains and became a civic and ecclesiastical leader. Reed Smoot grew up in the turbulence of the federal government's antipolygamy campaign; he saw his father arrested

"About Time This Book Was Opened and Aired," *Chicago Journal*, 17 December 1904. As the hearings were about to begin, this cartoon in the *Chicago Journal* reflected the public's sense that an investigation of Mormonism was long overdue and that the light of publicity from the investigation of Reed Smoot's right to a seat in the Senate would reveal the filthy and poisonous character of the L.D.S. Church. Courtesy of L. Tom Perry Special Collections, Harold B. Lee Library, Brigham Young University, Provo, Utah.

and tried for plural marriage to his mother.[6] Though the son chose not to practice plural marriage, he espoused it in principle. As late as 1902, in a meeting with other apostles, Smoot said that plural marriage "if universally practiced, would save the world much sorrow and distress," adding that he "looked for its restoration."[7] Married in 1884 to Alpha M.

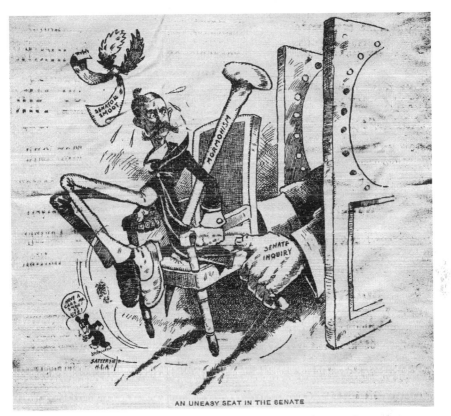

"An Uneasy Seat in the Senate," *American Affairs*, 17 March 1904. Smoot's credentials were accepted by the Senate, but his case was immediately referred to committee for an investigative hearing. For the next four years, as depicted in this cartoon, testimony from the hearing would make his position in the Senate insecure. Courtesy of L. Tom Perry Special Collections, Harold B. Lee Library, Brigham Young University, Provo, Utah.

Eldredge, Smoot remained monogamous, however, even though by the time he rose to that level of leadership where plural marriage was considered a duty, he had had years of opportunity to follow his father's example. It is unknown why Smoot remained monogamous, especially after becoming an apostle in 1900. Given that he attempted to run for the Senate in 1901, it is probable that his political ambitions were a contributing factor. Of course, federal law and the church's public acceptance of it had caused a decline in the practice of plural marriage and made monogamy a respectable choice for the faithful generally.[8] In addition, one can surmise

"The Most Characteristic Pictures of Smoot Ever Published," *San Francisco Chronicle*, n.d. (probably 1904). The new senator was not what the nation expected of a Mormon apostle. These sketches by journalist Kate Carew contrast Smoot with "the popular conception" of his co-religionists. Courtesy of L. Tom Perry Special Collections, Harold B. Lee Library, Brigham Young University, Provo, Utah.

Smoot family portrait. Portrayed here several years into the senator's tenure, Smoot's family was a model of domestic propriety. Married nearly twenty years, Reed and Alpha Eldredge Smoot brought six children with them to Washington in 1903. Courtesy of L. Tom Perry Special Collections, Harold B. Lee Library, Brigham Young University, Provo, Utah.

that, with the passing of time, the church had a need for monogamous men in public positions of church leadership, giving members of even the leading quorums a greater range of choice in their marital status.

In 1900 Smoot was elevated to the position of apostle to the surprise of many in the church, including himself. His personal proclivities and reputation had been more temporal than spiritual in nature. He was best known for his success in banking, real estate, mining, manufacturing, livestock, and merchandising ventures. He had traveled broadly, meeting men of affairs both within and outside the West. A founding member of Utah's first Republican Club, Smoot had been appointed director of the Utah Territory Insane Asylum, member of the statewide jubilee celebration of the pioneering of Utah, and trustee of Brigham Young Academy. Thus, when called to the upper echelon of church leadership, Smoot was already a wealthy, influential, and politically active man.[9] Church service was not as strongly represented in his credentials, however. Particularly noticeable, in a church where proselytizing defined religious commitment, was Reed's failure to serve a mission until 1890, after declining two previous invitations. Accepting the third call, Smoot was assigned to the church's European headquarters, where he managed immigration to Utah and was allowed to return home after ten months when his father was believed to be on the verge of death. For Smoot's critics inside the church, his mission service would later be seen as too little, too late.

Yet Latter-day Saint commitment to kingdom building left little room for distinctions between temporal and spiritual talent. Hence, it is deceptive to separate these proclivities in Smoot himself. Smoot's early church assignments in Utah and later apostolic portfolio in the U.S. Senate were perfectly consistent with responsibilities given other members of the church's Quorum of the Twelve Apostles. By the time he became an apostle at the age of thirty-eight, Smoot had run the church's woolen mills, the largest in the mountain West, for fifteen years. In fact, his early release from the mission field was caused by his aging father's inability to manage church-related businesses.[10] Thus his truncated mission, like his later one to the Senate, is best understood as the church's recognition that Smoot's "genius is practical and progressive," showing a "rare business aptitude." [11] Before sending Smoot to Washington, President Smith placed his hands on Smoot's head and gave him "a special blessing, in which the blessing and favor of the Lord was sought for his success in obtaining a seat in the senate of the United States Congress." [12]

Many of Smoot's contemporaries and later interpreters misunderstood the nature of Smoot's assignment in Washington and consequently characterized his religious commitment as lackluster. Even his biographer concluded that business, not the apostleship, was Smoot's "real life." [13] This conclusion seems justified in light of Smoot's own testimony at the hearing that he was "not a very active" Latter-day Saint.[14] Smoot's religiosity must be understood, however, in the context of the nature of L.D.S. religious life, where devotion was often expressed in digging irrigation ditches and trading commodities for a cash-poor pioneer economy. Smoot's self-representation must be read in its political context as well. It behooved him to be "not a very active" Mormon. For the same reason, church president Smith had testified that Smoot "does not attend to the duties of the apostolate . . . while he is here [in Washington]; he can not." [15] This was true only in the most technical sense, given that the duties of Smoot's apostolic calling were in the Senate. These and other such statements were designed to and did make Smoot appear for the remainder of his tenure in the Senate a less than engaged member of his apostolic quorum and his church.

While this reputation helped in the Senate, it hurt him in the church. B. H. Roberts, member of the church's third highest governing body, felt strongly enough to suggest that Smoot not seek a second term. "Whatever order of abilities may be claimed for him," Roberts opined, "there is no one who will seriously undertake to say he is qualified to meet the responsibilities of both offices, and those who urge the two positions upon him are merely making him a candidate for ridicule, and riding him under whip and spur to a humiliating failure."[16] Time would prove Roberts not only uncharitable but also wrong. Eventually Smoot was accepted into the inner circle of Senate leadership and "during the first third of the century . . . became what might be called the quintessential Mormon."[17] A magazine editor who observed him for many years was closer to understanding Smoot when he denominated him "Pontifex Babbitt."[18] Smoot was an astute choice to represent modern Mormonism, replacing its reputation for anarchical fanaticism with bourgeois patriotism.

Underneath Smoot's Babbitlike demeanor, however, was a very anxious man who suffered from various stomach ailments and sleeplessness throughout the hearing.[19] This seems only natural given the circumstances under which Smoot was learning his new job. But the level of stress he experienced also indicated internal conflict. Apostle-senator Smoot held loyalties to two apparently incommensurate communities, each with its own imperatives and each demanding full allegiance. That he held these competing loyalties sincerely made Smoot the ideal mediator between the Mormon church and the American state. In the meantime, though, his two identities required him to serve two contrary masters. The tension was sufficient that after two months in the Senate, Smoot returned to Salt Lake City and reported to his apostolic brethren "that he always had in mind Zion and her people. Her interests are my interests; whatever hurts Zion, hurts me." Acknowledging the degree of concern within the quorum over the Senate hearing generally, Smoot assured church leaders of his priorities, saying he "desired to be in harmony with the presidency and his brethren. If it were thought advisable for him to resign from the senate, he would not hesitate a moment."[20]

Particularly troubling to his church brethren were Smith's public statements on plural marriage, notwithstanding the fact that he was acting under Joseph F. Smith's direction to "keep cool, say little. Keep facts prominent. There have been no plural marriages by the Mormon Church since the manifesto."[21] Others, however, wanted him to say more in defense of the church's doctrines or thought he was misrepresenting them. Ben Rich, president of the church's mission in the southern states, said of the apostle-senator, "When his case is [s]ettled, he is to be taken hom[e] and taught the gospel."[22] Even among church witnesses at the hearing, some were not as willing as Smoot to abandon the practice of plural marriage. Elderly apostle John Henry Smith's testimony both embarrassed the senator and damaged his case. Born in 1848 during the Latter-day Saint exodus from Illinois, "John Henry" was a life-long veteran of the anti-polygamy campaign in Utah and could not change his tune so late in life; he testified, "I expect . . . while breath shall remain in this body to believe that the principle itself is correct." He also admitted that even if an apostle were guilty of practicing polygamy, the church would take no action unless it were compelled by the government.[23] John Henry's admission against his own and Smoot's interests was a rare public expression of Progressive Era Mormonism's continuing commitment to plural marriage.

Because the Latter-day Saints' defense of their "peculiar institution" was necessarily aimed at countering the accusations of their opponents, the believers' own reasons for living in plural marriages can be difficult to understand. Of course, the willingness of large numbers of Latter-day Saints to forfeit respect, property, liberty, and life in order to maintain the practice of polygamy between 1841 and 1906 is an easy measure of the significance of plural marriage.[24] Less noble, but equally telling, is the longer history of deception about the practice by an otherwise sternly ethical people.[25] No doubt persecution made the Latter-day Saints hold to the principle less critically than they might have done. More than the psychology of sacrifice and persecution, however, is required to explain their persistent effort to maintain such a unique—in America, at least—form of family life.

Several forces contributed to the church's stubborn conflation of religious faith and marital practice. Each of these forces had to be dealt with if Joseph F. Smith and his apostle-senator were to change the church's practice without destroying its faith. The first can be characterized as historical. Joseph Smith spent the last three years of his life implementing a theology and ecclesiology of temple worship that made celestial marriage, as its preferred name indicates, the highest sacrament of the church. As Smith's final prophetic effort, celestial marriage was necessarily given added significance by those who had entered polygamous unions under his tutelage. Thrust into leadership by Smith's murder, these early initiates organized the Utah church according to their understanding that celestial marriage constituted the fulfillment of Smith's mission to restore the fullness of the gospel. Smith himself called plural marriage "a new and an everlasting covenant . . . instituted for the fullness of . . . [God's] glory," and Brigham Young agreed.[26] In 1852, shortly after the grant of territorial status to Utah and the arrival of the last refugees from Illinois, the decision to make plural marriage a churchwide practice was justified on the grounds that it was a revelation "given [by God] to our Prophet, Seer, and Revelator . . . only about eleven months before he was martyred for the testimony of Jesus."[27] Later, when the Reorganized Church of Jesus Christ of Latter-day Saints, led by Joseph Smith's son, identified itself in opposition to polygamy and denied that Smith had ever practiced it, the Utah church's identity became further defined in terms of plural marriage. Not only for the nation but for the Latter-day Saints as well, to be a true follower of Joseph Smith was to be polygamous. Any successful attempt to stop the practice of polygamy had to find within Joseph Smith's life and thought an equally powerful expression of the church's restorationist claims and an equally differentiating belief from other churches.

A second force sustaining the practice of polygamy arose from the church's long contest with the federal government. Though not all the Latter-day Saints practiced polygamy, all were subject to and affected by government sanctions against it. Raided by federal marshals and accused of barbarism and immorality by Protestant ministers and dime novelists, the entire church population lived for decades in an atmosphere of fear, antagonism, and shame. After the failure of the U.S. Army to effect sufficient change in midcentury Utah, the forms and forums of American law were increasingly employed to impose the nation's moral sensibilities upon the L.D.S. Church. As federal law became the instrumentality for enforcing Protestant morality, the Latter-day Saints' resistance became framed increasingly in legal terms—not merely in scripture and sermon, but in political declarations. For example, in 1870 when antipolygamy legislation was tightening its hold over the Utah Territory, the following resolution was adopted by the Latter-day Saints: "The doctrine of Celestial Marriage or plurality of wives was revealed to the prophet Joseph Smith and by him established in the Church . . . as a revealed law of God, therefore be it. Resolved that we the members of said Church, in general mass meeting assembled do now most earnestly and solemnly declare before Almighty God that we hold that said order of marriage is a cardinal principle of our religious faith affecting us not only for time, but for all eternity and as sacred and binding as any other principle of the Holy Gospel of the Son of God."[28]

Beyond any theological significance it may have, this resolution was an explicit claim to constitutional protection for religiously informed action. The way the Latter-day Saints saw it, "free exercise of religion" could only be preserved by the government's ceasing to criminalize church-sanctioned marriages. Six years later, as the Poland Act's efforts to make the anti-polygamy laws effective were being felt, the Latter-day Saints strengthened their legal argument by canonizing Joseph Smith's revelation on celestial marriage. The 1876 edition of the church's *Book of Doctrine and Covenants* added the revelation, which was written in 1843. Thus, canonization of the doctrine in scripture occurred thirty-three years after the doctrine's inscription by Joseph Smith and twenty-four years after its publication by Brigham Young, but contemporaneous with renewed efforts by Congress to quash the practice. The choice to formalize in scripture their belief in celestial marriage strengthened the Latter-day Saints' legal claim that plural marriage was dictated by religious belief. That choice also complicated further the succeeding generation's task of deposing of the practice: proscription of plural marriage would have to be established with equal legitimacy and formality as had its prescription.

Finally, in addition to the history of polygamy and the effects of litigation on it, the Latter-day Saints' marital practices were thoroughly integrated with their doctrines of personal salvation and church administration. During Joseph Smith's lifetime, plural marriage was practiced secretly and only among the leadership elite. At the time of Smith's death in 1844, the doctrine was not well developed by sermon or other public exposition. This omission had been thoroughly corrected by the turn of the century. Indeed, thirty years prior to inheriting the burden of doing away with the practice, then-apostle Joseph F. Smith had said in sermon, "I understand the law of celestial marriage to mean that every man in this Church, who has the ability to obey and practice it in righteousness and will not, shall be damned. I say I understand it to mean this and nothing less, and I testify in the name of Jesus that it does mean that."[29] To the Latter-day Saints, damnation was to cease to progress. Though not equivalent to traditional Christian notions of hell, damnation did mean not going to heaven. For nineteenth-century Latter-day Saints, monogamy constituted a rejection of Joseph Smith's canonized teaching that "there are three heavens. . . . And in order to obtain the highest a man must enter into this order of the priesthood [meaning the new and everlasting covenant of marriage]; and if he does not, he cannot obtain it."[30] The bracketed definition was inserted into the text of the published scripture and, hence, made explicit the relation of "this order of priesthood" to the revelation that followed in the text, namely, plural marriage.[31] Thus, this definition makes explicit also the doctrinal connection between the plural marriage and priesthood, as well as salvation. The stubbornly enduring practice of polygamy within the leading counsels of the church until approximately 1905 is based theologically in this aspect of Latter-day Saint doctrine. Because plural marriage constituted for the Latter-day Saints an "order of the priesthood," not to practice it was to lack a form of priesthood or certain mediating authority prerequisite to church leadership.

No wonder, then, that the Senate tribunal found that four members of the present apostolic quorum had taken additional wives after the Manifesto in 1890 and at least two members had continued to perform plural marriages for others.[32] It was generally believed that others in the quorum had performed marriages, including President Smith, but evidence was only circumstantial.[33] Many years after the fact, a post-Manifesto polygamist wrote defensively to Joseph F. Smith's successor, "I never talked directly with President Smith about it [marrying polygamously after the Manifesto] because I supposed he didn't want to know, but he let me know as well as I wanted to know, that he approved of my family affairs, and therefore I do not consider myself in a bad 'fix'. Neither do I think any of the brethren sustained in these Church positions are in a bad fix, nor the authorities of the Church who place and sustain them there. The thing I am most concerned about is the ill-will among the brethren over this matter."[34] It would take many years for the "ill-will among the brethren" to pass, often only after their own passing.

As with Latter-day Saint loyalty to plural marriage, the nation's abhorrence of polygamy must be understood in terms of the practice's relation to church order. "Polygamy welds the Mormons together in a solid unity inasmuch as it separates between the Mormons and the rest of the world; and inasmuch as having permeated Mormon society it cannot be condemned without disgrace either in one's self or kinfolks," wrote the Reverend Thomas Cary Johnson.[35] The choice of "weld" to describe the bond of polygamy resonates with the Latter-day Saints' own characterization of "sealing" family relations "for time and eternity" by divine authority. Opponents of plural marriage, however, believed the Mormon family was united by shame, not God. Family members had no recourse to moral society because polygamy "shuts the door of Gentile sympathy against the Mormon," concluded Alfred Henry Lewis, a prolific writer on the subject. For Lewis, Mormonism's continuing existence could only be explained in terms of polygamy's "act[ing] as a bar to the member's escape"; without polygamy the church would "instantly dwindle away." Thus, polygamy not only made the Mormons morally reprehensible, but it made their ties to the church too strong, even involuntary. "Without polygamy," Lewis argued, "a Mormon might leave his or her Church and become a Gentile with no more loss of standing in the community than results to one who leaves the Congregational Church to unite with the Methodist." Polygamy was the means of Mormonism's refusal to conform to the American idea of a church, or in Lewis's words, "serve[d] to mark the church members and separate and set them apart from Gentile influences."[36]

Latter-day Saint loyalty to church was a central issue for many Americans during the Smoot hearing. For the Senate, Smoot's election forced a deliberation on whether the "visible" nature of the L.D.S. Church constituted a coercive monopolistic expression that threatened democratic institutions or the legitimate expression of special interests within a political democracy. Smoot's job was to convince the Senate of both the innocence and the political advantage of Mormon cohesiveness.

Most Republican senators were willing to defend Smoot because they had been told to do so. Their party and their president believed that Smoot held the key to new votes in the West that were disturbing old relations of regional political power in national elections. When Smoot won his seat as the first native-born Utahan in the Senate, he arrived at the peak of the transfer of political strength from East to West. The demographics of a westward-moving population had caused only marginal change compared with that of the westward movement of the republic itself. Eleven states lay beyond or along the intermountain corridor of the Rockies. Seven of them were the particular domain of the Mormons, and the remainder were subject to Mormon influence. At a time when electoral colleges determined the presidency and state legislators elected senators, it was feared that the Mormon vote could make the difference in national politics.[37] The significance of this was not lost on anyone, least of all the political parties. Thus, ironically, while some in Congress argued the L.D.S. Church had too much power, others sought to exploit that power.

Rumors abounded in Washington that the Republicans had promised to defeat any new antipolygamy legislation in return for the previously Democratic Mormon vote. Smoot's election seemed proof of the rumor to his contemporaries, and his correspondence confirms it today. As the hearing was about to begin in the winter of 1904, Smoot advised church leaders in Utah that Theodore Roosevelt's expected contest with Mark Hanna for the presidential nomination meant Roosevelt "is relying on me to control the convention for the nomination of delegates to the National

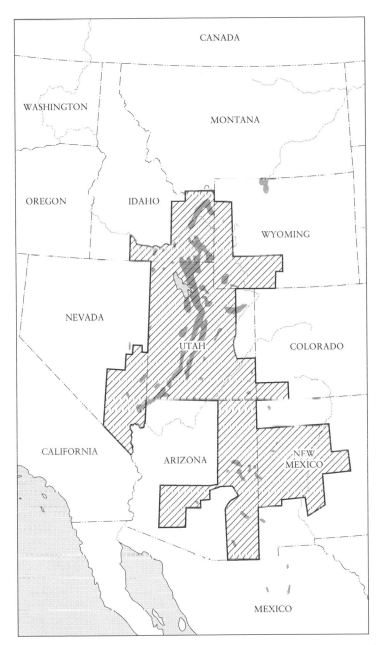

The Mormon Corridor, ca. 1900. Church-directed settlement patterns had already created a "Mormon Corridor" of political influence in five western states by the end of the nineteenth century, and statehood for Arizona and New Mexico was debated during Smoot's first month in the Senate. Concern over Mormon political power was a contributing factor to neither state's being admitted until 1912.

Convention, and I ask you to help me to accomplish the same, for if I do not I may just as well go home, as far as any influence I will have with the administration."[38] With Roosevelt's support, it appeared that the Senate could be counted on to vote for Smoot. "Politics rules here," wrote Utah congressman Joseph Howell to the church's leadership, "and with Senator Hanna a candidate for the Presidency, the outlook is very close, so that while Utah is but a small State, even her few votes are worth looking after. That is about the key to the situation, and I believe sets the tide in our favor."[39] The church delivered its vote as promised, but for Smoot the tide did not come in.

The Republican-dominated Senate Committee on Privileges and Elections would not be controlled by the administration, giving Smoot reason to complain that "every Republican anti-Mormon Senator . . . is on this Committee."[40] Smoot was only able to convince his Republican brethren to remove a very hostile Senator Eugene Hale, "representative of the great protestant religious organizations of this country."[41] The final appointments to the hearing panel were Republicans Julius C. Burrows (Michigan), George F. Hoar (Massachusetts), Louis E. McComas (Maryland), Joseph B. Foraker (Ohio), Chauncey M. Depew (New York), Albert J. Beveridge (Indiana), William P. Dillingham (Vermont), and Albert J. Hopkins (Illinois) and Democrats Edmund W. Pettus (Alabama), Fred. T. Dubois (Idaho), Joseph W. Bailey (Texas), Lee S. Overman (North Carolina), and James P. Clarke (Arkansas). Two others, both Progressive Republicans, would join the panel later and play a significant role in the Senate's plenary vote. When Senator Hoar died in September 1904, during the first year of the hearing, he was replaced by Philander Knox (R-Pennsylvania), a man of more progressive sentiments and closer connection to Roosevelt. In 1905 Senator McComas was replaced by Jonathan P. Dolliver (R-Iowa), a Methodist leader and favorite of his state's women's groups. Smoot's monogamy may have gotten him past the threshold of the Senate at large, but these men would make the recommendation on whether to keep him notwithstanding the estimated 3 million voters begging for him to be sent home.

The hearing panel was a powerful collection of some of the best-known political figures of the day. Twenty-five-year veteran George Frisbie Hoar was dean of the Senate as well as overseer at Harvard, eminent Unitarian descendant of framers of the Constitution, and respected interpreter of constitutional law. As recently as 1901 he had supported an antipolygamy amendment to the Constitution and was rumored to see the hearing as an opportunity to "take a fall out of the Church."[42] Likewise, Senator Julius

"The Senate Committee on the Mormon Question in Session at Washington,"
Harper's Weekly, 15 March 1904. In this photograph, *Harper's Weekly* posed the
accused Senator Smoot in the midst of the Committee on Privileges and Elections
with Chairman Burrows on his right and Senator Hoar on his left. The lawyers are
seated in the foreground on Smoot's right. Robert Tayler, protestants' counsel, is
nearest the camera, with Smoot's counsel, A. S. Worthington, on Tayler's left and
Worthington's associate, Valdemar Van Cott, behind Tayler. Courtesy of L. Tom
Perry Special Collections, Harold B. Lee Library, Brigham Young University,
Provo, Utah.

Caesar Burrows, chair of the Committee on Privileges and Elections, had
a lingering distaste for Mormonism. Working on antipolygamy legislation
two decades earlier, he had introduced a bill to make polygamists ineligible for a seat in the House. Now in the Senate, Burrows had not changed
his mind but expanded the scope of the hearing to include all allegations
against the L.D.S. Church, however unrelated to Smoot. Burrows's antipathy for the Latter-day Saints may have an earlier and more personal origin,
however. His uncle converted to Mormonism in the nineteenth century
and may have been excommunicated.[43] Burrows's chief ally on the panel
was Democrat Senator Fred T. Dubois, an old antagonist of the Mormons
from his days as an Idaho federal marshal assigned to ferret out Mormon
polygamists. Dubois was also chief strategist for the protestors and liaison
with women's groups. "This is the fight of my life," he said. "I have been

engaged in it practically for twenty years, and have organized this present contest, and am in complete control of it."[44]

Though less politically or emotionally wedded to the issue, panel member Chauncey Depew, former head of the Vanderbilt railroad empire, was another Republican on record against Mormonism. Speaking a few weeks after Smoot arrived in Washington, Depew had warned his fellow senators against granting statehood to New Mexico and Arizona because of the political influence of the L.D.S. Church in the region. "Nothing," he said, "so illustrates the power of concentration or the ability of concentrated power as the history and the present dominance of the Mormon Church." Theoretically, all in Depew's audience were opposed to "concentrated power" because it seemed inimical to democratic institutions. In practice, however, the New York senator himself represented powerful private interests, though in his case they were commercial. Nor was he alone in this respect, since concentrated power is a natural product of majoritarian politics. Especially prior to the democratic election of senators, political parties existed to aggregate power within a diverse electorate. Thus it may have been ironic, but it was not impolitic that the Republicans were attempting to benefit from the "present dominance of the Mormon church" even as they were about to try it for having such dominance. As Depew said jokingly when charged with as much during his speech on the statehood bill, the Democrats would have done the same if they could have.[45] Like Republicans who hoped to exploit the church's power in the West, the ministers' protest was ironic. For many years the Protestant churches and their reform agencies had combined politically to remove the L.D.S. Church from politics. Smoot's lawyer delighted in making Protestant witnesses confess the political means and goals of their reform activities and the routine concentration of their powers to select non-Mormon candidates for office, observing wryly to one witness, "I understand you consider it politics for religious organizations to get a man into the senate, but it is not politics to try to get him out."[46]

In February 1904, when Smoot was called upon to publicly defend his senatorial and apostolic offices, he stood between two demanding taskmasters, the U.S. Senate and the L.D.S. Church, and condemned by a third powerful force, American Protestantism. All three came to the hearing with competing goals. The protestors wanted to put an end to the L.D.S. Church because of their sincere conviction that it was destructive of home and nation. The Latter-day Saints wanted to be "known to the world in our true light" and believed the political leverage of a Senate seat would make that possible.[47] In the middle and sometimes falling on either side was the Senate, whose greatest concern was the L.D.S. Church's capacity for civil disobedience. The Senate wanted proof that the church was willing to submit finally to U.S. law, even if that meant disobeying the law of their god. The Senate wanted the church to conform to "religion according to the American idea and the United States constitution."[48] The conflicting interests of these groups appeared irreconcilable as the hearing commenced.

The protestors' hope of unseating Smoot and obtaining an antipolygamy amendment to the Constitution lay in proving that the L.D.S. Church had not changed and would not change. This required them to attack broadly and lobby heavily to ensure that the church's leaders would be forced to testify in defense of their religion and, thus, against Smoot's interest in retaining his seat. Unrestricted by the rules of civil courts, including that most common sense limit of relevance, the Senate proceedings supported the protestants' strategy. The Smoot hearing would range far beyond the senator's qualifications for office. Smoot did all he could, even compromising his defense, to stave off the movement to subpoena the church hierarchy. Apologizing for his weak written response to the formal protest filed against him, Smoot explained to Joseph F. Smith, "I could have made it much stronger by making specific allegations and explanations, but I was afraid to do this for the reason that an allegation made by me would compel me to prove it, and it might be that in order to prove it to their entire satisfaction, they might require some of the Presidency to testify. I contented myself with simple denials and admissions."[49] Smoot's sacrifice was to no avail. On the eve of the hearing, Chairman Burrows "very frankly" told Smoot that he "was not on trial, but that they were going to investigate the Mormon Church."[50]

On 24 February 1904 the first set of subpoenas arrived in Salt Lake City. Included on the list were church president Joseph F. Smith and seven of the church's twelve apostles: Francis M. Lyman, John Henry Smith, Hyrum M. Smith, George Teasdale, John W. Taylor, Matthias F. Cowley, and Marriner W. Merrill. Utah's reaction to the subpoenas ranged from feisty optimism to angry dread. Some, both in and outside the church, were furious with Smoot for bringing unwanted attention to the church and to Utah. The Democratic *Salt Lake Herald* believed that "the senator has invited the very thing Utah people do not want—an investigation on the drag-net plan which will involve the state in publicity of a kind and to an extent that Gentile, Jew and Mormon alike will deplore."[51] The church's official position was that the hearing would redound to the

"First Presidency and Quorum of Twelve Apostles," 1904. The L.D.S. Church leadership in 1904 is shown here with President Smith in the center, flanked on the right by counselor John E. Winder and on the left by counselor Anthon H. Lund. Clockwise, beginning with Reed Smoot in the lower left corner, the Quorum of the Twelve Apostles consisted of Hyrum M. Smith, son of Joseph F.; George A. Smith; Francis M. Lyman, president of the Quorum; John Henry Smith; George Teasdale; Heber J. Grant; John W. Taylor; Marriner W. Merrill; Matthias F. Cowley; Abraham O. Woodruff; and Rudger Clawson. Courtesy of LDS Family and Church History Library.

church's benefit. "Whatever may grow out of the present uproar against it, one result is certain; the Church will be the stronger, the world will be attracted towards its principles and its power, and the purposes of the Almighty will be accomplished, no matter what may happen to individuals and their desires."[52] As it turned out, there were some positive effects on the church's missionary work. On 26 February 1904 the *News* reported that anti-Mormon speeches by the protestants and the plethora of news arising from the hearing were increasing attendance at missionary meetings, if only inspired by curiosity. The next month a Pittsburgh newspaper reported that, after reading the Smoot hearing testimony, "Gottlieb Gassman, his wife and three children left here today for Salt Lake to join the Mormon Church."[53] The Gassmans were a rare breed, however. Most thought the testimony "show[ed] a condition of affairs in Utah more horrible than anything previously imagined."[54]

In response to speculation that the named witnesses would flee, the editor of the church-owned *Deseret Evening News* assured the nation that "all who are well and at home will respond, and be at Washington when required."[55] As it turned out, however, several were not well or not at home. Of the church's top leadership, only President Smith, his apostle-son Hyrum, and chief apostle Francis M. Lyman responded to the subpoenas. Two apostles were prevented by illness from responding, though one testified at a later date. Another four apostles avoided subpoena by leaving the country. They included seventy-three-year-old George Teasdale, who arrived in Colonia Dublan, Mexico, on 18 February 1904, a week ahead of the subpoenas. Apostles John W. Taylor and Matthias Cowley fled to outlying Mormon settlements and continued to confound attempts to serve their subpoenas by circulating through Canada and Mexico on church assignments.[56]

A fourth apostle, Heber J. Grant, was already beyond the Senate's reach in England, heading the church's European mission. When he donated $150 to the state university the preceding November, Grant had publicly announced that the amount represented $50 for himself and each of his two wives. It was a very bad time for a joke, coinciding with the Senate's demand that Smoot answer the protest. When Smoot asked President Roosevelt's support for an expedited hearing, Roosevelt mentioned Grant's "unfortunate" donation and that "delegations wait upon him calling attention to the remarks and claiming they disclosed the true attitude of the Church toward the Government, that the people were still defiant and law-breakers."[57] Though Grant had already been called on a foreign mission, his indiscretion greatly accelerated his departure and kept him out of the country until the end of the Senate investigation.[58] While the church's newspaper downplayed the subpoenas as providing "a rare opportunity for a spring vacation at Washington without expense to their individual pocket-books," there was growing fear about the scope of the investigation.[59] Joseph F. Smith seemed unconcerned, however. He dropped by the marshal's office—twice—to get his subpoena. A Republican colleague reported to Smoot in code that local "politicians view with alarm . . . the protracted hearing which it now appears plain has been outlined, but Alrota [Joseph F. Smith] does not seem alarmed."[60] Smith was among the few "pleased to have another opportunity of presenting the doctrines of the Church Jesus Christ before the World." His march-ing orders to Smoot were "Don't shrink from the issue, tell them to come ahead . . . the more thorough the better in all and everything that belongs to us."[61]

Smoot's senatorship was Smith's personal gambit, though it was "a bold game for the Mormon leaders to put Smoot in front of the cannon."[62] Nevertheless, Smith remained committed to keeping Apostle Smoot in the Senate. It was Smith who engineered the church's alignment with the Republican Party, and he was Smoot's chief advocate against those who called for his resignation rather than endure the scrutiny of a Senate inves-tigation. To one who disagreed, he said, "in the most forceful and positive manner: 'If ever the Spirit of the Lord has manifested to men anything clear and plain and positive, it is this, that Reed Smoot should remain in the United States Senate. He can do more good there than he can anywhere else.'"[63] As far as Smith was concerned, Smoot was in the Senate for the church's benefit, and God would ensure he stayed there.

Though Smith appeared prepared for a fight and confident of ultimate victory, he tried to satisfy the Senate prior to the hearing with official state-ments designed to counter concerns about the church's economic and po-litical power. Two months before the trial was scheduled to begin, Smith responded publicly to the Senate protest. Titled *The Kingdom of God*, Smith's published address was an extraordinarily plain and economical statement of what would become Smoot's defense. The senator received a copy of it prior to publication and did not deviate from its direction at any point during the four-year hearing.[64]

The essential point of Smith's proclamation was that "the system called 'Mormonism' . . . is solely an ecclesiastical organization . . . separate and distinct from the state."[65] Using biblical references to reassure his audi-ence that the Latter-day Saints did not constitute a political threat, Smith likened the role of his restorationist church to that of John the Baptist, whose job was to announce that "the kingdom of God is at hand." Con-temporary attacks on the church, Smith said, were merely "history re-peat[ing] itself with the old cry of 'treason' . . . and the charges that the 'Mormon organization is imperium imperio.'" The L.D.S. Church was not the kingdom of God but merely preparatory to it, he explained. He added that any "sermons, dissertations and arguments by preachers and writers in the Church" implying church dominion over temporal affairs were "in-correct, no matter by whom set forth."[66] This was a public renunciation of nearly sixty years of church teaching.

The remainder of the address described the ways in which the church was "solely an ecclesiastical organization," both as it operated vis-à-vis other social institutions and in the lives of its members. Smith repeated the Latter-day Saints' argument for statehood, namely, that the unity of church and state in Utah was a historical, not a theological, phenomenon. Because the Latter-day Saints were the first and, for a significant time, the only nonindigenous people in the territory, it was natural, he argued, that they would occupy the offices in the government and industry that they had created. The United States recognized as much when it made prominent churchmen the first territorial officers. Unfortunately, Smith explained, the unanimity of political voice consequent to these developments "favored the impression abroad that they voted as they were required. . . . But the ecclesiastical and political systems were kept distinct."[67]

Testimony at the Smoot hearing showed that this was largely true. Though exceptions could be found, they were susceptible to convincing rebuttal. The protestants relied heavily on the 1897 case of former apostle Moses Thatcher, who had been released from his position after insisting on running for the Senate in opposition to the wishes of his brethren in the quorum. Though called by the protestants, Thatcher testified in support of Smoot's contention that the requirement of high church officers to obtain church permission to run for office was neither an infringement on the right to run, were permission denied, nor an endorsement for election, were permission granted. Rather, he said, denial signaled concern for loss of time devoted to church concerns and approval was merely a leave of absence from church responsibilities.[68] Evidence at trial of the numbers of non-Mormons elected to office at the expense of Mormon candidates and testimony of non-Mormon party leaders from Utah and Idaho depicted both states as independent commonwealths that operated on the basis of party, not religious loyalties.[69] In sum, such dominance, if any, possessed by the church in Utah politics was the function of democratic principles coupled with human affinities. Yet Smith's argument and the evidence proffered in support of it did not address the ultimate question posed by the Smoot hearing: Could the Mormons be counted on to obey the law of the land, even when their god counseled otherwise? The Senate wanted Smith to answer this question directly and under oath.

Is not a man's duty as a citizen perfectly consistent

with any conception that exists in this country of

his religious duty?

—Senator Joseph W. Bailey, Proceedings *(1904)*

SUBORDINATING TO THE STATE

On Wednesday, 2 March 1904, the president of The Church of Jesus Christ of Latter-day Saints was called to the witness stand and placed under oath. The typical first questions introduced the witness better than most could appreciate: Name? "Joseph F. Smith." Place of residence? "Salt Lake City." Duration of residence? "Fifty-six years." [1] Each of the witness's answers was a critical marker of both his identity and the crux of the matter before the Senate committee. "Joseph" was the patriarchal name in the family, having been shared by Joseph F. Smith's grandfather and uncle, the church's first president. "Fielding" was the surname of his English immigrant mother, with whom he had made the forced march from Illinois to the Rockies. He had lived in Salt Lake City for fifty-six of his sixty-five years, making him an original citizen of the Mormon kingdom and firsthand participant in every phase of the nation's Mormon Problem. In both his personal history and his ecclesiastical office, Joseph F. Smith embodied the conflict of authority between a nation with the soul of a church and a church with the soul of a nation.

Joseph F. Smith's character and personality were shaped in an environment of extraordinary personal sacrifice and by experiences of abject loss and extreme terror. Born in 1838, Smith was immediately caught in the Latter-day Saints' brutal flight to Illinois, catalyzed by the Missouri governor's extermination order. Over the next few years, Smith saw the Latter-day Saint utopia, Nauvoo, Illinois, created out of a swamp on the Mississippi River and soon evacuated by force of mob violence. Three decades later, on his thirty-sixth birthday, Smith wrote in his journal, "My soul has never thoroughly dispelled the darkening shadows cast upon it by the lowering gloom of that eventful period."[2] The church's second forced exodus in six years and arduous trek to Utah was precipitated by the murder of both Smith's father and uncle while they were in protective custody of the governor of Illinois. The event so traumatized the five-and-a-half-year-old Smith that he did not visit the site of his father's death until 1906, notwithstanding his having been in the vicinity several times. Of this visit, a traveling companion reported that Smith "sank down in a chair and wept in the little jail room."[3]

The more immediate effect of the mob violence on Smith is implied in a letter he wrote to his wife when he passed through Nauvoo on his way to England in 1860. "I could pick out nearly every spot that I had known in childhood," he said, including "the little *Brick Out house* where I shut myself up to keep from going to *prison*—as I supposed."[4] Throughout his six-day ordeal on the witness stand in the Smoot hearing, Smith wore on the lapel of his coat a miniature of his father. One can only guess its significance, but it must have reminded the son that no sacrifice was too great for the family faith.[5] To others, the button on his lapel communicated the conviction that the Mormons continued to be a persecuted people in this tribunal, as they had been for the preceding sixty-six years of Smith's life.

Joseph F., as he was called within the church, matured in the Utah Territory under circumstances that continued to school him in the destructive antagonism between his church and the United States. His mother died from the hardships of homesteading the barren Salt Lake Basin, making him an orphan at thirteen. Two years later Joseph F. was expelled from school for beating a schoolteacher who had threatened to discipline his sister with a whip.[6] This precipitated the imposition of church discipline on the boy in the form of an early mission call to the remote Sandwich Islands. When he returned five years later, he found "all Utah . . . aflame with the war spirit . . . preparing to resist the impending invasion of Salt Lake Valley." The U.S. Army had been sent to subdue the Mormon kingdom, and Smith's first night home was spent, he said, "molding rifle bullets from a pig of lead. . . . I then proceeded to the front."[7] For the next forty

Joseph F. Smith. Taken during Smith's testimony before the committee, this photograph was published in *Harper's Weekly* on 15 March 1904. Courtesy of L. Tom Perry Special Collections, Harold B. Lee Library, Brigham Young University, Provo, Utah.

years, though the battle between his church and nation shifted to legal and political forums, Smith remained on the front line of the church's defenses.

Smith was a curious combination of frontier toughness, political sophistication, and religious certainty. He had participated in every stage of the church's colonization of a vast territory in the American West and had traveled widely throughout the United States, the Pacific Islands, and Europe. For a self-educated frontiersman, he had a surprising breadth of knowledge and facility with argument, as the Senate committee would discover. While he was his people's undisputed leader in spiritual matters, having served in the highest counsels of church government since 1867, he was also captain of the church's many industrial and commercial enterprises. Politically, he had served both his church and state as colonist, city councilman, legislator, Washington lobbyist, and drafter of Utah's constitution. No wonder, then, that the Latter-day Saints regarded him as "a reflex of the best character of the 'Mormon' people—inured to hardships, patient in trial, God-fearing, self-sacrificing, full of love for the human race, powerful in moral, mental and physical strength."[8] When he came to Washington in 1904 with a lifetime of personal trials coterminous with

Joseph F. Smith's family, 1904. Taken shortly after his testimony in Washington, this family portrait shows Smith seated in the center with three wives to his right and two to his left. His first wife, Julina Lambson (m. 1866; 13 children), is on Smith's immediate right, and second wife, Sarah Ellen Richards (m. 1868; 11 children), sits immediately to his left. Next to Julina is her sister and Smith's third wife, Edna Lambson (m. 1871; 10 children), followed by wife number four, Alice Ann Kimball (m. 1883; 7 children). To the left of second wife Sarah is fifth wife Mary Taylor Schwartz (m. 1884; 7 children). After being absent on church missions for five of the first six years they were married, Smith was divorced by Levira Annett Clark (m. 1859; no children) in 1866; she apparently objected to his marriage that same year to Julina. Smith's forty-eight children included five who were adopted. Courtesy of LDS Family and Church History Library.

the history of the church, Smith embodied the church no less than his martyred father, whose portrait he wore on his lapel during the trial. As the chief hierarch of the L.D.S. Church, husband to five wives and father of forty-eight children, Joseph F. Smith served an equally representative function for the protestants, however.

Newspapers for 2 through 7 March described the trial's atmosphere, as well as Smith's testimony, in great detail. "The Mormons sit in a stolid row . . . on the right-hand side of the great table that extends down through the middle of the room," said the *New York World*. The protestants and their attorneys, Robert Tayler and John Carlisle, sat opposite Smoot and his brethren. The Senate Committee on Privileges and Elections was arrayed at the head of the table, and spectators were crammed into every nook of the remaining space. How they viewed the defendants is conveyed by the *World*'s "Graphic Pen Picture": "Nearest the door is President Joseph F. Smith, a man of five feet eight or nine, with broad shoulders, a short neck and a general appearance of squattiness. . . . His eyes are small and shifty. They sparkle behind his glasses and are never still. . . . His words are well chosen. It is evident that he has had much practice in talking to the public. His temper is not well in hand, for at times he flares up and answers questions sharply. He rarely moves when other witnesses are on the stand. He watches each man closely, but betrays neither satisfaction at nor disapproval of the testimony."[9] Smoot's witnesses were read in terms of the anti-Mormon literature of the day. Here, Smith is portrayed as the personification of the Mormon viper on the hearth.[10]

Having projected their fears of religious authority and sexual activity onto Smith, most Americans were transfixed by the spectacle of his six-day cross-examination by some of their finest lawyers. A Salt Lake City paper reported, "The gallery corridors on the senate side of the capitol building were lined with people anxious to catch a glimpse of the men who had a multiplicity of wives."[11] Likewise, a stringer for the Associated Press concluded, "At times, the trend of questions indicated that counsel for the protestants proposed to lift the bed curtains in the homes of every official of the Church."[12] The *Washington Evening Star* headlined in bold type, "NOW HAS FIVE WIVES / Admission by 'President' Smith of Utah," adding that the interest in Smith's testimony made it "necessary to post policeman at door; no one allowed in except those directly interested; others blocked the passageway."[13] Directly behind the Mormon hierarchs sat forty or more representatives of the women's groups in a section reserved for their use.[14] Notables included Margaret Dye Ellis, general superintendent of and chief lobbyist for the Woman's Christian Temperance Union; Teunis S. Hamlin, treasurer-general of the Association of Women's Clubs and wife of the pastor of Washington's Church of the Covenant; and Iowa suffragist Phoebe Cousins.[15] Everyone else had to scramble for a seat. On any given day, as many as twenty members of the House as well as several senators not on the committee were in attendance; some were forced to stand along the walls of the hearing room.

Directly across from the "stolid row" of Latter-day Saints, the protestants took their seats at the table, "more sanguine of success than at any time heretofore during the campaign," reported the *Baltimore Sun*. The protestants' "campaign has now progressed to the point where the church, rather than one of its apostles, is about to be placed on trial before the nation."[16] On the eve of the hearing, the Senate committee had permitted the protestors to modify their complaint to charge that "the President [of the L.D.S. Church] and a majority of the Twelve Apostles now practice polygamy and polygamous cohabitation and some of them have taken polygamous wives since the Manifesto of 1890; [and] that these things have been done with the knowledge and countenance of Reed Smoot."[17] Joseph F. Smith and the church's apostolic quorum were now the express object of the Senate's investigation. Though it was doubtful that their conduct was legally relevant to a determination of Smoot's qualifications, the political nature of the hearing overwhelmed such scruples. After a year of having his objections to relevance overruled, Smoot's lawyer could only find comfort in sarcasm. "It would be well," he observed to the committee, "in the course of the investigation to have his [Smoot's] name mentioned once in a week at least."[18]

The Senate continued to look past Smoot to his church, however. Because the government was concerned primarily with the extent of L.D.S. Church power and its exercise at the expense of republican institutions, the Senate committee was willing to hear any evidence of the church's ability to control those who came within the sphere of its influence. Economic and political matters were of especial interest to the senators on the hearing panel, and they interjected their own questions into the examination of the witness by the protestants' attorney Robert Tayler. Tayler was the ideal advocate for the protestants' case. Not only was he a former prosecuting attorney, but Tayler had served as Ohio's representative in the U.S. House, where, as chair of the Committee on Elections in 1899, he led the successful campaign to deny B. H. Roberts a seat in Congress.

The first substantive question Tayler asked Smith concerned the extent of his business holdings. The answer covered four pages and included references to major commercial and financial institutions operating in the intermountain region: banks, utilities, railroads, newspapers, manufacturing plants, and retail outlets. It was soon established that Smith's engagement in these businesses was as president and that the boards that supported him were also comprised of Latter-day Saint ecclesiastical officers. This information shocked and dismayed his audience. The 1887 Edmunds-Tucker Act had dissolved the church and confiscated its property, not returning it until 1894 and only in part. Yet from Smith's testimony, merely ten years later the church appeared to be no worse for the experience and was back in control. Such testimony could have only added to the fear of the church's imperviousness to federal authority and the suspicion that it was less than forthcoming about the actual extent of its holdings.[19] Neither does it appear that the church was averse to extending its economic power. In December 1903, one month before the Smoot hearing began, Smith directed the consolidation of transportation and power companies in Salt Lake City and Ogden that gave the church control over street railways in two of Utah's most populous cities and electric power plants in the state's two most populous counties.[20]

Equally as distressing as the church's commercial dominance was its apparent political control in the West. Judge Orlando W. Powers, Gentile lawyer, resident of Utah for nineteen years, and former associate justice of its supreme court, testified that "from the earliest history of the Mormon Church it has been more or less a political institution." Powers explained that the church's history of conflict with the American people and government made it at best disinterested in and at worst hostile to "our national policies." Moreover, since most church members had emigrated from the "Old World" and were, therefore, "unacquainted with our institutions and our system of government," there was no impediment to their being "taught to look up to and follow the leaders of the Mormon Church." They were, he said, easily instructed in "the necessity of obeying counsel . . . of not questioning that which may be said to you by men claiming to be inspired." As evidence, Judge Powers described naturalization hearings of Latter-day Saint immigrants who insisted repeatedly that they would obey the authorities of the L.D.S. Church, even if in conflict with the law of the United States.[21]

The most electric revelation from the hearing was that polygamy was still practiced. Despite efforts by the church to keep it secret, examples of post-Manifesto polygamy were generally known by Utahans. Several witnesses testified to the post-Manifesto marriages of four of the quorum and to cohabitation by virtually all of the rest. In addition, the protestants produced testimony that four apostles had performed plural marriages for the general membership: John W. Taylor, George Teasdale, Matthias Cowley, and Marriner W. Merrill.[22] Evidence of new polygamy shocked the country and produced an emotional response that swamped Smoot's defense. Utah's delegate in the House of Representatives warned a friend in Utah, "It looks more serious for the Mormon people than they seem to realize at home. It is summed up in this: The question is not, Shall Reed Smoot keep his seat in the Senate? but, Shall the Mormon Church be declared an alien organization, and its members unfit to hold the rights of citizenship?"[23]

It was not a given, however, that Smoot should be held accountable for the actions of his co-religionists. Even those unsympathetic to him thought this a violation of his rights and corrosive of religious liberty for all. "Mormonism is bad if not rotten," opined the *Independent* magazine, "but bad men have political rights. The cure for Idaho or Utah is religious, and educational, and social, not political."[24] *Harper's Weekly* worried,

> In other words, a majority of the Committee on Privileges and Elections will ask the United States Senate to declare that no man holding a post of honor and power in the Mormon hierarchy is eligible to a seat in either House of the Federal Legislature. This, although he is admitted to be personally innocent of any violation of a State or Federal law. Is the establishment of such a precedent by the Senate reconcilable with the third section of Article VI of the Federal constitution, which provides that no religious test shall ever be required as a qualification to any office or public trust under the United States? . . . Where religious duty and duty to civil power conflict, as might conceivably be the case in the minds of Roman Catholics, could more be required constitutionally of a Catholic citizen than personal obedience to the law? This is a question the seriousness of which will be recognized by statesmen who have an eye to future contingencies.[25]

Opponents were not without a persuasive rebuttal, however. An exchange between competing editorialists in Poughkeepsie, New York, captures the contrasting views inspired by Smoot's trial. The *Daily Eagle* announced, "We think it is high time that the American people . . . realized just what all this talk means. It means simply that a man is to be excluded from public office because he believes things which we do not believe." The *Eagle*'s voice was the minority. Two days later the *Poughkeepsie Press* retorted, "Much that the *Eagle* says about the rights of men to freedom of conscience is excellent, although there are a few left in this bigoted age who do not recognize freedom of conscience as a license to violate the statutes and outrage the decent sense of the whole nation."[26] As in Poughkeepsie, so also in the Senate and the nation. Minority scruples over personal conscience and religious liberty were overwhelmed initially by the majority's fear of Mormon lawlessness. As Chairman Burrows told Smoot, "It is the Mormon Church that we intend to investigate, and we are going to see that these men obey the law."[27]

Two kinds of unlawful conduct were put at issue by the protestants: polygamy and unlawful cohabitation. Polygamy had been statutorily forbidden since the Morrill Act of 1862.[28] Because the church claimed that it did not keep written records of marriages, however, polygamy was practically impossible to prove, and convictions were virtually nonexistent. Latter-day Saint juries were disinclined to find guilt on any evidence, much less the circumstantial kind, and cooperating witnesses were not to be found. Consequently, in 1882 Congress passed the Edmunds Act, which created a category of crime named "unlawful cohabitation" and which was provable by inferences from social conduct.

The ultimate goal of the antipolygamy laws was not merely to proscribe sexual activity among multiple partners but also to enforce the regnant concept of American marriage as a partnership between one man and one woman. Certainly, polygamy's sexual dimension was its most scandalous and titillating aspect. But antipolygamy sentiment was equally aroused by the assumed negative social and psychological effects of plural marriage on women, the moral wellspring of the home and, thereby, of the nation. Consequently, antipolygamy law was intended to delegitimize plural marriage in all its dimensions as a domestic partnership. This was the purpose of the new crime of unlawful cohabitation and its application to a variety of behaviors that permitted the inference of a marriage. As one exasperated Utah judge instructed an otherwise law-abiding Mormon lay bishop, "You shall not cohabit and live with your plural wives as your wife, must not hold her out to the public, and your associations must not be such as the people who are unacquainted with your relations would naturally infer that you were husband and wife." The judge insisted, however, that the defendant's duty as a father was unchanged because "the limitations on your conduct that the law imposes are not such that you shall not visit there to look after your children in times of distress and sickness, but you are expected to give them your care and attention." In sum, a father must maintain his relationship with his children but not with his children's mother. "The law does not expect and will not permit you," the judge emphasized, "to go and cohabit with the woman as your wife and rear children by her; to be plain about it, to occupy the same couch and live and sleep with her and associate with her as your wife."[29] Visiting as a father but not as a husband was easier said than done, of course. As one non-Mormon witness testified during the Smoot hearing, "If they go there, if they visit the home, this other thing is bound to occur."[30] The protestants did not take such a lenient view of human nature, however, and believed any argument to the contrary a ruse to mask sexual license. Robert Tayler, counsel for the protestants, demanded of Joseph F. Smith, "Do you consider it an abandonment of your family to maintain relations with your wives except that of occupying their beds?" Smith replied, "I do not wish to be impertinent, but I should like the gentleman to ask any woman, who is a wife, that question."[31]

Smith would not budge from his assertion that pre-Manifesto marriages, including his own, were legitimate and that the families produced by them had a higher claim on the Latter-day Saints than did the civil law. The fact that these unions, including Smith's, had continued to produce children was especially galling to Senator Burrows, chairman of the committee, who challenged Smith's representation that he was law-abiding. Burrows interrupted Senator Beveridge to demand of the witness, "Do you obey the law in having five wives at this time and having them bear you eleven children since the Manifesto of 1890?" Smith attempted to answer, "Mr. Chairman, I have not claimed that in that case I have obeyed the law of the land." The chairman interposed, "That is all." Smith doggedly continued, "I do not claim so, and I have said before that I prefer to stand my chances against the law." To which the chairman huffed, "Certainly." But Smith hung on for the last word: "rather than abandon my children and their mothers. That is all there is to it."[32] The newspapers reported that Smith's testimony "displayed a spirit of defiance to the Senate and to the United States government. He said almost in so many words that it was none of the business of the rest of the world what the people do in the state of Utah so long as they do not actually contract plural marriages."[33]

Smith's sore temper on the subject of plural marriage was a function of his experience. During the 1880s, increased numbers of federal agents conducted "cohab hunts" or raids on Latter-day Saint settlements to arrest polygamists. Julina Lambson remembered it as a time when "our families were scattered and, to obey the laws of the land, changes were made in our family customs, which grieved us all."[34] Her husband, Joseph F. Smith, called it "the reign of Judicial Terror."[35] Eventually more than 1,300 L.D.S. men and women were fined and assigned to prisons in Arizona, Michigan, South Dakota, Idaho, and Utah.[36] The extent of the practice of polygamy in the Latter-day Saint community was virtually impossible to calculate under the circumstances. Modern scholars have arrived at various estimates. A reliable summary is provided by Thomas Alexander: "At present, perhaps the best estimates of the number of polygamous families among late-nineteenth-century Latter-day Saints range between 20 and 30 percent. Nevertheless, studies of individual communities show a wide variation in the incidence of plurality."[37] By 1904 these percentages had been reduced, but it is impossible to tell by how much. Understandably, the issue was hotly contested during the Smoot hearing. Smith testified that "only about 3 or 4 percent of the entire male population of the church have entered into that principle." Senator and former federal marshal Fred Dubois argued that this was merely the number convicted.[38] Popular belief among the Latter-day Saints reversed this percentage. A relative confided in Smoot's secretary that "when he went into polygamy, it was popular 'all the rage'; all worthy men entered 'the principle', and monogamy was a badge of unworthiness. . . . He said this tack about 2% of the people only having gone into polygamy was all untrue; that at one time that was nearer the proportion of the marriageable persons not polygamists."[39]

Pursuing information on domestic arrangements was a thankless task for some and a satisfying crusade for others in Latter-day Saint communities. "Mind your business" became part of the Latter-day Saint creed during a time when bribes were offered to anyone who would testify against another, the credibility of accusers went untested, and the presumption of innocence was reversed.[40] Because bounties were offered for information leading to arrest of church leaders, the majority lived in hiding or out of the country for years at a time. Wives, too, "went on the underground" to avoid federal marshals who would force them to testify against their husbands. The effects of the law were, as intended, thoroughly disruptive of Latter-day Saint society and morale. A polygamist wife later described the period in her autobiography:

> It is difficult to picture the unsettled conditions in Utah and Idaho during the raid against polygamists. Homes were broken up and families scattered among relatives or friends. . . . Some had secret hiding places in their own homes; others trained the children to watch for the Deputy Marshal, and to evade or deceive when asked questions by strangers or deputies about family relations. If people were at any public gatherings and the federal marshal entered the town, there was a scattering of local Church authorities. . . . Mothers ran with their babies to the neighbors; old men took to the fields. . . . It was almost impossible for a stranger, who may have had only innocent motives, to get any reliable information about resident members of a town, because of the suspicious attitude of the citizens and their aversion to answering questions.[41]

One mother instructed her children to say that, if asked, "they didn't know what their name was; they didn't know where they lived; they didn't know who their dad or mother was."[42] Church officials, too, engaged in "double speak" about the doctrine of plural marriage, especially after the 1890 Manifesto. Increasingly, they avoided reference to it where non-Mormons were likely to be present and denied its practice when asked. Obfuscation and even prevarication appears to have become commonplace when dealing with federal officials and the national press. The campaign for and against polygamy made Utah a society of deceivers and snoops.

As the majority of polygamous families aged, cohabitation was increasingly a crime of relationship inferred from otherwise innocent conduct, such as visiting too often or too late, giving gifts to ostensibly unrelated children, or being seen at public gatherings with different women. Persons best able to observe such quotidian events were also least inclined to prosecute. J. W. N. Whitecotton, attorney for Smoot's bank in Provo and sympathetic non-Mormon witness, explained to the Senate committee, "When it comes [to] . . . making complaint against a neighbor . . . it calls up to us all these things of an unpleasant character among neighbors; throwing the only support the women have into the penitentiary maybe, or taking the substance of the man to pay the fine. It makes a man hesitate, and a man who would do that must be a man peculiarly made for seeing nothing but the law."[43] The non-Mormon chair of Utah's Republican Party expressed an even more lenient view when cross-examined by Senator Dubois, who asked him incredulously, "Mr. Booth, do you not understand that these children who are now being born into the world in this polygamous relation come into the world contrary to the laws of God and man?" Booth replied, "Well, they do contrary to the laws of man. The other law is not so well defined and definitely settled as to enable me to testify concerning it. . . . I would despise a man who would abandon these women."[44] Even the otherwise anti-Mormon witness Orlando Powers said of the Latter-day Saints, "They are a God-fearing people, and it has been a part of their faith and their life. Now, to the eastern people their manner of living is looked upon as immoral. Of course it is, viewed from their standpoint. Viewed from the standpoint of a Mormon it is not. The Mormon wives are as sincere in their belief in polygamy as the Mormon men, and they have no more hesitation in declaring that they are one of several wives of a man than a good woman in the East has in declaring that she is the single wife of a man."[45]

While they did not endorse polygamy, most non-Mormons who lived among the Latter-day Saints believed in their sincerity and agreed with them as to their familial duties. Moreover, these neighbors were convinced that the practice of polygamy was moribund and, if not given further energy by persecution, would be quashed by the church's younger generation. They believed time, not prosecution, was the preferred cure for polygamy. The national reform movements, however, were convinced that local tolerance was the cause of new polygamy. They advocated a more exacting standard of enforcement. As Burrows told Smoot, "If a man was seen with a plural wife he was guilty of polygamy."[46] To the Senate committee chairman and the protestants, Joseph F. Smith's defense of cohabitation was an act of defiance and his homes were "houses of prostitution."[47] The reformers recognized, however, that Utah could not be compelled to enforce laws against polygamy and unlawful cohabitation. Having joined the union of states, Utah's citizens had the power to govern themselves within constitutional limits.

As the testimony of post-Manifesto polygamy and cohabitation continued to mount during the trial, those concerned about Utah's lackadaisical enforcement called for revocation of the state's charter on the grounds it had entered the union on false pretenses. No one knew exactly how to do that, however, and few, even among those willing to punish Smoot for his church, wanted the entire state penalized.[48] Most were content with demanding a constitutional amendment, modeled on the Idaho test-oath statute, that would disfranchise persons who belonged to an organization that espoused the practice. The *Buffalo Express* editorialized, "The facts brought out by this investigation call, not so much for the expulsion of Smoot, as for a constitutional amendment which will really stop the practice of polygamy in Utah."[49] By separate letters, two of Smoot's political contacts advised him that a constitutional amendment was likely. One had information that the committee would recommend "passing Constitutional amendment providing that 'Congress shall be given exclusive jurisdiction over all matters pertaining to marriage and divorce, with power to legislate in any manner to carry out its provisions' and that TR has seen draft amendment."[50] The other warned that some were lobbying the committee "to the effect that the only way to solve this Mormon problem is to disfranchise our people. There is but very little question, but the majority of these fellows are working for a Constitutional amendment to that effect. If they fail in the attempt to unseat you they hope to have raised such a storm that the committee will be forced to recommend an anti-polygamy amendment to the Constitution."[51]

The protestants' hope that the Smoot hearing would galvanize the public over Mormon lawlessness was being realized in the early months of 1904, during Joseph F. Smith's testimony. *Goodwin's Weekly* observed, "The people of this country are being stirred to the depths over this attempt to push into the Senate a man who holds another government as more binding upon him than the government under which he is born."[52] The Senate, too, was outraged. "The admissions made by President Smith were received with astonishment by the committee," reported the *New*

"Portrait of a Latter-day Saint," *Collier's Weekly*, 26 March 1904. Joseph F. Smith's testimony in defense of plural marriage did not endear him to the public. In this cartoon, illustrator Charles Dana Gibson captured the animosity directed toward Smith by portraying him as a dissipated and convicted criminal. Courtesy of LDS Family and Church History Library.

PORTRAIT OF A LATTER-DAY SAINT
DRAWN BY CHARLES DANA GIBSON

York Times. "Evidently the Senators had not believed the allegations that had been made against the Mormons."[53] Of course, Senator Smoot had been working the halls for months to achieve this end, but Smith's testimony undid his efforts in a matter of days. "If a vote could be taken at the present time," reported the *Chicago Daily Tribune*, "Senator Smoot would be expelled almost unanimously. There might be a few on either side of the chamber who would hold out for certain legal forms, but it is believed few senators could resist the strong tide of public opinion."[54]

The day before the hearing began, Smoot's young secretary Carl Badger wrote in his journal, "The answer [to the protestants' new charges against church leaders] seems a very difficult one to meet. The contradictions at home are peculiar, and if they hold the Senator responsible for them out he will go."[55] "Contradictions" was Badger's euphemism for the fact that, while the church maintained an official policy against polygamy,

CARL A. BADGER.

Carl A. Badger. Badger, Smoot's secretary, was a witness to each day's proceedings and privy to most of the negotiations between the senator and his colleagues in Washington and Salt Lake. Badger's letters to his wife Rose and his personal diary show the extremes of defiance and chagrin the hearing inspired in young, upwardly mobile Latter-day Saints. Courtesy of L. Tom Perry Special Collections, Harold B. Lee Library, Brigham Young University, Provo, Utah.

its members continued to practice it. The Latter-day Saints had lived with such contradictions for a long time. Only the young among them, like Badger, could think the contradictions "peculiar." They did not have the history to recognize in these contradictions the church's traditional defense for its practice of plural marriage. As early as 1835, church officers had issued a formal statement on marriage, providing in part that "inasmuch as this Church of Christ has been reproached with the crime of fornication and polygamy, we declare that we believe that one man should have one wife, and one woman but one husband." [56] The assertion was true only in the most technical sense. If "we" were construed to apply to the church collectively and not its members individually, "we" were not practicing polygamy. Similar denials were published in 1837 and 1838. [57] Church president Joseph Smith appears to have practiced polygamy as early as 1833, but he did not institutionalize the practice until the early 1840s and, even then, only among a select group of church authorities. Smith was absent when the articles on marriage were announced and endorsed by an assembly of the church, but he knew of them and probably directed others to draft them.[58]

In 1890 a similar strategy was used in the Manifesto, which provided, "I [Wilford Woodruff] hereby declare my intentions to submit to those laws, and to use my influence with the members of the Church over which I preside to have them do likewise."[59] By its terms, the Manifesto did not explicitly commit the church to any course of conduct. It merely advised church members to obey the law of the land. The logical and, no doubt, intended inference to outsiders was that Woodruff was acting in his official capacity as president to dictate church policy. To insiders, the message was simply a continuation of the policy under which many had lived for fifty-five years. It was an announcement that members were to take personal responsibility for deciding whether to obey the law of their god or their government. Thus, in 1899 the apostolic quorum could agree that "a man must take care of his family, but he must be responsible for his own acts."[60]

Records of quorum meetings show also that, as late as October 1903, Apostle Marriner W. Merrill exhorted his younger brethren to take additional wives.[61] Though President Joseph F. Smith had left the meeting prior to Merrill's comments, based on the remarks of others and evidence of marriages authorized by him after the Manifesto, it is probable he would not have objected to Merrill's exhortation. For example, Matthias Cowley instructed a local church leader "in confidence that it was not the policy of Prest. Joseph F. Smith to censure any man for entering the order of plural marriage since the days of the Manifesto, provided he had acted wisely and done so with the sanction and by the authority of the proper authority."[62] Many such indications exist in private letters and journals that polygamy was being preached and practiced by Latter-day Saint leadership in the early twentieth century. Probably the most telling evidence is from quorum minutes taken on the day after Smoot filed his answer to the protest and eleven days before opening arguments. One of the eight apostles present reported, "The principle topic of discussion was the present agitation in Congress. . . . The brethren were cautioned not to exercise the keys of sealing in plural marriage at present and to be wise and prudent in all their doings."[63]

The consequences of exposure were clear. "'Anyone who enters the Principle [of plural marriage] these days must bear his own burden,'" Apostle John W. Taylor is reputed to have said. "'I have been charged. If I can't protect myself, I will be dropped from the Quorum.'"[64] He was right. When evidence of new polygamous marriages was produced at the Smoot hearing, church lawyer Franklin D. Richards wrote Smoot, "I feel sure of one thing that if half of what is rumored . . . is true, they [Apostles Taylor and Matthias F. Cowley] have done a great wrong to their brethren and to the church and they, not the church, will eventually have to answer for it. I feel sorry for them, but they must take the consequences, I must defend the church."[65] Although evidence during the Smoot hearing showed that four apostles had performed new plural marriages, Teasdale's and Merrill's advanced age and ill health had made Taylor and Cowley more suitable targets for Senate attention. When Taylor and Cowley gave no reason for avoiding Senate subpoena power, the "great wrong" of new polygamy was attached to them with additional force. For Latter-day Saint attorney Richards, however, the wrong of performing new plural marriages was compounded by getting caught. Taylor and Cowley had committed the "great wrong" of putting the church at risk.

In addition to attempting to protect the church by treating it as a corporate entity with an existence separate from the activities of its directors and officers, church leaders endeavored also to shield the church's president and his counselors from both direct knowledge of and public accountability for the continuing practice of polygamy.[66] As a consequence, the church's presidency could advise Smoot, "We telegraphed you to deny knowledge of violations of law on the part of the Presidency and Apostles. We did so judging you by ourselves, for we could not say that *we knew* of any one of them violating the laws of the State and we did not think you knew of any either. If there be violations they are not by the counsels of the church, but contrary to our counsel, and therefore the law-breakers, if any there be, must be held responsible for their own acts."[67]

Because Smoot's diary for these years is missing, his feelings about this defense cannot be known. Seven years later, however, when the church was again accused of new polygamy, Smoot recorded in his journal that his brethren "seem to think that the fact that the church has not approved or sanctioned the marriages [means] it cannot be held responsible for them."[68] Smoot did not "seem" to agree, but he did not break ranks publicly during the contest over his seat. His formal answer to the protest stipulated that *the church* had abandoned "belief in the practice of polygamy and belief in and practice of polygamous cohabitation. . . . Where continued it is on the sole responsibility of such persons, and subject to the penalties of the law."[69]

Though church leaders were intent upon maintaining the defense that they were acting individually in exercising their priestly authority to perform marriages, church control over these men and their constant counseling with one another made their position untenable. For those who heard the testimony, it was simply unbelievable that this close-knit group of fifteen men, bound by work, faith, and even familial kinship, did not know the identity and number of one another's wives and whether their marriages had occurred after 1890. More than unbelievable, the testimony was at times absurd. When Apostle Marriner Merrill was proved too ill to testify, his adult son Charles Merrill was put in the docket. Asked whether his father had married him to his plural wife, Charles testified, "I do not know that he knew that I was living with a wife [already]." Charles had to admit, however, that he and his plural wife lived across the street from his mother, one of his father's six wives, who did know of her son's domestic arrangements. Charles could "not remember him [his father] ever being present when she [Charles's plural wife] was there."[70] Hearing such testimony made Smoot's secretary admit, "I feel sick sometimes and sometimes I just feel unwell. The Committee is insisting that John W. [Taylor] and Brother Cowley come and they ought to, but I do not want them to come and lie, and I do not know whether I want them to tell the truth. So there you are,—the devil and the deep sea."[71]

Since trial attorneys are schooled to ask only those questions to which they know the answer already, witnesses are given only a choice between confession or perjury. Thus trials, especially political trials, foster those "forms of lying [that] are ethically permissible and [demonstrate] how to lie in the most enlightened, constructive, successful, pleasurable, and humane ways possible."[72] For all the litigants, the Smoot hearing was rife with moral dilemmas, the more so because each party felt the stakes were high and each thought the other was a superior power. The church saw in its opponents the might of the national government and a cabal of Protestant agencies. The protestants believed they were tackling "an oligarchy working under an autocrat beside whom the Czar is a weakling."[73]

Moreover, each side was conscious of being at war with the other. The Senate decided not to subpoena polygamous wives and their children because "it was not desired to 'make war on women and children.'"[74] For their part, the Latter-day Saints referred to Washington as "the seat of war."[75] This attitude affected their assumptions of what was morally permissible under the circumstances. A few years later, on trial before his brethren for his church membership, Apostle Matthias Cowley reminded them that the church's ethics were situational: "I am not dishonest and not a liar and have always been true to the work and to the brethren[, but] . . . we have always been taught that when the brethren were in a tight place that it would not be amiss to lie to help them out."[76] But for the fact that the Latter-day Saints are a religious group battling on religious grounds, their deception on the subject of polygamy would be so predictable as to escape comment. As Sissela Bok concluded in her classic study on the subject of lying, "If the designation of a foe is open, as in a declaration of war, deception is likely to be expected on all sides. While it can hardly be said to be consented to, it is at least known and often acquiesced in."[77] Or, as observed by the press during the hearing, "the non-Mormon witnesses in the rear of the committee room chuckled as the clever parrying proceeded and the head of the church was brought nearer and nearer to where he must make a direct reply." Even Robert Tayler's "impassive countenance lighted up at the clever maneuvering."[78] The Smoot hearing provides a classic example of deception by foes or "clever maneuvering."

Only one of the protestants was placed in the docket: Edward B. Critchlow, a former assistant U.S. attorney who drafted and signed the Smoot protest. Thus the protestants' vulnerability under oath was limited. Still, no less than the accused, Critchlow exemplified the witness who is led to make admissions against his own interests. For Critchlow this meant testifying that Protestant churches were active in Utah politics and some Latter-day Saints had opposed Smoot's election without suffering church sanction. He admitted to campaigning for polygamist apostle John Henry Smith and for failing to prosecute polygamists during his tenure as U.S. attorney. He contradicted himself on the extent of L.D.S. Church control over its members. Finally, he admitted that the protest against Smoot was religiously motivated and dominated by clergy.[79] Secretary Badger was there to record Critchlow's undoing: "In regard to church influence it was made strongly to appear that the Salt Lake Ministerial Alliance has been just as much in politics, and as successful, as it is claimed the Mormon church has been. I, for one, felt like forgiving Critchlow for all of his meanness when he gave away his case with such readiness, he owned up like a gentleman even though it knocked a hole in the bottom of his tongue, he had a rather sickly smile on his face before he got through though."[80] In their conduct of the case, however, the protestants were not so "gentlemanly." For example, though they had stipulated in 1903 that Rev. John Luther Leilich's claim of polygamy against Smoot was false, the protestants later used the same allegation to reopen the hearing. They also padded the evidence. Smoot's only recorded outburst during the entire hearing came when Charles Mostyn Owen, the protestants' investigator and Utah's resident rumormonger, introduced a list of persons whom he represented to be polygamists. At that point, Badger was delighted to tell his wife, the always reserved Smoot "leaned over and called Owen a 'liar' and Owen told the Senator he was not a gentleman." Though Owen "said [his list] did not contain any mistakes. The truth," Badger claimed, "is that it contains many."[81]

Press reports show that even among the Senate committee, veracity was sometimes challenged: "The hearing was enlivened by a controversy between Senators Hoar and Foraker, who renewed their recent scrap on the floor of the Senate, and each informed the other in parliamentary terms that he was not speaking the truth."[82] Later, Senator Beveridge would call his chairman "'a damn liar'" for inferring that Smoot had a second wife and telling the committee that the rules permitted it to gather "secret evidence, not under oath, and which the Senator [Smoot] has no opportunity of meeting by cross-examination."[83]

There is no question, however, that the Latter-day Saint witnesses were most often backed onto the moral ropes of the fight. A close reading of the record permits the conclusion that Joseph F. Smith was sufficiently concerned for his personal integrity and skilled in casuistry to avoid lying outright. But it is obvious that he intentionally misled his interlocutors and used every conceivable strategy to deceive and frustrate them. For example, Smith was asked whether he performed the rumored plural marriage of then deceased apostle Abraham H. Cannon. Burrows phrased the question carefully: "When you were in Los Angeles and went out to an island [with Cannon and company] . . . was any ceremony performed by you?" The reference to "any ceremony" was an attempt, no doubt, to prevent evasion on whether and what kind of a marriage was performed. Yet Smith was able to answer absolutely, "No, sir . . . none whatever," because Cannon's marriage appears to have been performed in Salt Lake City by Smith.[84] And so it went throughout all six days of Smith's testimony. When asked to enumerate the wives of absent apostle Grant, Smith answered, "only two that I know of," telling the committee only what it already knew from Grant's indiscreet donation four months earlier. Chairman Burrows interjected, "Only two?" Smith replied tersely, "Only two. Pardon me for saying 'that I know of,' Mr. Chairman. I am like other men; I only know what I know."

It appears that Smith's standard of knowledge was rigidly empirical. Smoot's attorney returned to the issue three days later, and Smith answered, "All I know about it, sir, is that these men who are in the polygamous status with myself take their own chances individually as to the consequences of living with or abstaining from living with their families.

They are amenable to the law." Worthington noticed the evasion and replied, "That does not answer my question. . . . What knowledge [do] you have . . . in any way—as to whether or not they are actually cohabiting with more than one woman?" Smith responded, "Not having inquired into the matter at all, I am really not in a position to say. I do not know." As indicated, it is also clear that Smith did his best not to know. In 1900 Smith had written a colleague, "I know nothing about his [Benjamin Cluff, who would be come a subject of the Smoot hearing] domestic arrangements nor do I want to, the less I know about some things the better for me at least and perhaps for others concerned. . . . My motto is and always has been to protect to the uttermost in my power the rights and the secrets, if secrets there may be, of my friends and the friends of the kingdom of God."[85]

With respect to the critical question of whether the L.D.S. Church continued to practice polygamy, Smith testified repeatedly that "there never has been a plural marriage by the consent or sanction or knowledge or approval of the church since the Manifesto."[86] Later he said, "I wish to say again, Mr. Chairman, that there have been no plural marriages solemnized by and with the consent or by the knowledge of the Church of Jesus Christ of Latter-Day Saints by any man, I do not care who he is."[87] The next day he repeated, "Let me say to you, Mr. Senator [Beveridge]— I have said it, but I repeat it—there has not [been] any man, with the consent or knowledge of approval of the church, [who] ever married a plural wife since the Manifesto."[88] Thus, to the critical question of whether post-Manifesto polygamous marriages had been performed, Smith employed repeatedly the traditional distinction between the church and its members. In doing so, he belied the fact that he himself had performed such marriages. As protestor E. B. Critchlow testified, "When he [Smith] says that plural marriages have stopped, I understand him to use the words in a different sense from what I would use them, or anyone else would use them."[89] But neither opposing counsel nor the committee was able to shake Smith from his testimony.

Smith was equally sophisticated and resolute in answering a second set of questions that put him between a meaner devil and a deeper sea than did concerns about post-Manifesto polygamy. These questions had to do with the nature of church authority in general and Smith's power in particular. The protestants had placed these issues at the heart of their complaint against Smoot. L.D.S. Church leaders exercise, said the written protest, "supreme authority, divinely sanctioned, to shape the belief and control the conduct of those under them in all matters whatsoever, civil and religious, temporal and spiritual."[90] Polygamy was only the most obvious example of the strength and perversity of Mormonism's priestly hierarchy. The real problem, according to the protestants, was the prophetic and priestly character of the L.D.S. Church. The insult of the Latter-day Saints' "visible oneness" was directly related to the political injury of their conflation of the temporal and spiritual. This allegation required the committee to consider matters normally exempt from political inquiry—sometimes to the discomfort of its own members. Senator Bailey, troubled by the extended cross-examination of Smith on matters of belief, interjected, "Before we proceed any further, I assume that all these questions connected with the religious faith of the Mormon Church are to be shown subsequently to have some relation to civil affairs." Senator Hoar, without disagreement from his colleagues, simply instructed the senator from Texas that "what we might think merely civil or political they deem religious matters."[91]

The problem of Mormonism's "externality of the kingdom of God" was compounded by the Latter-day Saints believing themselves led by one who spoke for God. Though titled "president," the head of the church was considered by the faithful to have all the rights and powers of an Old Testament prophet, priest, and king. It did not matter that all male members of the church were considered priests. Because they were organized hierarchically in a system that culminated in the designation of a living prophet, the Latter-day Saints seemed to have achieved a "visible oneness [that] is the very essence of popery."[92] To Protestants, this "foreign," even "barbarian" conception of church, analogous to Roman Catholicism but worse, natively American, made the Latter-day Saints primarily loyal to their prophet and, thus, fundamentally disloyal to their nation. "The only reason why they do not rise up in revolt against the United States government is because they are too infinitesimally weak. At heart they are all traitors," said a non-Mormon resident of Utah to a Michigan newspaper.[93]

That the Latter-day Saints espoused a different order of marriage may have put them in violation of law. That they violated the law in obedience to a higher authority—not in heaven, but on earth—made them lawless. And it made Smoot a representative of a competing authority in the national legislature. America's Mormon Problem was a conflict of laws, not merely of morals. While the battle was joined over differences in marital ethic and order, the war itself was over the Saints' nondemocratic, nonrational system of authority expressed through prophets and prophecy. Hence the senators found themselves uncomfortably, but necessarily, entangled in questions of "religious faith" when trying to determine whether the Saints were loyal to their god or their country.[94]

The subject of conflicting authorities was introduced by prosecuting attorney Tayler, who questioned Smith "as to the method in which a revelation is received and its binding or authoritative force upon the people." Smith responded that the "guidance" he received from God was "the same as any other member of the church."[95] Moreover, he said, all members of the church were free to accept or reject any revelation presented to them by their prophet. Revelation was not binding upon the church by virtue merely of its enunciation by the hierarchy, but only upon acceptance by vote of the congregation, and even then some latitude was allowed. Smith emphasized that all may receive divine guidance through "the spirit of revelation." Similarly, he portrayed Smoot's authority as "no more than [that of] any other member of the church, except as a body or a council of the church."[96] With the unwelcome help of Senator Hoar, Smith admitted he knew of no revelation from church leadership that had been rejected by church members as a whole.

Chairman Burrows and Senator Overman wanted to know what happened to individuals who disagreed: Are they "unchurched"? To the extent they were, Smith answered, they "unchurched themselves . . . by not accepting [the revelation]." The remainder of the exchange bounced back and forth between equally frustrated and frustrating answers and questions. Finally Senator Hoar declared, "The point is, which, as a matter of obligation, is the prevalent authority, the law of the land or the revelation?" Smith replied, "Well, perhaps the revelation would be paramount." Hoar erupted, "Perhaps? Do you think 'perhaps' is an answer to that?" Smith tried again: "With another man the law would be accepted, and this was the condition the people of the Church were in until the Manifesto settled the question." At this point Smoot's attorney Worthington tried to bail him out: "Let me ask you a question in that connection." Hoar would not allow it. "I had not quite gotten through, Mr. Worthington," Hoar warned. Worthington begged the senator's pardon, and Hoar resumed: "I want to go a little farther. Suppose you should receive a divine revelation, communicated to and sustained by your church, commanding your people to-morrow to do something forbidden by the law of the land. Which would it be their duty to obey?"[97]

To answer this question, Smith had to find a way to rationalize convincingly the subordination of prophecy to democracy and do so without undermining L.D.S. Church order. Theoretically, all Americans would have agreed with the Latter-day Saints, as Belva Lockwood pointed out in a public letter of refusal to sign an anti-Smoot petition: "You say that the Mormon church claims to be superior to the government. So do all orthodox churches, and the thirteen united colonies were founded on the principle that conscience is superior to law, and I say to you that although a law-abiding woman and a lawyer by profession for twenty-five years, whenever a law impinges on my conscience, as the old Fugitive Slave law did, it is conscience first and not the law. God is above the law and the constitution."[98] What the Smoot hearing makes clear is that while God may be above the Constitution, churches are not.

As devout men themselves with strong ties to their respective denominations, the senators on the committee could pursue their questioning of Smith and other Latter-day Saint witnesses because they had a naive confidence in the compatibility of church and state. Senator Bailey spoke for his colleagues when he asked rhetorically, "Is not a man's duty as a citizen perfectly consistent with any conception that exists in this country of his religious duty?"[99] The committee's lack of identification with the predicament of the Latter-day Saint witnesses may also reflect the senators' low opinion of Mormonism as a religion. "Any conception" of religious duty that conflicted with U.S. law was per se not truly religious or, in Rev. Meade Williams's terms "utterly foreign to that on which our Christendom has been built." Thus there could be no point of identification with the question posed to the Latter-day Saint witnesses: "Suppose you should receive a divine revelation, communicated to and sustained by your church, commanding your people to-morrow to do something forbidden by the law of the land. Which would it be their duty to obey?"[100] Smith gave the only possible answer under the circumstances: "They would be at liberty to obey just which they pleased."[101]

Smith's answer turned the protestants' argument back upon itself: the church could not force its members to obey the law of the land. Smith assured the committee that church members were "at liberty to obey just which they pleased. There is absolutely no compulsion." As has been described, this was the church's traditional, public position on plural marriage. In addition, Smith asserted that Latter-day Saint obedience to civil authority was one of its doctrinal tenets. He proffered scriptural support from Latter-day Saint canon: "Let no man break the laws of the land, for he that keepeth the laws of God hath no need to break the laws of the land."[102] This statement, like so much else in the trial, was a definitional bait-and-switch, however. What the committee heard and what Smith meant were most certainly two different things. In 1882, the same year the Edmunds Act was passed, Smith had interpreted this scripture differently for church members gathered in general conference. "The law of the land, which all have no need to break, is that law which is the Constitutional law of the land, and that is as God himself has defined it," said Smith. But, he noted with particular emphasis, "if lawmakers have a mind to violate their oath, break their covenants and their faith with the people, and depart from the provisions of the Constitution where is the law human or divine, which binds me, as an individual, to outwardly and openly proclaim my acceptance of their acts?"[103] In short, the divine injunction to the Latter-day Saints to obey U.S. civil law was limited to those laws that comported with the divinely inspired Constitution. Since the antipolygamy statutes violated the First Amendment, Smith stated in 1882, they need not be obeyed. Clearly, the Smoot hearing was not the place for Smith to state his theory of broken oaths of governance and nonbinding legislation.

Smith was answerable not only to the Senate committee but also to the Latter-day Saints, for whom his words were of critical importance. For their benefit and his own sense of integrity, no doubt, Smith consistently refused to apologize for his own family relations or, more generally, the Latter-day Saint belief in and practice of plural marriage. He reiterated also that the church's belief in plural marriage was based in revelation to its founding prophet. Antipolygamy law, he said, "did not change our belief at all."[104] Furthermore, when asked why the church was now willing to obey civil law instead of the revelation, Smith asserted that even the change in Latter-day Saint action was a response to their god, not their government. Senator Beveridge wanted to make sure he understood, asking, "Is the committee to understand that you and your church regard the law of the land as more binding upon your actions than your religious beliefs?" Smith responded, "No, sir: not in that sense. I understand that we are under injunction by the Manifesto not to practice plural marriage . . . not to continue plural marrying. Under that injunction we refrain from teaching it, inculcating it, and advocating it, and out of respect both to the law and to the Manifesto of President Woodruff."[105] In this manner, Smith attempted to appease the committee and not displease his people. As we shall see, in achieving the former, Smith failed at the latter. Publication of his characterization under oath of his office as inspirational, not revelatory, created a crisis for Smith when he returned home.

Moreover, the ten witnesses who followed Smith during the remainder of March 1904 were not as successful in walking the line between perjury and confession. Each in his or her own way provided evidence that plural marriage was still a way of life among many in the L.D.S. Church, especially its leadership. The witnesses included a woman who testified that an apostle performed her post-Manifesto polygamous marriage, an apostle who testified that he would have to defend the principle of plural marriage if it were assailed, and a former bishop who argued that he had committed adultery rather than admit to polygamy and gave Smoot the credit for his arrest. Of course, Smoot won a few victories, such as the testimony of the anti-Mormon Utahan who had to admit there was no difference between "good Methodist brothers" and Mormons with respect to political interference, except the latter were "more effectual."[106] At times even the participants could not resist laughing at the absurdity of the situation and the answers it inspired. But no one was amused by the increasing evidence during the first phase of the hearing that the nation still had a Mormon Problem. Indeed, through Smith's testimony the protestants had shown that the church's political, economic, and polygamous kingdom was largely intact though diminished since its zenith under Brigham Young.

The protestants squandered their advantage, however. Smith had set a high standard of sensational disclosure, and the protestants had trouble sustaining public interest in the witnesses who followed. Much of what was said was simply repetitious, and repetition robbed the case of its power to titillate. The public was further distracted by a hiatus in the proceedings. For fear the hearing would prejudice Roosevelt's campaign, Chairman Burrows's fellow Republicans convinced him to adjourn on 24 April 1904 and resume after fall elections. Democrats concurred for their own political reasons. In particular, the protestants' chief ally on the committee, Democratic senator Dubois of Idaho, hoped to use anti-Mormon sentiment to help his own reelection and, therefore, supported the delay.[107] The eight-month interruption in the proceedings broke the protestants' momentum and gave the Latter-day Saints much needed time to control the damage done in Washington and Salt Lake City during the first phase of the hearing.

The Church exists for the State, to maintain that

righteousness that exalteth a nation.

—*Rev. Bishop E. R. Hendrix*, Church Federation

THE COMMON GOOD

When the Senate committee reconvened in December 1904, the public's attention was elsewhere and had to be recaptured. The L.D.S. temple ceremony offered the best means for doing so. The original protest included the charge that Smoot had taken an oath in the Mormon temple that was incommensurate with his duties as a senator. All Latter-day Saint witnesses were adamant that there was nothing about the temple liturgy that affected their ability to serve the country, but they simultaneously refused to disclose the ceremony. To the Latter-day Saints the ceremony was sacred and not to be divulged to the uninitiated. To others it was a conspiratorial secret. Even those who were not suspicious were curious. When J. H. Wallis Sr., a disaffected church member, took the stand, the committee was poised to throw open the doors not only to Mormon bedrooms but to its temples as well, and most of America wanted a look.

Detective Charles Mostyn Owen catered to public curiosity by posing in temple clothing for the national press. The women's reform groups provided forums for his performance of the ceremony to the general public.[1] No doubt the protestants enjoyed ridiculing Mormon worship practices.

They had, however, a more serious point to make than Mormon eccentricity. Wallis was prepared to testify that temple-going Mormons took an oath of vengeance for the murder of Joseph Smith. Wallis restated the oath as best he remembered it: "That you and each of you do promise and vow that you will never cease to importune high heaven to avenge the blood of the prophets upon the nations of the earth or the inhabitants of the earth." Wallis returned to the stand two days later to correct himself, saying the oath applied not to the inhabitants of the "earth" but to "this nation."[2] There was much confusion throughout the hearing over whether the disputed practice was a vow or a prayer and, in either case, whether the protestants had produced an accurate representation of it. Nor was there evidence that the alleged sentiment had ever been acted on, at least recently, and certainly not by Senator Smoot.[3] Nevertheless, the apparent existence of the sentiment and its enshrinement in liturgy, even as an artifact from the Latter-day Saints' past, evidenced a continuing antipathy toward the nation and, even in its most benign form, showed a desire for anything but the common good. By the time the hearing adjourned for the Christmas holiday, most Americans were again convinced that the Utah senator should lose his seat. Carl Badger reported, "I have just read sixty-five clippings, and out of that number I find only about five that think that Senator Smoot would retain his seat."[4] An observer from the majority editorialized, "If Senator Smoot has been obliged . . . to take such oaths as described by witnesses, he cannot be received in the senate as one whose fidelity to country is undisputed. It is no longer a question of personal chastity with him. Whether the doctrine of polygamy is still upheld by the church leaders and followers is now a subordinate matter of the greater question of the relation of the church toward the country."[5]

Like polygamy, the temple ceremony represented a definitive aspect of the Mormon Problem. Whereas, for the protestants, plural marriage revealed Mormon lawlessness, the temple oath revealed the fundamentally flawed "relation of the church toward the country."[6] The Mormons did not share in the vision of America as the righteous empire and did not work for its establishment. To the contrary, the oath of vengeance showed that Mormons sought the triumph of their own institutions at the expense of the nation's. This was a direct reversal of the way religion was supposed to work in America.

American Protestantism's denominational variety was counterbalanced by its unified commitment to build a Christian nation. Contributing to this objective defined America's churches as good citizens and tacitly qualified them for the privileges of citizenship, namely, free exercise at home and protection abroad. The impulse to build an ideal Christian state had been expressed first in America through the sectarian efforts of the Puritans in the seventeenth century. One hundred and fifty years later, when the union of states required an accommodation of religious diversity, the Puritan ideal was invested in the nation as a whole by all Protestants. In particular, nineteenth-century American Protestantism found common cause in reviving the nation's religious sensibilities. Conversion not only saved the individual soul but also strengthened the nation's institutions and enlarged its boundaries. In particular, the attempt to convert America's frontier populations created a shared missionary enterprise that, for all its sectarian competition, expressed solidarity of purpose.[7]

In 1905 the Progressive Era version of Protestantism's common cause was given at the initial meeting of the Federation of Churches. The chair of the federation's business committee explained, "The Church exists for the State, to maintain that righteousness that exalteth a nation."[8] "Righteousness" for the nation was defined in terms of the various moral reform initiatives of the time, such as prohibition, Sunday closing laws, and various other efforts to "outlaw sin."[9] Dedication to these shared objectives was a principal means by which members of mainstream Protestantism both expressed their establishment credentials and recognized one another as legitimate constituents of America's religious economy and, hence, worthy of religious liberty under U.S. law.

The Latter-day Saints' estrangement from reform purposes was apparent in their iconoclastic mores and parochial sensibilities. In 1908 young Claton Rice, a recent graduate of Princeton Seminary, was assigned to the Presbyterian mission in southern Utah. Upon arriving he found it "doubly clear that the Mormon church with its constantly iterated statement that all other churches are apostate churches, would not cooperate with Protestant Christian bodies." Individually, too, the Latter-day Saints preferred to remain aloof from members of other faiths. In his memoir written several years later, Rice recalled, "'We are a peculiar people' was still a dominant theme in Mormon ward [congregation] meetings when Senator Smoot went to Washington. 'We are a persecuted people' continued to create emotional reactions which kept the gulf which divided Mormons and Gentiles dangerously deep." As a result, he concluded, "the average Mormon wanted to dress in his [temple] 'garments', pay his tithing, go on his mission, raise his family and center his loyalties in his church, and let the rest of the world go by save as he went out among the 'gentiles' on his mission."[10] Isolated by geography and religious conviction, the Latter-day

Anti–Woman's Christian Temperance Union rally in Provo, Utah, n.d. Utah
citizens did not appreciate being the targets of various reform movements.
A gathering in Smoot's hometown of Provo held its own counterrally to protest
the protest against its senator. Used by permission, Utah State Historical Society,
all rights reserved.

Saints had developed a closed community with an ethic of self-reliance
that made them appear selfishly interested only in their own welfare. Of
course, their goodwill toward the nation was further dampened by the
nation's treatment of them. Regardless, while they may have been generous and helpful in their personal relationships with outsiders, the Latter-
day Saints did not have a sense of shared purpose with other American
churches, and they certainly did not like the idea of a Protestant Christian
America.

Latter-day Saint inwardness was all the more obvious for its contrast
to mainstream Protestant investment in broad social welfare initiatives.
"We believe," said the organizers of the National Federation of Churches,
"that the great Christian bodies in our country should stand together and
lead in the discussion of, and give an impulse to, all great movements that

The Common Good 85

'make for righteousness' . . . [namely] the saloon, marriage and divorce, Sabbath desecration, the social evil, child labor, relation of labor to capital, the bettering of the conditions of the laboring classes, the moral and religious training of the young, the problem created by foreign immigration, and international arbitration."[11] The Latter-day Saints shared many of these concerns and used their influence locally to combat activities they deemed social vices. Nationally, however, they had a reputation for injuring the cause of righteousness by their marital practices, including relatively easy divorce, and by sponsoring immigration. These injuries were aggravated by the Latter-day Saints' failure to cooperate in such basic reform initiatives as public schooling.[12] Of course, the Latter-day Saints and other marginalized religions were not invited to participate in the Protestants' joint venture, and they were hesitant to participate for their own reasons, such as the Catholics' ambivalence toward modernism. Obviously, however, mutual antagonism was the chief cause of nonparticipation by non-Protestants. Or as noted by one editorialist, "For intelligent Mormons to find a common cause in the industrial upbuilding of the country with unembittered Gentiles has been made increasingly difficult."[13]

The Protestants had cause to distrust the citizenship skills of a group that had exploited its own outcast status so effectively as to create vigorous sociopolitical institutions that competed directly with those of righteous America. The Latter-day Saints had spent the nineteenth century building their church within the nation, not building the nation through their church. Countless Latter-day Saint sermons to this effect can be found, and many were introduced into the record of the Smoot hearing to show that the L.D.S. Church did not seek the welfare of America as an end in itself but to build its own kingdom within America and with the intention of eventually ruling the nation.[14] For the Smoot protestants and their sympathizers, Mormon nationalist aspirations were not yet history. Though statehood had dampened the church's hopes of complete autonomy, as recently as 1903 the flag of the "State of Deseret," the original ensign of Latter-day Saint pioneer government in the mountain West, was flown at the funeral of Apostle Brigham Young Jr. in Salt Lake City.[15] To be sure, this was a last gasp of political chauvinism, but it showed nevertheless that Mormons stood apart from, not together with, the American denominational churches whose purpose was to Christianize the nation.

Ironically, Protestant commitment to "social reconstruction in the interests of equity and justice" was a means of making room for the Latter-day Saints and other outsiders.[16] Once the Protestant missionary impulse was directed abroad to foreign missions and channeled into social welfare activities at home, marginalized American churches could more easily sponsor similar welfare initiatives that brought them within the definition of good citizenship. For example, the Latter-day Saints were praised for their quick reaction with food, clothing, and $100,000 in cash for victims of the 1906 San Francisco earthquake. During Joseph F. Smith's administration, the church began to make its welfare resources available for national emergencies and cooperated with international relief agencies such as the Red Cross. The church also began to accept aid from governmental sources, further harmonizing itself with the American way of life.[17]

As the Latter-day Saints showed a willingness to act for the common good, it became more difficult for mainstream Protestants to argue that Mormons were un-American and ought to be excluded from the privileges of citizenship. Meanwhile, representatives of other marginalized religions began to see that they had a stake in the outcome of the contest over Smoot's seat in the Senate. Catholics and their friends were especially quick to see the broader significance of the Smoot hearing. Former Senator McConnell of Idaho wrote to L.D.S. Church president Smith, "I consider this . . . a crisis in the history of our government. If we close the doors of the Senate today against Smoot why not against the members of the Catholic Church next session."[18] The Catholics, however, were not seeking to place one of their hierarchs in the national legislature. Therefore, the issue of conflict of laws and loyalties was embodied in the person of Apostle-senator Smoot.

The solution to the conflict, attorney Tayler suggested to Smoot, was for the apostle to abandon his church position to retain his Senate seat. Smoot responded, "I do not see any reason why I should resign. It does not interfere with my being a good citizen of the United States in any way, shape, or manner."[19] That was his story, and he was sticking to it. Smoot's apostolic mission to the Senate was to show that there was no conflict between his church and nation and that the Latter-day Saints could be fellow travelers with American Protestantism: patriotic, religiously tolerant, independent citizens who were committed to and capable of contributing to the commonwealth. Thus when Smoot began his defense, it was not only incumbent upon him to show that his church did not sanction post-Manifesto polygamy. He had to demonstrate also that the church was comprised of good citizens, both willing and able to promote American institutions and values.

Like representatives of other causes in Washington, Smoot was earnest, confident, optimistic, and even a little opportunistic. He believed in both material and spiritual progress and saw little distinction between the two. He was convinced that the new century should and would bring improvements in the human condition, through a strong domestic economy, an integration of industrial power with scientific discovery, and the discipline of managerial professionalism. Indeed, he was reared to believe there were no limits to human progress, except those imposed by sin, and thus he held himself to rigid moral standards and was a famously hardworking man.

In addition to his moral scrupulosity and Herculean capacity for work, Smoot had demonstrated a strict party loyalty that provided an acceptable alternative to his apostolic identity. His Senate colleagues found him "an apt pupil, safe, sober and steady" and "recognized that he was a lion for efficiency, a tiger for economy and a worm for detail."[20] They were pleased to learn that Smoot had performed few church assignments of a noncommercial nature and that these had been of short duration. "The only particular office that I ever held in the church," he testified, "was that of counselor."[21] This meant, secretary Badger rightly observed, that "viewed at close range . . . the Senator is reassuring in appearance."[22] Smoot himself must have been elated by news reports like the one in the *Brooklyn Eagle*, which looked past the shocking testimony by his brethren to observe, "Senator Smoot is well liked by his associates in the Senate. His quiet, reserved and dignified conduct have favorably impressed all."[23] When the senator began his defense on 10 January 1905, he hoped to convince the nation there was nothing to fear from his church either.

Smoot called a series of witnesses, mostly non-Mormon or lapsed Mormon, who swore that a majority of the Latter-day Saints were opposed to polygamy and few had ever practiced it. The witnesses agreed also that the Latter-day Saints "pride themselves on independent suffrage." Such control as the church might have had belonged to a bygone era, "like the Pilgrim fathers in early times." Moreover, the witnesses testified, Utah's non-Mormons experienced no restriction of opportunity in commercial or political activities; even former prosecutors of polygamy had been elected to local office. All agreed that younger Latter-day Saints would rebel if any attempt were made to control them in politics or reinstate the practice of plural marriage. As for the antipolygamy agenda, it only served to "drag religious matters into our State politics." Smoot's witnesses painted a picture of a modern church with a new, progressive generation anxious to take it into the twentieth century.[24]

Modern Mormonism was personified by Brigham Young's grandson and local church leader, Richard W. Young. Brigadier General Young was

Brigadier General Richard W. Young. Spanish-American War veteran Young provided important credentials to support Senator Smoot's declaration of the church's capacity to make good citizens and to act in defense of the nation's interests. Courtesy of LDS Family and Church History Library.

introduced to the committee through his credentials as a West Point graduate and Spanish-American War hero who had a law degree from Columbia and had been appointed president of the criminal branch of the occupied Philippine supreme court. A devout Mormon, Young joined Smoot's non-L.D.S. witnesses in testifying that the Latter-day Saints were "decidedly hostile to polygamy." When pressed on cross-examination as to the alleged unanimity of feeling against polygamy, Young responded, "Well, Mr. Tayler, there are all sorts of Mormons, as there are all sorts of people belonging to various organizations, and I believe that there are people and always have been people in the Mormon Church who have not accepted that revelation."[25] In other words, the Mormons were just like everybody, and if given enough time, their church would be, too. This testimony was meant to establish the factual basis for the senator's second point, which he pressed during his own testimony. Since the Latter-day Saints were like other Americans, they should have the same privileges and protections as their fellow citizens.

Smoot's objective on the witness stand was to call attention to the religious liberty issues that had been minimized during the hearing. He characterized his church affiliation as a matter of personal conscience that had no controlling influence over his actions. Specifically, he testified that Joseph Smith's revelation on plural marriage was "permissive not mandatory"; that the people, not the president, are supreme in the church; and that to violate civil law was to violate the law of the church. He took care to emphasize his lack of knowledge of and accountability for the actions of others in his church. He said that he had no personal knowledge of the marital status of other church leaders, that he could not remember the temple ceremony, and that "political matters . . . are never discussed in the quorum of the twelve apostles." He represented that, as a senator, he acted independently of his church superiors and that "my first duty would be here."[26]

Meanwhile, on the floor of the Senate, Smoot supported his testimony with unvarying party discipline. Two weeks after testifying, he joined his party in opposition to the statehood bill for New Mexico and Arizona. The *Chicago Evening Post* concluded that the vote proved Smoot could act contrary to his church. More accurately, however, Smoot's vote was a matter of priorities. A seat in the Senate meant more to the L.D.S. Church than did immediate statehood for the Southwest territories, notwithstanding the presence of many Latter-day Saints in the area. Regardless, Smoot's party vote showed the nation that, in addition to his useful work habits and business expertise, he brought to the Senate his people's characteristic respect for authority and capacity for solidarity. When employed in pursuit of national interests, these attributes signaled good citizenship, not slavish obedience. As requested by his party, Smoot organized a pro-Roosevelt delegation to the Republican convention and delivered Utah's votes in the presidential election of 1904. Some saw in his endeavors a conspiracy of church and party interests, but to most it was simply American politics. As one commentator saw it, the Latter-day Saints were no longer building their kingdom but acting in "common cause in the industrial upbuilding of the country."[27]

Tayler was too good a lawyer to let Smoot's testimony end with the generalization of the senator's own characteristics to his co-religionists. Before his three days on the stand were finished, Smoot was forced to concede that his prophet, Joseph F. Smith, was a lawbreaker; that B. H. Roberts, the polygamist ousted from the House of Representatives, "would not have been elected if I could have helped it"; that he did not agree with certain statements made by his fellow apostles; and that he would seek their removal if any had married after the Manifesto.[28] Thus while Smoot made as good a case for himself as was possible under the circumstances, his testimony did not exonerate his church, nor, in fairness to Smoot, could it have. Senator McComas, one of the church's severest critics on the committee, congratulated Smoot but warned that he could still lose his seat because of the church's failure to produce the testimony of those apostles who were alleged to have married polygamously or performed marriages for others after the 1890 Manifesto. Smoot relayed the message to Smith, adding that, according to McComas, "it was a lucky thing for the church that I [Smoot] was sent here as Senator for I was liked by both Democrats and Republicans and for that reason he did not expect I would be unseated."[29] As self-serving as this sounded, it was largely true, but not entirely. By itself, goodwill toward Smoot was insufficient to overcome the nation's antipathy toward his church. The continued tolerance of post-Manifesto polygamists in church leadership countered all the goodwill Smoot was seeking to create for the church. It signaled Mormon disrespect for U.S. law and intent to break new promises made by Smith during his testimony to the Senate.

Though the committee had not gotten a confession from Joseph F. Smith, it had obtained a promise. He had been forced to agree that the church would discipline members who married plurally after the Manifesto. In response to verbal pursuit from the former "cohab hunter" and now Idaho senator, Fred Dubois, Smith had said, "If any apostle or any other man claiming authority should do any such thing as that [marry polygamously after the 1890 Manifesto], he would not only be subject to prosecution and heavy fine and imprisonment in the State under the State law, but he would also be subjected to discipline and excommunication from the church by the proper tribunals of the church."[30] Smith must have regretted making such a promise, but by the logic of his own argument, he had no choice. After taking the position that new plural marriages were unsanctioned, he had to admit that grounds existed to sanction the persons performing them. This the church had never done. In the fifty-year history of antipolygamy law, no Latter-day Saint had ever been subjected to church discipline for practicing plural marriage.

Smith first attempted to satisfy the committee through a public pronouncement. Immediately after he returned from Washington, Smith presided over the April 1904 general conference of the church, where he called for a sustaining vote on the proposition that "all such [post-Manifesto plural] marriages are prohibited, and if any officer or member of the Church shall assume to solemnize or enter into any such marriage he will be deemed in transgression against the Church and will be liable to be dealt with, according to the rules and regulations thereof, and excommunicated therefrom."[31] It was unclear from its terms, however, whether this "Second Manifesto" was any more reliable than the first. Moreover, Smith did not implement his policy against new polygamists identified during the hearing. Not surprisingly, then, the response from Washington was negative. In March, three weeks after the hearing recessed pending fall elections, the church's lawyer F. S. Richards returned to Salt Lake City to report that Smoot's case was in crisis and the only cure was to "discipline such men who have brought reproach upon the Church." The Senate wanted deeds, not words. Richards was sufficiently concerned that he recommended "Bro. Smoot put a stop to these proceedings by resigning." But "this Pres. Smith feels should not be done unless the Church is put in jeopardy," reported one member present at the meeting.[32] As bad as things were for Smoot within the Senate, his most serious challenge came from within his church. He had to convince his fellow apostles that, if they wanted him to stay in the Senate, they would have to act against those among them who continued to practice plural marriage.

In particular, John W. Taylor and Matthias F. Cowley had been singled out during the hearing as symbols of what was wrong and dangerous about Mormonism. Evidence had shown that both men had taken additional wives after the 1890 Manifesto and as recently as 1901. They appeared also to be the most open in their advocacy of plural marriage and most likely to be the officiators for unlawful marriages.[33] Taylor's and Cowley's refusal to respond to Senate subpoenas and Smith's refusal to produce them were deemed proof of the church's defiance of the law. The committee had heard evidence that George Teasdale and Marriner W. Merrill also had taken additional wives and performed plural marriage ceremonies for others, but their advanced age made them less representative of new polygamy.[34] Moreover, they were not deemed in contempt of the Senate's subpoena power because their absence had been excused by sworn affidavits of ill health.[35] Heber J. Grant was relatively young, but his move beyond the Senate committee's jurisdiction was apparently not as aggravating to the senators because Grant had not been charged with performing plural marriages for others or taking additional wives himself after the Manifesto. Ultimately, the public and its political representatives reduced the trial's burgeoning mass of conflicting evidence and legal theory to a simple proposition: If the church were telling the truth about itself, it

Matthias F. Cowley (left) and John W. Taylor. The refusal of Apostles Taylor and Cowley to respond to Senate subpoenas not only evidenced their guilt but also illustrated for most Americans Mormonism's defiance of the law. Courtesy of LDS Family and Church History Library.

would not keep Taylor and Cowley within the highest ranks of its leadership.

In January 1905, immediately prior to putting on their defense, Smoot's attorneys met with Smith in Salt Lake City to impress upon him the gravity of the situation. They told him that without punitive action against Taylor and Cowley, the case for Smoot would certainly fail and the church risked "a constitutional amendment and perhaps confiscation." Two weeks later the apostles, too, were told that "a constitutional amendment is sure to come." Some of them thought it was too late to do anything; others believed "we should leave no stone."[36] Pressure from legal counsel appears to have resulted in a brief thaw at church headquarters. Another letter was released from Taylor stating emphatically his refusal to appear and, consequently, drawing the Senate's attention away from the church itself and onto Taylor and Cowley. But the apostolic quorum remained divided on how to respond to the committee. Apostle Hyrum M. Smith, son of Joseph F. Smith, stated in a meeting with his colleagues that he "regretted that the brethren of the quorum had differed somewhat in their views regarding a certain question." He voiced their low spirits by adding, "The church has been brought prominently before the world, and as to whether the hand of the Lord was in it all, he could not say."[37]

If given a choice of whom to sacrifice, several in the quorum would have chosen Smoot. After the furor over Smith's testimony, Smoot had offered to resign, rather than subject the church to further investigation. Lyman wrote his son that the apostles "'were at their wits end to know what to answer.'" To this his son replied, "any guilty man would be."[38] The next year, after Smoot had been placed on the stand, a "very anxious" Badger wrote home, asking how the senator's testimony had been received within the church. "I understand," he said, "there have been some severe criticism of the Senator. . . . I expect that we will have some trouble before we get through."[39] As late as January 1906, writing from exile in England, Apostle Heber J. Grant lobbied on behalf of Taylor and Cowley. "With all my heart I plead for these two brethren," he wrote Joseph F. Smith, "that they may be protected no matter what the enemy may ask. What they have done I have also done or intended to do. . . . From the bottom of my heart I plead for my brethren—even if Reed has to resign if that would do any good in their case."[40]

Outside the quorum, too, important church leaders argued that Smoot was the real liability. Ben Rich, president of the church's largest mission and friend of Theodore Roosevelt, grumbled to Smith, "It will take a magnifying glass, in my estimation, for us to find the good that has been done to our cause by Brother Smoot's election to the Senate. . . . It would be better for him to resign." Rich concluded his objection to Smoot by observing that "God has told me that this principal [plural marriage] is true, and I don't care what Reed Smoot says to the contrary."[41] The senator himself was sometimes driven to opposite but equal hyperbole, such as telling Badger that "if 'these things' [plural marriages] did not stop he would go out of the Church."[42] Badger could "not see how Senator Smoot can stay in the Senate, and I do not see how he can stay in the quorum of Apostles. . . . His path is strewn with thorns and he must crawl the whole length."[43]

The increasing outcry over Taylor's and Cowley's post-Manifesto polygamy and the wide publication in Utah of conflicting testimony by church leaders was creating a separate crisis within the church. "I dread to think of another crusade against our people, and if it should come," Smoot advised Smith, "we must remember we have not the full sympathy of our own people behind us."[44] Even the most faithful Latter-day Saints were struggling to find a way to rationalize the surprising disclosures from the Smoot hearing and to rebut charges of duplicity relayed through the national press. Some praised their leaders' courage under fire and were proud of their evasive testimony. All had been variously embarrassed, humiliated, confused, or angered by caricatures of church representatives and beliefs. In the spring, however, an even higher level of calamity was inspired by the hearing.

When the committee's adjournment left the anti-Mormon *Salt Lake Tribune* without news in March 1905, the paper began publishing the transcript of Smith's testimony from the preceding spring.[45] For the first time, the Latter-day Saints read in full Smith's disavowal of plenary power and denial of ever having received revelation. He had been president of the church for only two and one-half years when he told the committee, "I have never pretended to nor do I profess to have received revelations. I never said I had a revelation except so far as God has shown to me that so-called Mormonism is God's divine truth; that is all."[46] Though Senator Burrows pressed the witness to state whether this conviction was based on a divine manifestation, the witness would only admit to "inspiration."

The senator's frustration and the witness's stubborn demurrer were based in a definitional contest over the nature of prophecy and Smith's influence over his people. From the point of view of the protestors and the senators sympathetic to their case, if Smith claimed to be a prophet, then he claimed also God's power and could exercise that power over his followers in opposition to civil authority. Since Smith's goal was to show the contrary, he consistently minimized his role in church government. When, after giving his name and address, Smith was asked to state his title for the record, he answered, "president of the church." Attorney Tayler pressed him: "Is there any other description of your title than mere president?" "No," said Smith. This was an absurd answer, given what everyone familiar with the church and certainly opposing counsel already knew. Smith was much more than a president to his people. Tayler tried again: "Are you prophet, seer, and revelator?" Smith responded that he "suppose[d]" he was. Afterward, in private correspondence, Smith explained his answer in terms of the dictum "a fool should be answered according to his folly." In doing so, he revealed not only his scorn for the hearing process but his litigation strategy. "Had I replied, '*I am*' to the sneering question of the Synical prossicuter [*sic*] . . . it would have been construed as blasphemy!"

Better, he said, to answer as Jesus had to a similar question: "'Art thou the Christ?' Jesus answered 'Thou hast said?'"[47] To whatever extent the strategy was successful in Washington, it failed in Salt Lake City.

The *Tribune*'s publication of Smith's testimony coincided with the church's semiannual general conference where members gathered to receive direction from their prophet, seer, and revelator. Smith's demurrer to revelatory power assaulted the faithful's understanding of the role of prophets and the duty to obey them. Disaffected Latter-day Saint and *Tribune* editorialist Frank J. Cannon announced that Smith had "argued him[self] and his particular church out of any reason for existence. . . . The Mormons are no more entitled to claim that they are led by direct revelation from God through Joseph F. Smith than are the members of any other church whose ministers claim that, by leading a good and prayerful life, they can discover the truth and be saved."[48] Cannon was a former Utah representative in Congress and son of one of Mormonism's most respected and powerful church leaders, the late George Q. Cannon. As chief editorialist for the *Tribune*, Cannon taunted Smith mercilessly over his testimony, calling him "Earthly King" and "A Prophet Who Hates." In response, Joseph F. referred privately to Frank J. as "furious Judas" Cannon, adding, "The very devil himself must be ashamed of him."[49]

The resulting trauma to the Latter-day Saints from his published testimony was sufficient that Smith tried to explain himself at a local conference. He said that in denying he received revelation, he was only trying to avoid the "trap" designed by his "inquisitors." He reassured the audience that God "has made manifest to me a knowledge of his truth by and through spirit of revelation."[50] To some the explanation was worse than the admission. The next day Cannon denominated Smith "God's Appointed Liar" for contradicting his Senate testimony. Cannon elaborated by telling his readers that they had to decide whether Smith was "prophet to smite the Nation with law or truth at his pleasure; or . . . a shallow pretender." In the same issue, news coverage of Smith's speech was headlined: "By Command of God the Prophet Lied / Law Defier Admits Perjury. Joseph F. Smith has New Revelation." The article reported, "President Joseph F. Smith declared in the Tabernacle yesterday, in the presence of about 4000 people . . . that he had purposely prevaricated in his testimony at Washington in the Smoot investigation . . . to thwart the 'inquisitors,' as he called them, in their design to entrap him, as he knew that none of them would understand what a revelation is. He said that it is not true that he had received no revelations."[51]

The exchange over Smith's testimony caused some Latter-day Saints to

Frank J. Cannon. Cannon's excommunication from the L.D.S. Church was trumpeted in the national papers. The story accompanying this photograph in the *Washington Post* on 15 March 1905 links Cannon's ouster to a plan to formally charge Joseph F. Smith with apostasy during the upcoming general conference. Courtesy of L. Tom Perry Special Collections, Harold B. Lee Library, Brigham Young University, Provo, Utah.

conclude that Smith was a fallen prophet. The local ecclesiastical leader in Smoot's hometown reported that "apostates from the Church of Christ [of Latter-day Saints] have joined hands and hearts with the sectarians. . . . Many people have believed or pretended to believe, that elder Joseph F. Smith . . . would be destroyed from the earth, and another man would be appointed to his position as president of the Church. Writing to this effect has been sent to all parts of the State of Utah."[52] It was rumored that Frank Cannon had been excommunicated because he was attempting to organize a movement to charge Smith with apostasy during the April church conference.[53] In their visits to local conferences, the church apostles were forced to respond by preaching "upon the necessity of being in line with the Authorities."[54] For church members who had expected that the Smoot hearing would present their beliefs to the world, this was indeed a sad day. A friend in Salt Lake City wrote Badger that "the air is heavy with misrepresentation, falsehoods of the most diabolical kind are daily published by the *Tribune*. The air seems tainted with a spirit of hatefulness, causing the people to wonder what will happen next."[55]

At the opposite extreme were members whose faithfulness put them at risk of martyrdom. Smith was receiving reports that the hearing and related debates on statehood had catalyzed in Arizona the arrests of Mormon polygamists, including the church's local leaders, Smith's cousin among them.[56] Delighting in the crisis, the *Salt Lake Tribune* announced to spring conference attendees, "More sacrifice of the things which they esteemed as the high idealities of their religion and its priesthood, and more sorrow for the shameful attitude in which men were compelled to stand before the world, have come to the Mormon people through this Smoot case than has come through any other situation in their history."[57] For once, the Latter-day Saints could agree with "Furious Judas."

In addition, published transcripts of the testimony of church witnesses on plural marriage created confusion on church policy and administration. With their home constituency, the witnesses were damned if they did deny the practice of plural marriage and damned if they did not. There was a growing population within the church who wanted plural marriage abandoned and, understandably after a decade of official statements, believed that it had been. This constituency was pained by admissions and additional rumors of polygamy at high levels. Smoot's secretary Badger was among them, writing to wife Rose, "I do not want to see polygamy reestablished, and I want to see the Church leaders tell the truth. It is absolutely impossible after the many declarations made by the leaders to tell just where we are."[58] There were at least as many members who knew that the practice had continued after 1890 and who felt alarmed and even betrayed by the denials. Thirty-four-year-old Sarah Pearson recorded her reaction to the testimony in a notebook she titled "Woman of Mormondom / Smoot Investigation." She was pleased that Smoot had shown himself to be "upright and capable in business, clean in morals, honest in religion, patriotic in sentiment, and law-abiding in everything." She was troubled, however, that he and the other church witnesses had taken the position that the revelation to Joseph Smith on plural marriage was precatory, not mandatory. "I cannot see," she wrote, "how anyone can believe in a prophet and accept his other revelations without accepting that also."[59]

Church leadership had cause to be especially concerned over the effect the hearing was having on younger members, particularly those in the East pursuing degrees and other professional honors who were troubled by the apparent duplicity of their leadership. Though his feelings were no doubt intensified because he sat at the epicenter of the hearing, Badger was not alone when he declared to his wife, "For one I can give up my belief in prophets where it comes to choosing between them and honest men."[60] If the intent of sending Smoot to the Senate was to ensure a future for the church, Smith could not afford to lose the confidence of this next generation on whom the church would rely for leadership in the twentieth century. The L.D.S. Church was in serious trouble, with both the nation and its own membership, and the way out was marked by hard choices. Indeed, to satisfy one set of problems only aggravated the other.

For nearly a year after his testimony, Smith stood pat, waiting for the public furor to blow over and hoping his policy initiatives would satisfy the Senate that the church had changed. Conditions continued to deteriorate, however. The Senate was impatient for action against the absentee apostles and getting increasingly querulous with Smoot. Members of the church were confused and embarrassed. The apostles, too, seemed in disarray and dispirited. Smoot especially was chagrined to have had to stand by silently while fellow Utah senator Tom Kearns railed against the church on the Senate floor. "If he had answered . . . he would have gone right into the trap laid for him. Burrows [and others] . . . were there ready to jump on him in any way, and there would have been raised a terrible row throughout the country," explained Utah's congressional representative Joseph Howell.[61] Even more mortifying, Smoot had to concoct a business trip to San Francisco during the church's April conference in order to avoid participating in its ritual confirmation of all church leaders, including Taylor and Cowley. Publicity over his absence necessitated his appearance at the next conference in the fall. In an act he later called the "sternest test of his

"Revelations Doom Mormonism to Extermination," *St. Paul Pioneer Press*, 8 January 1905. As indicated by this headline, by the second year of the hearing many believed that Mormonism—"This Most Strange and Peculiar Faith" and "Menace to Both Morals and Political Institutions of the Country"—would be destroyed by the Smoot hearing's evidence of new polygamy. Courtesy of L. Tom Perry Special Collections, Harold B. Lee Library, Brigham Young University, Provo, Utah.

life," Smoot abstained from the ritual in full view of the conference attendees, including his apostolic brethren.[62] Howell said it well to young Badger: "'The Senator is cowed, I am cowed, the leaders of the Church are cowed.'"[63]

The longer Joseph F. Smith delayed keeping his promise that he would discipline post-Manifesto polygamists, the more Reed Smoot's support eroded. The Washington papers, which had been favorable to the senator, were now opposed or cynical. Formerly sympathetic colleagues in the Senate, too, were impatient with him and his church. Many worried about the effect of the hearing on their upcoming campaigns. President Roosevelt groused that Smoot should "have the temple ceremonies abolished; they were 'foolishness.'"[64] Developments in Utah politics also undermined the senator in 1905. As a result of confusion in church ranks, Salt Lake City's municipal elections were carried by the anti-Mormon American Party, making Smoot look politically powerless and unable to deliver his state's votes to his party. As he waited for word on whether Taylor or Cowley would be censured, Smoot felt powerless in the church as well.

Joseph F. Smith's delay in punishing Taylor and Cowley was explained to critics in terms of the need for an internal investigation. In reality, there was no need to gather facts. Taylor's and Cowley's colleagues in the church knew at least as much as the protestants. The only question was whether the hierarchy could bring itself to take action against two of its own and subject church members to the sight. As the months passed and the demands for church disciplinary action increased, Smith must have felt he was holding the last of several losing hands in a high-stakes game begun in 1890. None of his earlier strategies had worked, and the only card left in the deck was schism. Smith would do all he could do to not draw it. This meant obtaining a consensus from a deeply divided apostolic quorum. Consensus was slow in coming: two years to be exact. While Smoot waited for word of action against the two infamous apostles, Smith spent the remainder of 1904 seeking alternatives to dropping them from the quorum and all of 1905 trying to convince the quorum that there was no alternative.

Given the church's hierarchical organization, it is easy to overlook the extent to which consensus rules action, both in the church at large and more particularly in the two ruling quorums of the church, its First Presidency and Quorum of the Twelve Apostles, which are equal in authority.[65] It is especially easy to disregard the role of consensus in Smith's failure to act, given that his own theological convictions made him loath to act against anyone who practiced plural marriage. These scruples were surely compounded by a sense of hypocrisy for punishing two apostles for what probably all, including himself, had enabled. Finally, Smith no doubt hesitated to act because he had great affection for Taylor and Cowley, who had devoted themselves to the church and were known for their charismatic gifts. Yet Smith's affection for his brethren was, like all else in his life, subordinated to his conviction that the church was to be defended at all costs, even death and certainly lesser martyrdoms of office and reputation. He had demanded as much from himself on the witness stand and would have expected others to endure similar forms of public humiliation if necessary.[66] Smith's ultimate concern was for the continuing viability of the church that was threatened by divisive tension within the apostolic quorum and the membership at large. But punishing two apostles for doing what many thought was their apostolic duty required more than the usual amount of agreement when it was in short supply.

As promised in his March 1904 testimony, Smith located the two apostles when he returned to Utah. Though he denied vociferously Chairman Burrows's claim that he had promised to produce them, Smith assured Smoot that he wanted Taylor and Cowley to testify and had advised them to do so. "I believe," he wrote the senator, "the two Elders . . . might fill their missions better before the anti-Mormon Inquisition at Washington than they can do, or are doing in their legitimate mission fields." [67] Nevertheless, three weeks later Smith informed Burrows that the two apostles "are unwilling, voluntarily, to testify in the Smoot investigation. As this is a political matter, and not a religious duty devolving upon them or me, I am powerless to exert more than moral suasion." [68] Smith's denial of the capacity to force compliance was a sly check to the protestants who had charged him with having despotic control over his flock.

But no one believed that Taylor and Cowley were beyond Smith's control. Even Smoot was exasperated enough to say to his secretary that Smith acted as if he were "a mother brandishing a stick to her flock hid in the willows and asking them if they want to come and interview a neighbor who has called to see about some windows who have been broken by stray stones, of course not." [69] It was not a faulty assessment, though it gave too much credit to Smith's intentions. According to Taylor's wife, the apostle had sent his president two letters, one agreeing to testify and the other refusing.[70] It was Smith's decision which letter to use. Available correspondence supports her claim. A month after Smith informed the committee that the apostle would not testify, Taylor ended a report to Smith of his activities by promising, "Any instructions you have to give me will be cheerfully complied with." [71]

Badger's journal also supports the conclusion that Smith's protestations notwithstanding, the absentees were instructed not to respond to the subpoenas. From three different sources Badger was told that Lyman had gone to Canada to encourage Taylor to testify and "John W. said that if Pres. Lyman thought that way he would go, but only because Pres. Lyman wanted him to." On the train home to Salt Lake City, however, Lyman had a vision that changed his mind. The promulgator of the first manifesto "President Woodruff appeared to him, and told him that he had best ask John W. what he was going to testify to before he had him go to Washington." Lyman returned to Canada on the next train to ask Taylor what he would say to the committee. "'Nothing but what will make my families, my wives, and children honor me,' Taylor answered. Lyman told John W. not to go," according to Badger's sources. Cowley, too, was contacted by Lyman and presumably to the same effect, since he never testified either.[72] Church leaders—both in this world and the next—seem to have effectively stymied the committee's efforts to command the presence of either apostle.

In the long run, however, Smith's representations were irrelevant. After so many empty promises, all that mattered were Smith's actions, and he had yet to invoke his Second Manifesto to discipline anyone known to have married or married others plurally after 1890. It is doubtful that Smith intended that the Second Manifesto do more than restate the "advice" given in the first one in 1890. As historian Michael Quinn points out, Smith may have sent a signal to conference attendees that he was preserving the status quo when he chose known post-Manifesto polygamists to second the motion in support of the proposition. They included, for instance, Moses W. Taylor, the brother of John W. Taylor.[73] It is, however, equally arguable that these men served as bona fides of Smith's intent. As symbols of past practice, they could be interpreted as placing their fidelity behind a new policy. The historian's difficulty in parsing the actions of church leadership mirrors that of the participants in these events. Did Smith mean to stop plural marriage or didn't he?[74]

Available records tip the scale in favor of the conclusion that Smith did not intend to change the church's policy.[75] Minutes of the briefing for those who were being asked to second the new manifesto include the following exchange: "Questions were asked which drew from President Smith the statement that this declaration was nothing more nor less than confirmatory of President Woodruff's of 1890; adding that if any plural marriages had been performed they were performed without his knowledge or consent, and that persons having entered into them, or solemnized them, must be held responsible for their acts to the law of the land, as well as the rule and discipline of the Church. With this understanding the position of the First Presidency was endorsed."[76] Thus it appears that Smith's Second Manifesto was meant merely to restate the traditional strategy for defending the church against civil sanction: church members who chose to practice plural marriage were liable, but the church was not. At least that is what Badger concluded, based on a comment from a member of the church's presidency that "the actions of the last conference . . . do not matter, or, since we cannot remain neutral in such vital concerns—that we will approve the lives and conduct of those who break the laws."[77] The conference actions did matter, however. Notwithstanding Smith's original intentions, the Second Manifesto would have to be enforced eventually.

The immediate significance of Smith's pronouncement lay in its reference to the prophet-president himself, not polygamy. Smith prefaced his declaration with "I, Joseph F. Smith, President of the Church of Jesus Christ of Latter-day Saints, hereby affirm and declare that no such marriages have been solemnized with the sanction, consent or knowledge of the Church of Jesus Christ of Latter-day Saints."[78] After reading the warning of discipline for those who entered new polygamous marriages, Smith said to the assembly, "They charge us with being dishonest and untrue to our word. . . . I want to see today whether the Latter-day Saints representing the Church in this solemn assembly will not seal these charges as false by their vote."[79] Thus it appears that Smith's 1904 antipolygamy statement was an attempt to consolidate support for his testimony at the hearing only two months earlier. His promulgation of a Second Manifesto was more an exercise in consensus building than in policy making.

Throughout the summer and fall of 1904, Smith applied himself to the task of authenticating his March 1904 testimony by keeping the apostolic quorum from performing plural marriages. In this he had an ally in Francis M. Lyman, president of the quorum and opponent of post-Manifesto polygamy. Lyman notified each member in July 1904 that he "must sustain the stand taken by President Smith and must not talk nor act at cross purposes with the Prophet. What has already been done is shaking the confidence of the Latter-day Saints. We are considered as two-faced and insincere. We must not stand in that light before the Saints to the world."[80] Two months later Smith took the first practical step to stop the practice of polygamy. He asked the quorum to agree that the authority to perform Latter-day Saint marriages could be exercised in the church's temples only.[81] This constrained the unofficial performance of marriages, since there were only four temples and all were within Utah. The obvious next step was to discipline post-Manifesto polygamists.

Smith had returned from Washington in the spring of 1904 convinced that Taylor and Cowley "have stated their own cases and they will have to abide the results themselves."[82] Meeting with the apostolic quorum two months later, he "was emphatic in having [Taylor] bear the weight of his own doings."[83] The quorum was not ready to act against the two men, however, and Smith had to wait for it. Not only was the quorum equal in ecclesiastical authority to Smith and, therefore, due Smith's deference. As a practical matter, the quorum's cooperation was also required for the effective administration of the church. Thus the actual work of obtaining consensus in favor of expelling Taylor and Cowley was left to quorum president Lyman, who was, luckily for Smith, an opponent of post-Manifesto polygamy.[84] For a year Lyman labored to enforce Smith's restraint of marital sealing powers to the church's temples and to convince his brethren of the danger in contradicting Smith's testimony in Washington. By the fall of 1905, the quorum appeared ready for the next step. At least Lyman had garnered enough support to gather the quorum for a formal consideration of the committee's demand that Taylor and Cowley be disciplined. In the company of the church's First Presidency, the apostles were briefed by George F. Richards, the church's lawyer, and B. H. Roberts, who made "a forceful presentation of the case as it affected the Church. It was made clear that it was necessary, under the circumstances, that the Church and the Presidency should be disassociated from the acts of individuals. . . . Only by that means could the firends [sic] of the Church [in the Senate] stand up in its defense."[85] The two advocates and the First Presidency then left the meeting.

For the next several days, the quorum discussed the "subject . . . in all its phases." Initially Taylor and Cowley argued that their personal acts should be "differentiated" from "the responsibility of the Church." They believed they should not be liable to the church for their acts and should be able, as Smith had said of himself during his Senate testimony, to take their chances with the law. They were preaching to the choir, however. No one in the quorum, except possibly Smoot and Lyman, felt Taylor and Cowley had done anything wrong. Smith refused their requests to meet privately before answering the quorum's questions, signaling his refusal to intercede in the quorum's deliberations and his probable conviction that the circumstances of — even the presidency's complicity in — their post-Manifesto marriages were irrelevant. All that mattered was protecting the church. As he wrote to Apostle Grant in England, though Smith was "sorry for" them, Taylor and Cowley had "unwisely brought trouble for both themselves and the church. And the enemy is after them fiercely. I scarcely see how they can escape." Again, however, Smith deferred to the prerogatives of the quorum, telling Grant, "Prest Lyman will no doubt inform you more fully on this matter."[86]

After six days Smith was brought back to hear Taylor's and Cowley's statements. He then gave his view of "the necessities of the case," telling the two apostles that they "were not on trial charged with an offense, but were present to hear the statement that had been made and to take such steps as they felt they were willing to take." He told them he thought they had three options: deny the committee's charges, if they could do so honestly; confess wrongdoing to the church and be excommunicated or dropped from the quorum; or "let things go on as they had gone and risk the consequences which might mean the disfranchisement of the Church." After defining the alternatives, Smith "left the matter in the hands of the brethren and of their quorum."[87]

The next day, having "modified their feelings," Taylor and Cowley "expressed their readiness to take the only step that appeared adequate to meet the situation." Their resignations were executed on 28 October 1905, demonstrating to the Senate and no doubt to church members as well that those who entered post-Manifesto marriages were "out of harmony with the Church . . . [and] were against the declarations of [church] Presidents."[88] Cowley later recalled that "our resignations were brought to us in the Temple all written, with no suggestion from us."[89] Both men were told that the resignations would not be used "unless matters came to the last ditch of necessity."[90] The reluctance with which the resignations were received can be measured by the fact that no decision was made about whether and when to use them. In this, too, Smith's deference to the apostolic quorum is evident. In November, about to return to the Senate, Smoot asked the church presidency how he was to handle the resignations, no doubt wanting permission to inform his supporters on Capitol Hill. Smith, though he felt it best to release the letters, "told Bro. Smoot to do as the Apostles had agreed."[91] The quorum, however, still did not want to sacrifice Taylor and Cowley and continued to look for alternatives to satisfy the Senate that the church was law-abiding.

After two weeks in Washington and at least three telegrams in twenty hours instructing him that "Taylor and Cowley should not be sacrificed unless required . . . [to] save you," on 8 December 1905 Smoot handwrote a lengthy letter reporting the condition of his case before the Senate. "I hear nothing but T and C, T and C, and why are they not handled. And [i]f the President of the Church won't stop polygamy we will," he told the church's presidency. "This feeling so freely expressed" caused the senator not to fear the loss of his office, he said, but the enactment of "legislation effecting our liberties, if something is not done by the Authorities of the church to show the country we are honest and that you meant what you said in your testimony." He had returned to Washington to find that even President Roosevelt and senators whom Smoot considered his friends were disgusted with the church's lack of action. When Smoot proffered a mild excuse for his church brethren, one friendly senator "showed anger at once" and demanded, " 'Why does the Church vote to sustain them and by so doing encourage and approve of their unlawful acts? Why do they show contempt for the Government . . . ? I am going to vote for you but I want you to know that this double dealing of the church authorities with the Government I will never stand for.'" The level of outrage caused by the church's inaction led Smoot to report that the time had passed for any effective use of the resignations in his own case. In fact, he said, announcing them at this point in the proceedings would appear disingenuous and "have an unfavorable effect."

The letter was Smoot's personal manifesto to rid himself of the burden of blame for Taylor's and Cowley's being asked to fall on their swords. Smoot was telling his brethren that he did not want and did not need the resignations. Indeed, he fumed, "I would rather be expelled from the Senate, go home and resign from the Quorum than have it said now, or hereafter, that Taylor or Cowley was sacrificed or resigned to save me." Conversations with his Senate colleagues had convinced Smoot that the committee vote would be against him by a narrow margin, though a tie was still possible. In either case, his fate would be decided by the full Senate, based on his answers during floor debate. Consequently, he told the First Presidency, the only use for the resignations was to give his supporters on the floor "some ground to stand on in case they would decide to say a word favorable to the church." [92] In sum, the church's liberties, not Smoot's seat in the Senate, were the determining factor on whether to discipline Taylor and Cowley. Perhaps because it was "very, very late" and he was "not sleepy, but weary," Smoot closed his long missive with an uncharacteristically critical, possibly even sarcastic statement: "You have decided not to use the resignations of Taylor and Cowley unless I say they are necessary to save my expulsion, or to save me. If it is not for the best interest of the Church to handle Taylor and Cowley . . . If [they] have done no wrong and their acts meet the approval of the Brethren for Heavens sake don't handle them but let us take the consequences." [93]

Even as Smoot labored over his letter, quorum secretary George Gibbs was writing another, which Smoot would receive the next day. In a tortured analogy to Isaac's role in the biblical account of Abraham's sacrifice, Gibbs informed Smoot in veiled terms that he must find an alternative to the sacrifice of his brethren. Just as Abraham's duty to obey God's command to sacrifice his son was fulfilled by the willingness to do it, "the sacrifice is already made," said Gibbs. He then instructed Smoot, "It's your business now to look about you and find the ram [the substitute for Isaac in Abraham's actual sacrifice]; and I can promise you that if you will go to work in this spirit you will find the ram, and then victory will be yours." Gibbs's instructions ended with a command. "This is the word to you," he told the senator, "if you will let the spirit of this note burn in your heart I will promise you again the ram will come, for come he must."[94] The promise was never realized.

For the common good of the church that needed to be seen as acting for the common good of the nation, Taylor and Cowley would have to be removed from the quorum. Smith knew it and left it to the apostles to resist the inevitable, while he turned his attention to preparing the church for the shock of abandoning the practice of polygamy.

It is difficult to see, in fact, how the
[L.D.S.] church could hope to exist and
retain the confidence of its own believers
after surrendering this one fundamental
doctrine which differentiates it from
other Christian bodies.

—Topeka Capital (*1904*)

RE-PLACING MEMORY

While an exasperated Smoot prepared for the hearing's final session and Lyman continued to struggle with his quorum, Smith dedicated himself to shoring up the faith of those who had staked so much on the principle of celestial marriage and were about to witness its abandonment. If Smith's ultimate goal in sending Smoot to the Senate was to "make [Latter-day Saints] assume our real position and standing in the midst of the earth," he first had to ensure that the changes precipitated by the hearing did not knock the church off its feet.[1] This meant renewing the members' confidence in the authority of founding prophet Joseph Smith and, thereby, sustaining Mormonism's coherence with its sense of divine origin. The Smoot hearing would, indeed, "abolish Mormonism without war," unless Joseph F. Smith could convince the faithful that the church was remaining the same even as it changed.[2]

Modern Mormonism's capacity to adapt to its social environment has been explained in terms of its belief in continuing revelation.[3] Revelation is not of itself sufficient to legitimize change, however. Removing a part of religious conviction, even by revelation, can easily remove the whole of it, as well as confidence in the revelatory process itself. This is especially true where the part is thoroughly integrated into the whole, as was plural marriage for the Latter-day Saints. As summarized by Jan Shipps, "The connection between plurality and the 'restoration of all things' underscores the importance of the *actuality* of polygamous marriages to the generative period in Mormon history. This, in turn, makes it possible to see that the fervor with which plural marriage was preached and practiced . . . took the Saints inside the biblical story, allowing experience to tie Old Testament accounts and everyday Restoration history together."[4] Smith's task was formidable. He had to remove his people's faith in one revelation without undermining their confidence in all revelation, as well as the revelator, namely, Joseph Smith and himself as Smith's prophetic successor.

Nothing to date had been adequate to separate the Latter-day Saints' belief in plural marriage from its practice. While the church had been drawn along the path to abandoning plural marriage since the Manifesto, the 1905 orchestrated resignations of two apostles for their practice of polygamy intensified to a heretofore unknown degree the need to obtain the Latter-day Saints' confidence in their church's revelatory foundations and present leadership. Conveniently, 1905 was also the 100th anniversary of the birth of Joseph Smith, the prophet whose status was in crisis. The dedication that same year of a monument to Joseph Smith provided the occasion for identifying what about him and his legacy mattered to the L.D.S. Church and what would be carried forward into the twentieth century to provide it with continuing confidence in both the original prophet and his twentieth-century successors.

On 18 December 1905 President Joseph F. Smith gathered what was left of the senior leadership of the church and boarded a train for Vermont to celebrate Joseph Smith's birth centennial by dedicating a monument to his memory.[5] Plans for the commemoration had been suggested to President Smith nine months earlier by Junius Wells, a member of the church who had made a pilgrimage to the area. By May property had been purchased near Joseph Smith's birthplace, and work was under way to find "a stone that would measure up over thirty feet, from which to get a polished shaft typical of a perfect man."[6] In the fall, instructions were sent to "all the Assemblies of the Latter Day Saints throughout the world" to celebrate memorial services on Sunday, 24 December. The monument itself would be dedicated on 23 December, the actual anniversary date. The dedicatory party of thirty persons included members of the leading families of Mormondom who had made the forced exodus to the Great

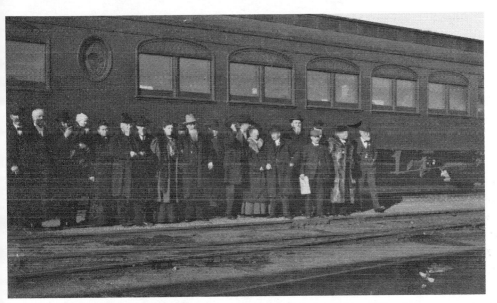

Travelers to Vermont. The dedication party left Salt Lake in a special train car reserved for their use. Conspicuously absent from these representatives of Mormonism's founding families were Joseph F. Smith's plural wives and those members of the quorum accused of post-Manifesto polygamy. Courtesy of LDS Family and Church History Library.

Basin from Illinois in the 1840s.[7] Before returning to the mountains behind which they had fled as children, this now-aging second and third generation of church leadership would travel 5,500 miles and visit carefully selected sites of Latter-day Saint history in the Northeast and Ohio.

Arriving on 22 December, the party from Salt Lake City, joined by Latter-day Saints from New York and Boston, must have nearly overwhelmed the little hamlet of South Royalton, Vermont.[8] Royalton's hospitality was equal to the occasion, however. The Mormons were greeted with a petition "recognizing the right of said [Latter-day Saint] persons to worship God according to the dictates of their own conscience" and, in a "broad spirit of toleration," were offered use of the town hall.[9] The welcome was no doubt warmed by the financing and entertainment incident to constructing and hauling overland to this remote place "the largest polished shaft we know of in America, and perhaps the world." The spectacle included planking roads, shoring up bridges, shearing off groves of trees when granite went awry, and hitching as many as twenty-two horses to a specially made wagon and, behind them, another four horses with a battering ram "for the last push."[10] Why all the effort? President Smith had stated their goal at the end of his semiannual conference address the preceding October. He said the Latter-day Saints must proclaim "that 'Mormonism' is a living, moving entity; that it is not dead nor sleeping, but that it is alive and awake, growing and advancing in the land; and let the world know it."[11] The effort to celebrate the legacy of Joseph Smith was meant to signal that the movement he founded had both the intentions and the resources necessary to carry on and to do so on a grand scale.

Of course, this message was intended for those critics who declared that "the Smoot case will abolish Mormonism without war."[12] Yet the outside world was not Joseph F. Smith's only audience. The monument to Joseph Smith also sent a message to the believing but demoralized Latter-day Saints. It was serendipitous that the centennial of Joseph Smith's birth occurred when the faithful needed something to celebrate—particularly to celebrate Joseph Smith as first in a succession of modern prophets. That Joseph F. Smith seized this occasion is remarkable for two reasons. First, the church was generally defensive about accusations that it worshiped Joseph Smith, not Jesus Christ, and celebration of Joseph Smith's birth could support such charges. This may have been a contributing factor to the monument's design, which was not of Smith's face or form, but an obelisk.[13] Second, for its first celebration of Joseph Smith outside the Mormon culture region, the church chose an occasion unrestrained by any theological or ecclesiastical associations except those the dedication party would bring with them. Memorialization of a birth is, after all, the blankest of slates upon which to write retrospective meanings. The monument erected in Vermont was susceptible to embodying not only the nature and the permanence of the Latter-day Saints' claims about their founding prophet, but their claims about the nature and permanence of their church. These claims were both inclusive and exclusive. The dedication ceremony celebrated the Latter-day Saints' identity with, as well as their difference from, their host nation.

Joseph F. Smith responded to the town's welcome by hosting a patriotic meeting and inviting everyone to the festivities the next day. Going east as they did in the midst of the crisis posed by the Smoot hearing, the Salt Lake City travelers were not unaware of the renewed attacks on their patriotism and never failed to remark on their identification with American origins. Calling the first Mormons "pilgrim fathers No. 2," chief apostle Lyman reminded his Vermont listeners that the Latter-day Saints were "descended of stock from New England—from Massachusetts, New Hampshire, Rhode Island and Vermont and from everywhere else."[14] In the Midwest this was echoed by one who could say, "Tonight we meet

WELCOME
DEC. 8 – 1955

Constructing the Joseph F. Smith Monument. The plan for a centennial monument commemorating Smith's birth was suggested and executed in eight months by dynamo Junius F. Wells, shown here in a fur coat to the monument's left. Taken two weeks before the anniversary date, this photograph records the raising of the polished granite shaft that measured 1 foot for every year of Smith's life, or 38.5 feet. Courtesy of LDS Family and Church History Library.

with you in my native state [of Illinois]—the state where the prophet found his sepulchre [*sic*]."[15] In Boston, apostle and future church president George A. Smith noted that "'Mormon' people have been the builders of a great commonwealth in the . . . Western country. And now for the first time they have turned their faces back, as it were, to begin to build in New England."[16] Like the decision to send Smoot to Washington in the first place, the monument erected to Smith's memory signaled the church's intent to come out from behind its mountain barrier and claim a place in America at large. Whereas Smoot's election constituted a claim to participation in America's future, the Joseph Smith monument staked a claim to America's past. For the Latter-day Saints, the dedicatory ceremonies in Vermont marked an attempt at homecoming and healing: "And now we come back," said Lyman. "The west and the east meet here. . . . We want your friendship; and you have ours."[17] These Utahans came to celebrate Smith's New England origins with New Englanders and express their shared history and citizenship with all Americans at every stop along the way.

There was, however, also an exclusivity to their Vermont celebration. Many in the dedicatory party reflected upon the historical significance of reversing their pioneering trek and remembered the losses that characterized their youth. One speaker noted that all the Latter-day Saints in memorial services held in congregations throughout the church were "reckoning the time from the birth of their prophet, leader and organizer."[18] According to that reckoning, he added, Mormonism's history not only "repeated the labors and successes of the Pilgrim Fathers" but was "the fulfillment of the dreams of the ancient prophets. . . . Jerusalem, Shechem, and Capernaum rise again from the great American Desert, and the Lord has remembered His promise to Jacob."[19] Rehearsals of church history, not just secular but also sacred, during the dedication were offered as proof that the church would survive its present travails and triumph in the future. While such claims are typical of exercises in communal memory, the Joseph Smith memorial revealed the particularities of a modern Latter-day Saint community that was coming into being at the beginning of the twentieth century.

Maurice Halbwachs inaugurated the study of collective memory, and many have built upon his foundational work.[20] Central to his thesis is the insight that commemoration is inevitably a function of selective memory and entails the equally important task of forgetting. As David Thelan has paraphrased Halbwachs, "People develop a shared identity by identifying, exploring, and agreeing on memories. . . . In the course of taking a picture or creating an album they decide *what* they want to remember and *how* they want to remember it."[21] In 1905 the Latter-day Saints were about to turn the American landscape into their scrapbook. During Joseph F. Smith's administration, the church began to recover and reconstruct the sites of its early history in New York, Ohio, Missouri, Illinois, and Iowa. Consistent with Pierre Nora's observation generally, the Latter-day Saints felt the need for "places of memory" at the very time when they felt at risk of a breach with their past.[22] The Utah church's claim to a piece of Vermont constituted a collective act of remembering that helped members forget a past they could not carry with them into the future.[23] They would be so successful that eventually they would hardly be aware that they were agreeing to forget and, if made aware, would tend to think they were forgetting Brigham Young. In fact, they were in the process of forgetting portions of Joseph Smith's legacy that Brigham Young and his successors had taken so literally.

Leaving the overt historicizing to others, during the two-hour ceremony Joseph F. Smith limited his remarks to his dedicatory prayer. In it he stipulated the elements of Joseph Smith's mission that would be carried forward into the twentieth century as inviolable, even to the consciousness of change. Thanking God for "the great Prophet and Seer of the nineteenth century," Joseph F. made an offering of each element of the monument in terms of its significance."[24] The huge cement foundation symbolized the primitive church, or "the foundation Thou has laid, of Apostles and Prophets, with Jesus Christ, Thy son, as the chief corner stone." Upon this foundation was laid a 4-foot thick, 30-ton granite base "typifying the rock of revelation." Finally, erected on the base and measuring a foot for each year of his life, a 38½ foot shaft of granite represented Joseph Smith himself. The shaft was polished to symbolize Smith's "reflecting the light of heaven" and was crowned to illustrate Smith's successful completion of his mission and the possibility for all to be similarly glorified. These three elements—a foundational restoration of Christ's church from apostasy, a base of continuing revelation from heaven, and an assertion of Joseph Smith's revelatory power and divine authority bestowed to those that follow—were the core elements of Latter-day Saint doctrine and continued to frame the church's identity within twentieth-century American denominationalism. In place of its nineteenth-century emphasis on theocratic and familial kingdom-building, the L.D.S. Church was prepared by crisis to return to less grandiose but still large claims regarding restoration of the primitive church, divine sponsorship, and living prophets. These principles constituted the generative and, hence, nonnegotiable core of Mormonism.

Junius F. Wells. Photographed on the day of the dedication, 23 December 1905, Wells posed in front of the inscription on the monument base that describes Joseph Smith's mission in terms of his first vision of God and Jesus Christ, restoration of priestly authority and the primitive church, and promulgation of a new canon. Courtesy of LDS Family and Church History Library.

They were carved in stone both literally on the surface of the Joseph Smith monument and figuratively in terms of the church's identity.

Inscribed on the monument's north side was a reference to Joseph Smith's first vision in 1820, when he was instructed to reject all existing churches. Other surfaces were devoted to Smith's subsequent experiences of angelic restoration of knowledge and authority to organize "the Church of Jesus Christ in its fullness and perfection."[25] Notions of restored truth, authority, and order, based in models both of Old Testament prophecy and New Testament apostolic witness, constitute the creative material out of which the L.D.S. Church has adapted itself over time. Moreover, they define the outside limit of what may be changed. They comprise both the boundary and content of Latter-day Saint identity in a sense of separateness from non-Mormons and sameness of being Mormon. Everything else is relatively fungible, making the church extraordinarily adaptable and identifiable at the same time. Indeed, Joseph F. Smith's efforts to adapt the church to the Progressive Era's demand for change demonstrate clearly that the ideals of revealed knowledge and restored authority constitute the creative and untouchable core of Latter-day Saint belief and identity.

Joseph Smith claimed to have received many revelations, all of which were to varying degrees indices of his prophetic calling among his followers and were mined for theological significance according to the needs of each successive generation. This is especially true of what is called "the First Vision," which occurred in 1820 when concerns caused by competitive revivalism motivated the fourteen-year-old Smith to try to choose a church. Relying on biblical injunction to pray for wisdom, Smith retired to the woods to ask "which of all the sects was right (for at this time it had never entered into my heart that all were wrong)—and which I should join."[26] The canonized account of the vision states that two divine personages appeared to Smith and identified themselves as God and Jesus Christ and "answered that I must join none of them, for they were all wrong."[27] Two definitive doctrines of Mormonism made their first appearance in this vision. Of greatest import in the nineteenth century was the instruction not to join any of the existing churches. This private message to Smith of Christian apostasy was publicly elaborated ten years later through the 1830 publication of the Book of Mormon. The second doctrine is implicit in the description of God and the Son as "personages," which marked an immediate and radical break with traditional Christian creeds. Yet, if noted at all by the church's early critics, the Latter-day Saints' belief in a godhead of three separate personages was considered only one among many unpleasantly distinctive elements of Mormonism and secondary in concern to Mormonism's new scripture, priesthood hierarchy, economic communalism, temple building, modern revelation, and of course, plural marriage.

Many factors contributed to the relative lack of interest in the First Vision by believers and nonbelievers. Most have been identified by Latter-day Saint scholars in a variety of articles attempting to validate the historicity of the event or its relationship to developments in Latter-day Saint doctrine.[28] Though these studies disagree on the theological implications of the First Vision, what matters for our purposes is that all agree, in the words of James Allen, author of the most extensive study, that "the weight of evidence would suggest that it [the First Vision] was not a matter of common knowledge, even among church members, in the earliest years of Mormon History."[29] Allen further concludes that this oversight continued until 1883 when the First Vision was first employed to teach the Latter-day Saint doctrine of deity. Even here, however, Allen can only characterize the 1883 sermon as having "implied" that a major purpose of the vision was to "restore a true knowledge of God."[30] While appreciation for Smith's First Vision continued to grow in the last decade of the nineteenth century, not until the early twentieth century did it move to the fore of Latter-day Saint self-representation. As Allen's research makes apparent, the turning point in the status of the First Vision occurred during the administration of Joseph F. Smith and was contemporaneous with the Smoot hearing and its immediate aftermath. The story was first used in Sunday school texts in 1905, in priesthood instructional manuals in 1909, as a separate missionary tract in 1910, and in histories of the church in 1912. Moreover, the Smith family farm in Palmyra, New York, was purchased by church members in 1907 and passed into church ownership in 1916. A grove of trees on the site where the young prophet is assumed to have received his First Vision became an increasingly popular pilgrimage site, culminating in centennial celebrations in 1920. By midcentury, Smith's account of his theophany was denominated "The Joseph Smith Story." Eventually it would be granted the status of "the beginning point, the fountainhead, of the restoration of the gospel in this dispensation."[31] In the First Vision, Joseph F. Smith had found a marker of Latter-day Saint identity whose pedigree was as great as—and would be made greater than—that of plural marriage for the twentieth-century Latter-day Saints.

The First Vision contained the elements necessary to fill the historical, scriptural, and theological void left by the abandonment of plural marriage. To the extent that plural marriage had captured the Latter-day

"THIS IS MY BELOVED SON. HEAR HIM!"

"This Is My Beloved Son. Hear Him!" Latter-day Saint rejection of trinitarian theology is displayed in this 1913 stained glass window of the First Vision in the Adams Ward Chapel in Los Angeles. A similar stained glass portrayal of this event was included in the Salt Lake Temple, dedicated in 1893. During the first years of the twentieth century, however, accounts of Smith's first theophany began to dominate sermons and course curriculum for all ages, as well as being represented in public spaces. "Joseph Smith's First Vision" (artist unknown), © by Intellectual Reserve, Inc., courtesy of LDS Museum of Church History and Art.

Saints' loyalties as Smith's last revelation, the First Vision, as its referent indicates, was equally appealing. It also, like polygamy, was both a historical event and an idea that could be characterized as attracting persecution. Nineteenth-century Latter-day Saints had not endeared themselves to their neighbors by claiming to be the only true church in a religiously plural society. Moreover, though it was not of as much note as the Book of Mormon or other doctrines, the Latter-day Saints' rejection of Trinitarianism appears to have been a source of some antagonism. Joseph Smith's mother remembered several confrontations with representatives of evangelical Protestantism over her son's claims to revelation, noting "the Methodists also come, and they rage, for they worship a God without body or parts, and they know that our faith comes in contact with this principle."[32] Whether the Methodists knew this from accounts of Smith's theophany did not matter to the twentieth-century Latter-day Saints. They believed it to be so.

Joseph F. Smith made the connection explicit between the vision and persecution, "The greatest crime that Joseph Smith was guilty of was the crime of confessing . . . that he saw those Heavenly Beings. . . . That is the worst crime he committed, and the world has held it against him. . . . He suffered persecution all the days of his life on earth because he declared it was true."[33] From here it was a small step to finding in the First Vision a source of the Latter-day Saints' continuing identity with their forebears. In 1909, still feeling the aftershocks of the Smoot hearing, Joseph F. told the Latter-day Saints, "From the day that the Prophet Joseph Smith first declared his vision until now, the enemy of all righteousness . . . the enemy to direct revelation from God and to the inspirations that come from the heavens to man has been arrayed against this work."[34] New emphasis on the First Vision maintained a sense of religious difference and, as such, provided the equally necessary sense of internal cohesiveness and historical continuity in terms of persecution.

Significantly, however, the First Vision changed the arena of confrontation over differences from social action to theological belief, a necessity created not only by the experience of persecution but by Supreme Court law. In *Reynolds v. U.S.*, the Court made clear that the Constitution protected only differences in religious thought, not religiously motivated actions that compete with social mores.[35] New emphasis on the First Vision successfully reframed the Latter-day Saints' necessary sense of otherness to fit safely within the politics of American religion. Jan Shipps, however, rightly warns students of Mormonism that "when Mormon history begins with the First Vision, the result tends to be an account of a religious movement which, even as it differs dramatically on basic theological and doctrinal issues from other sects and churches, is analytically yet one more subdivision of Christianity inaugurated through the efforts of a charismatic leader."[36] As we shall see in Chapter 6, this is exactly what the Senate panel was asking the church to become. For now, it is sufficient to note that unlike Joseph Smith's last vision, his first one placed his followers at odds only with other churches, not the state, and shifted the battle from issues of public morality to theological tenets.[37]

Finally, like plural marriage, the First Vision could be formalized as doctrine fundamental to the faith. An account of it had been added to the church's scriptural canon in 1880 on a motion of Joseph F. Smith, then counselor in the church's presidency. Thus this first revelation to Joseph Smith was susceptible to a role as formal and central as his last. Moreover, in 1902 under the direction of Joseph F. Smith, the text of Joseph Smith's autobiography was divided into chapters and verses and integrated by reference to the rest of Latter-day Saint scripture. This gave Joseph Smith's First Vision a status equal to that of the visions of biblical and Book of Mormon prophets. The formalization of Smith's First Vision and its placement at the core of Latter-day Saint identity is neatly summarized by an apostle called to fill one of the vacancies created by the dismissal of Taylor and Cowley: "One outstandingly distinguishing feature of this Church is divine authority by direct revelation. The appearing of the Father and the Son to Joseph Smith is the foundation of this Church. Therein lies the secret of its strength and vitality. . . . That one revelation answers all the queries of science regarding God and his divine personality. Don't you see what that means? What God is, is answered. His relation to his children is clear. His interest in humanity through authority delegated to man is apparent. The future of the work is assured."[38]

The "assurance" provided by the First Vision was in no small part due to its synthesis of those ideas so necessary to Latter-day Saint faith: an immanent God, modern revelation, and divine imprimatur for ecclesiastical authority. Notwithstanding such extravagant endorsement of the First Vision's theological substance, however, the significance to the church of Smith's account of his early experiences is not adequately understood if it is seen merely as a container for Latter-day Saint theology. In the twentieth-century Smith's autobiography could only be appreciated as a narrative, even a story of origins or a myth with the capacity to order the reader's experience of time. The Latter-day Saints had a particular need for order during Joseph F. Smith's administration, and so it was that during these years Smith's autobiography emerged not only as a source of doctrine but as the modern L.D.S. Church's master narrative.

Joseph Smith's autobiography covers only his early years and is commonly referred to as "The Joseph Smith Story." As indicated by the breadth of its title, the narrative is deemed to communicate the essence of Smith's life and work, notwithstanding its limitation to only a few events during a nine-year period that, significantly, preceded the organization of the church in 1830. The events around which the narrative is constructed are (1) Smith's 1820 First Vision of the Father and the Son; (2) several appearances between 1823 and 1827 of an angel named Moroni, who instructed Smith and directed him to the hiding place of an ancient record that he would publish as the Book of Mormon; and (3) an 1829 appearance of the resurrected John the Baptist, who ordained Smith and a colleague to priestly authority. While other versions of Smith's autobiography include additional events, and the contemporaneously kept record of Smith's life is voluminous, only these early events were canonized as Smith's "Story."[39] Why they are considered sufficient to constitute *the* Joseph Smith story and are deemed worthy of canonization can be deduced in part from the earlier discussion of the dedication of the Joseph Smith monument. Each of these three experiences corresponds directly to the three principles memorialized in the 1905 dedication ceremonies and lie at the core of Mormonism: a foundational restoration of Christ's church from apostasy, a base of continuing revelation from heaven, and an assertion of Joseph Smith's revelatory power and divine authority bestowed to those that follow.

As a narrative, however, the Joseph Smith autobiography places these principles in a plot that, by definition, is an ordering of events in time that allows its readers to experiment with the world offered by the plot. In theory, by sympathetic participation with a narrative and by interpreting the writer's offered order of events, readers construct meaning for themselves. "It is," Paul Ricoeur argues, "the very heart of reading [and hearing, one assumes] that explanation and interpretation are indefinitely opposed and reconciled."[40] Reconciliation of contemporary oppositions by its readers is anticipated by the other names given to the Joseph Smith story, namely, the "Joseph Smith Testimony" and in the most recent version of Latter-day Saint scripture, "Joseph Smith—History." In its appeal to these types of discourse—story, testimony, and history—Smith's autobiography signals narrative uses in excess of its theological message. Naturally, the "reconciled" meaning that the reader derives from any story will depend on the immediate questions that he or she brings to it. Thus one way to understand the appeal or explanatory power of a given narrative in a given time is to consider its community of readers and their circumstances. Achieving its popularity in the L.D.S. Church between 1905 and 1920, the "Joseph Smith Story" appealed to a church readership struggling—in the midst of external attack and on the verge of internal schism over abandoning nineteenth-century commitments—to know whether their church was still "the only true and living church on the face of the whole earth."[41]

From its first sentence there can be no doubt that Joseph Smith's canonized autobiography is an explanation: "Owing to the many reports which have been put in circulation by evil-disposed and designing persons, in relation to the rise and progress of the Church of Jesus Christ of Latter-day Saints, all of which have been designed by the authors thereof to militate against its character as a Church and its progress in the world—I have been induced to write this history, to disabuse the public mind, and put all inquirers after truth into possession of the facts, as they have transpired, in relation both to myself and the Church."[42] After a brief introduction, the narrative describes the tension inherent in Smith's search for religious certainty amidst competing truth claims. It ends ten printed pages later with the protagonist's receipt of heavenly endowments of power to organize a church. Compiled in 1838, this version reflects its contemporaneous circumstances: an organized and hunted church in combat with its neighbors. The account is, therefore, preoccupied with persecution, using the word seventeen times in its ten pages. The appeal of this aspect of the story to the early-twentieth-century church, embattled in another antipolygamy campaign and subject to national criticism, is obvious. By his own account, Joseph Smith's sense of persecution was aroused by accusations regarding his family's poverty and local treasure-hunting activities as well as other aspersions on his own integrity. For twentieth-century readers of the account, however, what mattered most were those portions of the story related to allegations of heresy by Protestant critics, as indicated by Joseph F. Smith's conclusion that persecution resulted primarily from his uncle's doctrine of God.

In addition, Latter-day Saints in the Progressive Era, small in numbers and capital relative to the larger population, must have been drawn to the story's portrait of endurance and certainty of purpose. "It caused me," Joseph Smith said, "serious reflection then, and often has since, how very strange it was that an obscure boy, of a little over fourteen years of age, and one, too, who was doomed to the necessity of obtaining a scanty maintenance by his daily labor, should be thought a character of sufficient importance to attract the attention of the great ones of the most popular sects of the day, and in a manner to create in them a spirit of the most bitter persecution and reviling. But strange or not, so it was, and it was often the cause of great sorrow to myself." After recounting the personal consequences of his experience, Smith asserted its ontological significance:

> It was nevertheless a fact that I had beheld a vision. I have thought since, that I felt much like Paul, when he made his defense before King Agrippa, and related the account of the vision he had when he saw a light, and heard a voice; but still there were but few who believed him; some said he was dishonest, others said he was mad; and he was ridiculed and reviled. But all this did not destroy the reality of his vision. He had seen a vision, he knew he had, and all the persecution under heaven could not make it otherwise; and though they should persecute him unto death, yet he knew, and would know to his latest breath, that he had both seen a light and heard a voice speaking unto him, and all the world could not make him think or believe otherwise. So it was with me. I had actually seen a light, and in the midst of that light I saw two Personages, and they did in reality speak to me; and though I was hated and persecuted for saying that I had seen a vision, yet it was true. . . . For I had seen a vision; I knew it, and I knew that God knew it, and I could not deny it, neither dared I do it.[43]

This is what made Joseph Smith the Latter-day Saints' "perfect man" worthy of memorialization in polished granite. He constituted the ideal seeker, the petitioner who becomes a prophet by means of theophany and unwavering public witness. It was this type of perfection under pressure that the Latter-day Saints themselves aspired to when they built the monument in 1905 and began reading his story with renewed interest.

The second, pivotal event in the narrative is Joseph Smith's vision of an angel who instructed Smith in the meaning of biblical scripture and directed him to new scripture, the Book of Mormon. The account of this event teaches the second of the three themes celebrated in the Joseph Smith monument: restored truth through divine communication. For twentieth-century leaders the numerous biblical references in Smith's account of the angel's instruction provided an additional basis for demonstrating the holy pedigree of several L.D.S. doctrines. Anthon Lund, Joseph F. Smith's counselor, taught that at the second vision . . . [a]mong the things that were revealed to him was the principle of vicarious work [in temples] for the dead, and the principle of the gathering of the people, principles of our Church that are unique to it. These were given by the angel Moroni . . . [who] read from the book of Malachi about the hearts of the children being turned to their fathers . . . [and] the eleventh chapter of Isaiah, which refers to the gathering; and other principles he explained to the young man [Smith]. Today [in the report on church expenditures] we have heard read how much has been given for temples and for temple buildings, and this shows that the Latter-day Saints believe in the principle revealed to the Prophet Joseph as early as 1823.[44]

As exemplified by Lund's remarks, the "Joseph Smith Story" validated the practice of performing ordinances vicariously for the dead, a particularly twentieth-century initiative of the church.[45]

Most fundamentally, the account of Moroni's appearance to and tutoring of Joseph Smith conveys the necessity of revelation and its triumph over worldly opposition. The narrative makes the latter point when it relates a failed attempt by Joseph Smith to validate the historical claims of the Book of Mormon by showing its purportedly ancient script to Columbia University professor Charles Anthon. According to the account, once Anthon realized the source of the characters, he withdrew his endorsement, "saying, that there was no such thing now as ministering of angels."[46] In Professor Anthon's reaction, later readers of the Joseph Smith story would see, as did Smith himself in his 1832 account, the fulfillment of the "learned man" prophecy of Isiah 29 and be reminded that they should not expect and neither would they need worldly assistance. In 1905, when the dedication party included in its itinerary a prayer meeting on the hill where Smith said he retrieved the Book of Mormon record, the travelers came away with a renewed conviction of "the truth of the latter-day work and the fortelling [sic] its ultimate triumph over opposing powers."[47] Thus the second of Smith's visions also was a useful source of interpretation of present events and a source of continuity with their past.

The third and final event in the canonized version of Joseph Smith's story occurred in 1829 and illustrated the same principles as the previous events: ongoing revelation in an atmosphere of opposition, but with promises of triumph. Motivated by questions during his work on the Book of Mormon and accompanied by his scribe Oliver Cowdery, Smith prayed again for guidance. Implicit in the result of the prayer is concern for authority. An account of baptism in the Book of Mormon had left the pair wondering how to receive remission of sin if, as they believed, no existing church was an acceptable agent of God. The short version of the story is that a resurrected John the Baptist appeared to Smith and Cowdery, ordained them with authority not only to baptize but also to organize a church, and promised that further authority would be bestowed in the future. The words Smith ascribed to the angelic visitor provide the pre-church origins of authority to receive continuing revelation: "Upon you my fellow servants, in the name of Messiah I confer the Priesthood of Aaron, which holds the keys of the ministering of angels, and of the Gospel of repentance, and of baptism by immersion for the remission of sins; and this shall *never be taken again* from the earth, until the sons of Levi do offer again an offering unto the Lord in righteousness."[48]

The endowment of authority and promises of permanence, like experiential knowledge of God modeled in the First Vision and continuing knowledge from God illustrated in the second, provided the foundation on which the Latter-day Saints could tolerate a changing church. Thus Smith's story was also denominated his "testimony." No less than other canonized narratives, Smith's autobiographical writing constitutes for the church "a history directed by a 'promise' and moving to a 'fulfillment.'"[49] When in the first decades of this century the Latter-day Saints broke finally with their immediate past, they found present stability—not merely theology—in Smith's testimony of promises made prior to the organization of their church. Herein lay the greatest strength of the church's new twentieth-century uses of the Joseph Smith story as a myth of Mormon origins.

To the extent that Smith's canonized story is concerned exclusively with events that occurred prior to the organization of the church but were foundational to it, the narrative's concerns are primordial. Thus, like other myths of origination, "in recounting how these things began and how they will end, the myth places the experience of [the reader or listener] in a whole that receives orientation and meaning from the narration. Thus, an understanding of [Latter-day Saint] human reality as a whole operates through the myth by means of a reminiscence and an expectation."[50] The Joseph Smith story captured the attention of the twentieth-century church because it "oriented" members *to* a possible future, not merely *within* the present crisis of authority.[51] Specifically, Smith's explanation of the church's origins promised that the Latter-day Saints' felt bond with the sacred would not be broken.

The most extravagant and comforting promise was the story's last, namely, that the authority by which the church could be organized (and, implicitly, susceptible to reorganization) "shall never be taken again from the earth" until it accomplishes its purpose of latter-day preparation for a millennial reign of Christ.[52] The believing reader of the Joseph Smith story was thereby assured that Smith's restoration was permanent. With this promise, Smith's canonized story cum testimony qua history of church origins climaxes in an affirmation of unchangeable ecclesiastical authority that has the capacity to mediate divine knowledge and power.

Richard Bushman concluded his biography of Smith's early years by asserting, "What distinguished Mormonism [in the nineteenth century] was not so much the Gospel Mormons taught . . . but what they believed had happened—to Joseph Smith, to Book of Mormon characters, and to Moses and Enoch. . . . Mormonism was history, not philosophy."[53] As implied by reference to Moses and Enoch and by the placing of Smith in such company, it is obvious to anyone familiar with Smith's reworking of the traditional Jewish and Christian canon that the Latter-day Saint sense of history is cosmological. Thus it is also possible to elaborate on Bushman's observation to conclude that what distinguished Latter-day Saints was the conviction that the cosmological order was expressed immediately in their everyday lives. Smith's canonized autobiography is placed in Latter-day Saint scripture immediately following the Latter-day Saint version of Moses' and Abraham's theophanies and is of a type with them—a type bearing promise of fulfillment in a new aeon in God's relation to his people. A sermon by one who participated in the revival of Smith's story illustrates Smith's relation to this biblical type: "There has been some reference here today to the First Vision of the Prophet Joseph, which we look upon as the dawn of this last dispensation, the dispensation of the fullness of times."[54] This sense of new time, a "fullness" of time given by Smith's narrative of churchly primordial events, contributed significantly to the Latter-day Saints' capacity to embrace change in church doctrines and programs without a sense of loss of identity or continuity with their past.

Progressive Era changes were ordered within a cosmology of promise and fulfillment, which lent stability to efforts to revoke the theocracy, economic communalism, and plural marriage of the previous generation. The Latter-day Saints' confidence in their cosmology may have been shaken by the defensive and prevaricating testimony of church witnesses at the Smoot hearing, by the confusion and disarray in church policy, and by the judgment and removal of Taylor and Cowley; but the history of the pre-church origins of their bond with the sacred, as explained in Joseph Smith's story, was a means of restoring that confidence through the constructive capacity of both the nineteenth-century writer and his twentieth-century readers. The Latter-day Saints managed the dislocating passage into the twentieth century by inscribing their present experience onto Smith's, which promised changeless duration, even the "fullness of times." In placing confidence not in particular practices or doctrines but in the promises of divine presence, revelation, and authority that, as the angel promised, "shall never be taken again from the earth," the believing reader of Joseph Smith's testimony could appropriate a future in which failure was impossible.

Finally, in the process of inscribing their own experiences onto his, the believing readers made of Joseph Smith the model of modern Sainthood. A church authority and major interpreter of church doctrine during this period wrote, "The whole latter-day work was initiated by Joseph Smith's search for truth. . . . Thus came the first great vision of Joseph Smith; and as a consequence of his search for truth came the other revelations, and the enduring light-giving structure of the Church. . . . It is understood that every worthy member of the Church must likewise seek and find truth for himself."[55] Thus Smith became the model for resolving doubts, even those about his own legacy. "If any of you lack wisdom, let him ask of God," Smith had read in the biblical book of James. By this means he had learned which church was true, and so could his followers who read these same words now embedded in the canonized version of his story.

The reshaping of Latter-day Saint theology, however, was not limited to forgetting Smith's last revelation and remembering his first. The itinerary of the dedication party on their way home to the West illustrates a second reordering of historical priorities. After they left Vermont the day after the dedication, Joseph F. Smith and his party traveled to Massachusetts and held public services in Boston in the afternoon and evening of 24 December 1905. On Christmas day they visited the Massachusetts homestead of the progenitors of Joseph Smith. From Boston the party traveled to Palmyra, New York, to pay homage at the Joseph Smith Sr. family farm and its "sacred grove," site of the First Vision. They held a prayer meeting at the Hill Cumorah, reputed discovery site of the Book of Mormon. From New York they went to Kirtland, a small town in northern Ohio, where Joseph Smith had gathered his followers on the new frontier in 1831, eight months after organizing the church in New York. This was the final site of commemorative activities related to Smith's role in the church. The travelers made only one more stop on their way home: Chicago. There they spent the majority of their two-day visit observing local

Joseph F. Smith in the "sacred grove." While other members of the dedication party explored the sacred grove near Palmyra, New York, where Joseph Smith was believed to have had the First Vision, his nephew posed for the trip photographer. Courtesy of LDS Family and Church History Library.

industries in nearby Kenosha and Racine and paying respects to business leaders.

Thus the travelers retraced the church's steps only as far as Kirtland, Ohio, and the final years of Joseph Smith's ministry were ignored. In geographic terms, this meant that the party did not visit Independence, near Kansas City, Missouri, site of the Latter-day Saints' first attempt to build an American Zion. Nor did they stop in Nauvoo, the town from which the Latter-day Saints had fled to the Rocky Mountains and that lies on the western border of Illinois midway between Chicago and Omaha. Both Independence and Nauvoo have powerful associations with later developments in Latter-day Saint doctrine. For example, plural marriage was first practiced in Nauvoo, as were the nascent forms of theocratic government that would find full expression in Utah. Similarly, the anticapitalist principles that had characterized Utah's economy were revealed in Kirtland but were first practiced in Missouri. Finally, though Kirtland was the site of the first Latter-day Saint temple, the ceremonies and oaths of such concern to the Smoot hearing panel were performed only later, in Nauvoo. In sum, those practices that placed the church in conflict with American institutions were largely a product of the Latter-day Saints' history in Missouri and Illinois, and to these sites the dedication party did not go.

While stopping at either Independence or Nauvoo would have been a detour for the travelers, it would have been no more of a deviation than Kirtland, to which they backtracked from Cleveland, "going at a slow pace, because of the condition of the road and of the hills and hollows, at the old-fashioned ox-team speed."[56] Moreover, in an itinerary that took them by train from Chicago to Omaha, they skipped Nauvoo and Council Bluffs, both of which were directly in their path. But for the fact that the travelers spent two days sightseeing in Chicago, one could explain the omission in terms of time constraints. Whatever the reason, their itinerary emphasized the less controversial stages of Smith's life, and similarly their sermons to church members and nonmembers alike emphasized his less controversial ideas.[57] In this respect, too, the dedication party illustrated a means by which Mormonism transformed itself during the period.

Avoidance of certain ideas was to be expected from the travelers. Since the 1880s, the Latter-day Saints had abandoned all efforts to defend their marriage practices to "Gentiles" and had become very careful even within the church. Only at local conferences, where outsiders were unlikely to overhear, had the subject been taught. It was no surprise, then, that the few allusions to polygamy made by these travelers were indirect and defensive. In Chicago, for example, Joseph F. Smith assured visitors, "We

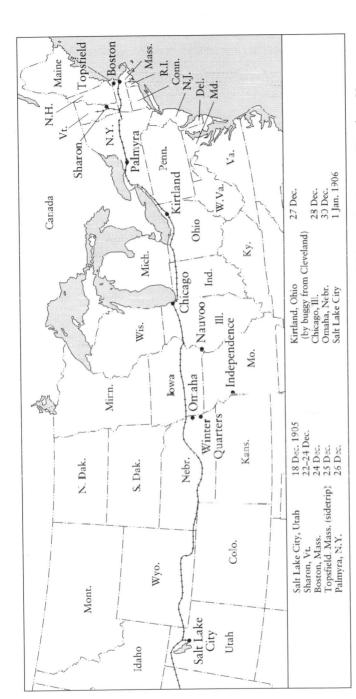

Salt Lake City, Utah	18 Dec. 1905
Sharon, Vt.	22–24 Dec.
Boston, Mass.	24 Dec.
Topsfield, Mass. (sidetrip)	25 Dec.
Palmyra, N.Y.	26 Dec.
Kirtland, Ohio (by buggy from Cleveland)	27 Dec.
Chicago, Ill.	28 Dec.
Omaha, Nebr.	30 Dec.
Salt Lake City	1 Jan. 1906

Joseph F. Smith memorial trip. The dedication party visited selected L.D.S. Church history sites between Royalton, Vermont, and Omaha, Nebraska.

are not seeking for women; we have women of our own and they are as good and pure as ever women were on the earth."[58]

On other subjects, too, the church became increasingly careful. Its public discourse changed on such subjects as theocracy, millennialism, and deification. For example, "fullness of the gospel" was sometimes employed to represent the complete primitive church, as opposed to the phrase's former comprehension of all ordinances and truths ever revealed and then some. Past emphasis on deification shifted to a kind of ethical perfectionism: "'Mormonism' is to benefit mankind. Obedience to it makes good men better, and bad men good. No man dare continue in wrongdoing and still claim membership in the Church of Jesus Christ of Latter-day Saints. That is one of the distinctive features of our people, and of this work."[59] So said President Smith to the Vermonters, and his companions repeated the message throughout their trip: "If the Gospel will not make us better, by obedience to its precepts, then it is no better than any other religion. . . . The religion that will make men the best of all in the world is the best religion and that religion has been embraced by the members of this Church, for it is the religion of Jesus Christ."[60]

Significantly, the message to member and nonmember became indistinguishable during this period. Instead of being admonished to do the works and receive the blessings of Abraham, the Latter-day Saints were encouraged to manifest Yankee virtues and Progressive Era values. Exhortations to missionary work overtook the other elements of nineteenth-century millennialism; growth, not gathering to Zion, became the rallying cry. During Joseph F. Smith's tenure, immigration to Utah was officially ended, and the church began to build centers of membership abroad. Finally, celestial marriage was redefined in terms of the longevity, not the multiplicity, of the marriage covenant. It became exclusively understood as "temple marriage" for time and eternity. The version of Mormonism lived publicly in the twentieth century was the version taught in the first years of Smith's life and preached in New York and Ohio. The more exotic doctrines from the Missouri and Illinois periods of Smith's work would be placed in temples and, thus, privately practiced. As Jan Shipps noted in her analysis of a conference address given by Joseph F. Smith ten years later, "By concentrating on what the Mormons regard as essential principles of the gospel—the nature of God, Christ's role as Savior, the restoration of the church and its place, and the place of the priesthood, in humanity's quest for salvation and eternal life—Joseph F. Smith conveyed to the Saints his confidence that the changes which had occurred during his tenure were not changes which had in any way diminished the strength of the relationship between God and his chosen people."[61]

Whatever discontinuities may have been created in church doctrine by the redefinition of plural marriage as temple marriage, gathering as growth, and deification as moral perfection were bridged by didactic restatement of the same claims made in the "Joseph Smith Story." The incidence of general conference sermons on the theme of an apostasy by the primitive church was nearly four times greater during this period than in the immediately subsequent or preceding decades. The number of assertions that the L.D.S. Church was the "only true church" was nearly three times greater than in the preceding and subsequent two decades. Mention of fellowship with other faiths was lower than at any other time, except between 1830 and 1859.[62] This pattern among the Latter-day Saints was contrary to that of other restorationist churches that were minimizing their claims to primitive Christianity and choosing between evangelical or fundamentalist identities during the early twentieth century.[63]

Finally, in addition to these interpretive strategies that minimized the significance of plural marriage, the church had to act more formally to reposition the founding prophet's last revelation within its canon, both because the Senate demanded it and because the Latter-day Saints needed it. In December 1908 the 1890 Manifesto was added to the *Book of Doctrine and Covenants* and titled an "Official Declaration." The *Deseret News* announced the new publication without fanfare: "A new edition of the Doctrine and Covenants has just been prepared and is for sale at the Deseret News Book Store. . . . [In addition to a concordance] the edition also contains the official declaration generally known as the Manifesto of President Woodruff. We call special attention to this edition of one of the four standard works of the Church."[64]

The inclusion of the Manifesto in scripture was never explained publicly, though it was much discussed privately by church leaders. For example, in 1908 Apostle Charles Penrose wrote to President Smith from Europe six months prior to the publication of the new English version of scripture. Penrose wanted instructions on whether to include the 1890 Manifesto in a Dutch version "now ready for printing." The individual responsible for the project had asked Penrose about "the insertion, at the close, of the manifesto," apparently because "the ministers in Holland are getting very much stirred up, and they accuse us of covertly teaching polygamy." But Penrose did "not feel at liberty to tell him what to do without consulting you, seeing that there is an idea out that you virtually promised [the Senate] to insert the manifesto. . . . Please let me know at your earliest convenience what your mind is on this matter." Penrose offered several alternatives: "We can go ahead and publish the work as it appears in English, or we can add the manifesto at the close in a separate chapter, or as an entirely separate article and let it stand for what it purports to be."[65] Publicly the decision to include the Manifesto was treated simply as an editorial determination, like the addition of a concordance.

Having so legitimated the 1890 Manifesto, the church now had to account for its fifteen years of disobedience to it. The official explanation was that the few violations occurred on individual initiative and were caused by understandable differences of interpretation: "Since that time [1890] the Church has not performed any plural marriages or authorized any violation of the law thus forbidden. But there were some persons who construed the language of that Manifesto to signify plural marriages within the boundaries of the United States, that being 'the land' wherein the laws spoken of extended. They, therefore, went or removed to Mexico and thus acted on that which they believed to be right without violating the Manifesto. They looked on plural marriage within the United States as *malum prohibitum* and not *malum in se*."[66]

Published in 1911 within church periodicals and in pamphlet form, this legalistic interpretation of the recent past and disclaimer of church involvement attempted to satisfy insiders and outsiders that the institution itself was not responsible for the continuation of polygamy into the twentieth century. Such had been the official position throughout the Smoot hearing, and the church never wavered from it. Eventually outsiders lost interest in the question, and insiders accepted the interpretation at face value. Those who needed particular reassurance received it privately. One very upset, post-Manifesto polygamous wife sent her brother to Joseph F. Smith to ask whether her marriage was legitimate. She turned to Smith not because he was president of the church but because he had performed the ceremony. In an interview years later, the brother said that Smith told him "to tell his sister that her marriage was o.k., but he had had to say what he did in Washington to protect the Church."[67]

Members who could not accept the change and who contracted plural marriages after Smith's 1904 injunction, including Taylor and Cowley, were subjected to church disciplinary courts beginning in 1911. For those who were willing to change, the effect of the abandonment of the practice was cushioned doctrinally by three strategies. First and most obviously, the church did not repeal Joseph Smith's revelation as contained in church scripture as Section 132 of the *Book of Doctrine and Covenants*. Instead the 1890 Manifesto was subordinated to it by placement at the back of the Book. Moreover, by calling the Manifesto a *declaration*, not a revelation, church authorities implied that the Manifesto was not of weight equal to material contained within the main text. As stated by its own terms, the Manifesto's addition to the *Doctrine and Covenants* was understood to memorialize only a suspension of church law and to do so merely out of respect for "laws enacted by Congress . . . pronounced constitutional by the court of last resort." True to the *Reynolds* decision, the Latter-day Saints would believe but would not act according to their belief.[68] Second, then, change in practice was palliated by continuing intellectual commitment to doctrine. Moreover, the church continued the practice of plural marriage to the extent that males whose previous wives were deceased were permitted to have subsequent marriages sanctioned by temple ordinance, which is believed to ensure marital status after death. Finally, through sermon and other doctrinal exposition, the doctrine of celestial marriage was applied in such a manner as to equate it exclusively with eternal marriage, rather than with plural marriage. Though this had been a defensive strategy in legal arguments since 1880, it was now universally applied within the church as well.[69]

By bypassing Independence, Missouri, and Nauvoo, Illinois, the 1905 dedication party avoided more than problematic theology. These were sites of martyrdom and persecution that had been the rallying cry to establishing an autonomous kingdom in the West. Missouri was legendary among the Latter-day Saints for "mobocracy" or state-sanctioned efforts to exterminate Mormonism. In Illinois, Joseph Smith and his brother Hyrum were murdered while in the governor's protective custody. While these places would not be forgotten and in the next few years would become developed as sites of pilgrimage, the 1905 centennial celebration's emphasis was not on justice and struggle but on forgiveness and progress, birth not death.

The conflict of emotions ran deep, however, and was apparent in the dedication ceremony. The unveiling of the monument to the martyred prophet was punctuated by a hymn that included the sentiments so criticized by the Smoot hearing panel: "Earth must atone for the blood of that man. Wake up the world for the conflict of justice."[70] Immediately afterward, the dedication party sang "The Star Spangled Banner." At home, too, celebrants mixed complaint and patriotism. Over the Salt Lake Tabernacle's organ pipes hung a portrait of Joseph Smith with "great festoons of national colors running toward the choir seats on either side."[71] The

Latter-day Saints entered the new century still trying to balance their patriotism with their losses.

Their new president, however, demanded a more positive offering from his church to the nation: forgiveness. It was one of the most consistent themes of Joseph F. Smith's counsel to the church during his seventeen-year tenure as president. Ignored by social and political explanations of what brought the Latter-day Saints into the twentieth century, Smith's emphasis on forgiveness was nonetheless a critical aspect of his leadership during the Smoot hearing crisis. Though the nation needed to be reassured that the church was not a threat to its legal and moral order, members of the church were no less concerned about "the bloodthirsty Christians of these United States" who had oppressed them lawfully for seventy years.[72] No summary list is adequate to capture the inherited and immediate sense of personal and collective injury and anger held by church members who heard Smith require them to "go from this conference to your homes feeling in your hearts and from the depths of your soul to forgive one another, and never from this time forth to bear malice towards another fellow creature, I do not care whether he is a member of the Church of Jesus Christ of Latter-day Saints or not, whether he is a friend or a foe, whether he is good or bad."[73] One measure of Smith's success as a leader during this period is the extent to which not only the Latter-day Saints but also their interlocutors have forgotten why this message was necessary in its day. It may be the best measure of his people's acceptance of him as "a worthy successor of the mighty men who preceded him."[74]

While these sentiments no doubt expressed Smith's sincere desire for peace with the American people and government, his efforts to satisfy the Senate were more than a defensive strategy. Smith wanted also to secure the political support necessary to take the church's religious message to a larger audience. The ultimate object of Smith's efforts to reconcile his church and nation lay beyond the existing borders of each. In August 1906 Smith became the first sitting president to tour the church's European missions. In the course of his travels he encouraged members in Germany, Holland, Belgium, Switzerland, France, and England not to come to America but to stay and build the church in their own countries. Smith's trip "symbolized," in the words of one scholar, that "the era of organized gathering to America was over. Building Zion all over the world could commence."[75] Smith's tour of Europe marked the end of the Mormon exodus from the world and signaled what would soon become formal church policy. It is in this context that, when giving Smoot permission to notify his Senate colleagues that Taylor and Cowley had resigned, Lyman cautioned Smoot that the resignations "were not given for your benefit, but for the relief of the Church, and for that purpose you may need to use them and need not hesitate." The final sentence of Lyman's exceptionally terse, three-sentence letter provides the only insight into why the forced resignations were deemed "relief" for the church, but it was enough and even obvious: "May the Lord bless you and keep you in your seat in the Senate."[76] At the very time that the United States was extending its sovereignty and exercising diplomatic influence in the internal politics of foreign nations, the L.D.S. Church placed an apostle in the Senate who could and did leverage his office to enable his church also to internationalize.

DEFINING DENOMINATIONAL CITIZENSHIP

While the Latter-day Saints were planning a trip east in 1905 to celebrate their identity with the rest of America, the protestants were in the West seeking evidence of enduring difference. The persuasiveness of their case had been diminished by Smoot's monogamy and his irreproachable conduct in the Senate. Even Chairman Burrows had to admit that "the Senator stands before the Senate in personal character and bearing above criticism and beyond reproach."[1] Though confident that evidence against the L.D.S. Church was sufficient to support antipolygamy legislation, the protestants lacked evidence that linked Smoot to the wrongfulness of his church and supported his removal from the Senate. In February 1906 Burrows reopened the hearing after a year's hiatus. He convinced his reluctant colleagues to reconvene based on the promise of proof that Smoot had a plural wife hiding in Mexico. The protestants' litigation strategy this time was to attempt to prove the charges in the formerly eschewed protest by Rev. John Luther Leilich that Smoot himself was a polygamist. In addition, they believed they had found a witness with a better memory of the

Mormon temple oath and capable, therefore, of demonstrating the incompatibility of that oath with Smoot's senatorial oath of office.

Monogamist Smoot was thoroughly exasperated by the new charges, telling his secretary "that it might be a wise thing for him not to go near the committee room again, and to let them do as they want."[2] His despair was aggravated, no doubt, by Burrows's refusal to disclose to either Smoot or his legal counsel the identity of the new witnesses, "claiming that if the names were known they would be gotten out of the way."[3] This meant Smoot had to rely on rumors and secondhand information from his friends on the committee to prepare his defense.[4] To make matters worse, the Republican Party had lost Salt Lake City's municipal elections, causing doubt in Washington that Smoot could deliver Utah's vote to the Republicans nationally. His opponents pressed their advantage by spreading the rumor that the election signaled loss of church support. Smoot's champion, Senator Albert Beveridge, received a letter from the manager of the *Salt Lake Tribune* telling him that the city election "was a knock out for Apostle Smoot, and he is about the most hated politician in Utah to-day. The Mormons are roasting him more vigorously than the Gentiles; in fact, he has been lambasted so hard by some of the Latter-day Saints that a few of us feel like taking sides with him just as a man will the under dog."[5]

Most aggravating of all, however, was the apostolic quorum's continuing vacillation on the status of the Taylor and Cowley resignations. As late as March 1906 and immediately prior to presenting his defense to the new charges, Smoot received letters from members of the apostolic quorum counseling patience but able only to promise, in the words of one earnest member, "Action may and I believe will be taken."[6] As long as the resignations were not announced, it was possible to preserve the status quo. This is exactly what some in the quorum wanted. Apostle Heber Grant wrote from his exile in England, "It has been my earnest and constant prayer that Brothers Taylor and Cowley might be preserved from the shafts of the enemy. I feel sure that if they were sacrificed that it would only be one more concession and that in the near future something else would be demanded. It seems impossible to satisfy a lion when he has once tasted blood."[7] Rather than be blamed by his church for the fall of two apostles, Smoot continued to face the "lion" while waiting for church leadership to achieve consensus.

As Smoot began the last phase of the hearing, his letters to church authorities expressed a mounting sense of indebtedness to his fellow senators as well as frustration with his fellow apostles. The strain of competing loyalties had taken its toll on the senator. He worried that he would lose his health over the ordeal and complained of stomach and bowel pains, sleeplessness, and loss of appetite. He felt humiliated by the accusations of public and press, unappreciated by his fellow believers, terrified by the prospects of failure, and abandoned by many of his church brethren. "I would also like to suggest that the [church's] general authorities . . . meet a day in the near future for fasting and prayer," Smoot wrote to Joseph F. Smith two weeks before the hearing reconvened. "I am sure some of the brethren would not care to pray for me; but I would like you to impress upon them the fact that it is not me that is in danger, but the church, and they certainly [illegible] pray for it. If they think it is my ambition that has brought this trouble upon the church, I think they ought to have charity enough to ask God to forgive me."[8]

Charges that his political ambitions were the cause of the church's troubles continued to bedevil Smoot. At the end of March 1906, while he was waiting for the committee vote on his fate, Smoot reported that he was the object of hostility among certain church leaders: "My letters from home often contain reports of unjust and untrue criticisms having been made by leading brethren of the Church against me. Coming from all parts of our State," he wrote, "it appears that these accusations are a premeditated plan to kill me politically and religiously with the Mormon people. . . . Some of the people at home do not seem to understand that my fight is their fight, and a victory for me means a victory for them."[9] Notwithstanding his anger and anxiety, Smoot's performance in the third year of the contest over his seat was as restrained as in the first two years. He conducted his defense within the limits set by the church, which often meant merely questioning the relevance and credibility of opposing witnesses and saying as little as possible in rebuttal to the facts.

The protestors' chief witness in this last phase of the hearing was Walter Wolfe, a former professor of botany and history at Brigham Young Academy, the Provo school where Smoot was a trustee. Wolfe had unofficially "severed connection" with the church "by refusing to comply with the demand for tithing."[10] At least he obediently understood it as a severance, since his church president had so denominated any willful failure to tithe. Like so many of the witnesses, Wolfe was not a non-believer but a disappointed one. His disappointments appear to have begun on an archaeological mission to South America led a few years earlier by the academy's president Benjamin Cluff Jr. It had been such a bad experience that afterward Wolfe had brought charges against Cluff in a church court. Cluff was, according to Wolfe, not only a tyrant but also a dilettante more interested in keeping company with his plural wife in Mexico than in pursuing the mission with his brethren. Or as Badger summarized in his letter home, Wolfe "thought Cluff would rather live with his new wife than with Nephite ruins, and, not making allowances for human nature, stirred up quite a fuss."[11] Wolfe's firsthand description of Cluff's polygamous conduct during Smoot's tenure on the academy's board of trustees undermined Smoot's claim to being a champion of antipolygamy within the church. Wolfe was also able to give circumstantial evidence of Joseph F. Smith's knowledge of Cluff's post-Manifesto marriage. Thus Wolfe could link both Smoot and Smith to post-Manifesto polygamy.

Smoot's case was vulnerable to Wolfe's testimony. The senior L.D.S. Church official in Mexico, Anthony Ivins, who had performed unlawful marriages at the direction of the church's presidency, declined the presidency's invitation to perjure himself on the church's behalf by testifying for Smoot.[12] Unfortunately for the protestants, however, their lawyer failed to maximize Wolfe's knowledge of church practices in its Mexican settlements, which had been established in the 1880s to sustain the practice of plural marriage outside the reach of U.S. antipolygamy law. Neither did counsel seek to obtain testimony from Ivins, whose records show he performed at least forty plural marriages in Mexico after the Manifesto and as late as 1904.[13] In addition to taking advantage of these omissions by the protestants, Smoot was able to show affirmatively that Cluff had been removed as president of Brigham Young Academy, reducing Wolfe's testimony to a historical anecdote.

In the failure to exploit Wolfe's knowledge and to subpoena Ivins, the protestors' case suffered from a change of counsel for the 1906 phase of the hearing. Conveniently for Smoot, Roosevelt had appointed Robert Tayler to the federal bench in 1905, leaving the case to his much less effective co-counsel John G. Carlisle, ex-secretary of the U.S. Treasury. Carlisle was initially listed as principal counsel for the protestors' case, but he took no active role until he replaced Tayler in the final phase of the hearing and closing arguments in the winter of 1906. Badger gleefully reported the effect of the change: "Tayler had a conviction as well as an ambition behind his work; Carlisle has neither, and we are profiting. His examination was listless and was confined to the bare outline of the story desired to be brought out."[14] Finally and probably most importantly for Smoot's success in the last phase of the hearing, the protestors were never able to find another Mrs. Smoot. This left the hearing panel where it had been at the end of closing arguments in 1905: having to decide whether to hold Smoot personally responsible for actions of others, and what appeared to be a very few others at that.

While Chairman Burrows was able to convince a slim majority to recommend Smoot's ouster, the minority report stated the position that would eventually prevail: "So far as the testimony discloses there have been but few plural marriages since [1890], perhaps not more than the bigamous marriages during the same period among the same number of non-Mormons."[15] Unsupported by data on bigamy, this conclusion was mere conjecture. To add insult to injury, it was possible to engage in such conjecture only because, as the majority's report showed, "shifts, tricks, and evasions" by the church had frustrated the protestors' access to records and persons, which could prove a more systematic practice of polygamy.[16] Nevertheless, it remained true that the protestants had not carried their burden of proof. They admitted as much by reversing themselves and endorsing Leilich's original allegation that the Mormon temple ritual made Smoot a traitor. If polygamy failed to motivate the Senate, perhaps sedition would.

Unlike their judicial counterparts, senators hold hearings primarily to find prospective remedies, not to apply retrospective punishments. If the L.D.S. Church, as Smith promised, was going to change its ways and, as hoped by those who supported Smoot, discipline wrongdoers Taylor and Cowley, new justification was needed for Senate action. By making the L.D.S. temple oath an issue in the third and final round of the hearing, the protestors hoped to provide that justification. They could show that Smoot himself had participated in the temple ceremony and was bound by the terms of the oath he had taken there not to disclose it. This refusal, like Taylor's and Cowley's defiance of the Senate's subpoena power, could condemn Smoot as one who placed himself above the law and in conflict with his oath of office. Smoot warned his church leaders, "This subject [of the oath] seems to have been revived in the Senate for some special purpose, and this purpose I believe to be the exclusion of all Mormons from holding Federal offices."[17]

Wolfe provided the most confidently detailed, firsthand account of the L.D.S. temple ceremony. "The law of vengeance is this," he said. "'You and each of you do covenant and promise that you will pray, and never cease to pray, Almighty God to avenge the blood of the prophets upon this nation.'"[18] Unlike previous witnesses who were confused on the point, Wolfe explicitly named the "nation" as the object of Mormon vengeance. The drama of Wolfe's disclosure of the "secret oath" was compromised, however, by the evidence of its scriptural basis in the biblical book of

Revelation, which all Christians believed but with no visible effect on their behavior. "I saw under the altar the souls of them that were slain for the word of God, and for the testimony which they held," prophesied the Revelator, observing that the righteous "cried with a loud voice, saying, How long, O Lord, holy and true, dost thou not judge and avenge our blood on them that dwell on the earth?"[19] In addition, the force of the protestants' argument was undermined when it was shown that the Latter-day Saints who took this oath did not act on it. Senator Knox asked one witness, "What did you ever do in the line of keeping that vow? Did you ever avenge the blood of the martyrs upon this nation?" "No, sir," the witness responded, "I have enlisted twice to try to defend the nation."[20] Though expressing an unpleasant sentiment, the oath was sentiment only and, because it was never expressed in action, was constitutionally protected, religious belief.

Moreover, the country was accustomed to secret societies of oath-bound men. Many in the Senate belonged to one and were routinely invited to join more. The Methodist Reverend Joshua Stansfield, D.D., had recently written Senator Beveridge inviting him to become a mason in "our Lodge—The Mystic Tie."[21] Latter-day-Saint-turned-Unitarian John P. Meakin characterized himself as a "joiner" when he testified on Smoot's behalf, and he was not exaggerating. "I belong to the Knights of Pythias," he told the committee, "and am the Past Grand Chancellor of our State. I belong to the Benevolent Protective Order of the Elks, and I served as chaplain for six months. I belong to the Fraternal Order of Eagles, to the Woodmen of the World, to the Maccabees, and I still have standing in the Odd Fellows, but not active."[22] Ultimately, the L.D.S. temple ceremony aroused less suspicion because of its easy comparison to the activities of other secret societies.

Meanwhile the committee had lost patience with its chairman. The hearing had taken on the appearance of an internecine squabble that threatened to be interminable. Roosevelt himself began to criticize Burrows publicly for not bringing the matter to a close, and some senators thought Dubois "had gone cranky on the subject."[23] Finally, when the protestors placed on the table thirty volumes of Latter-day Saint sermons, members of the committee rebelled. They refused to hear sermons on polygamy read into the record for the sole purpose of giving the president of the Reorganized Church of Jesus Christ of Latter-day Saints, the non-polygamous representatives of Joseph Smith's legacy, an opportunity to denounce his Utah cousins.[24] The senators demanded that their chairman bring the investigation to a close. Smoot obliged them by placing all seven of his rebuttal witnesses on the stand in one day. The senator had no interest in prolonging the ordeal.

Finally, after closing arguments on 13 April 1906, the hearing adjourned, but not before the much awaited disciplining of Taylor and Cowley. The historical record is too censored to reveal when or by what means the quorum achieved sufficient consensus to subordinate itself and the church to the Senate by following through on Taylor's and Cowley's resignations. It is known, however, that on 5 April 1906 at their quarterly meeting in the temple and on the eve of the spring plenary conference of the church, a formal vote was taken, and "it was agreed to present the resignations of J. W. Taylor and Cowley to the Conference."[25] Three days later, at the closing session, Lyman introduced the usual sustaining of church officers by announcing "the resignation of our beloved brethren, John W. Taylor and Matthias F. Cowley, from their positions . . . because they found themselves out of harmony with the Presidency of the Church and the quorum to which they belonged."[26] No further explanation was given. To replace them and the recently deceased Marriner Merrill, the third of five apostles guilty of post-Manifesto polygamy, three monogamous men were presented to the church for its sustaining vote.[27]

Even for some within the church, the action did not go far enough. Carl Badger wrote a long letter home to Rose after the conference vote: "The shame of the whole matter is that the congregation which accepted their resignations would just as gladly have sustained them. The truth of the matter is that they were put out for the sole purpose of allaying prejudice and shielding the Church."[28] The action was enough, however, for Smoot's supporters and apparently too much for opposing counsel. In his closing argument for the protestants, Carlisle made no mention of polygamy. It is difficult to know whether this was incompetence or a considered judgment that the church's action made testimony of post-Manifesto polygamy irrelevant. Whatever the reason, it provided a welcome opportunity for Smoot's lawyer to make his case. "When Mr. Carlisle undertook to discuss the matter which he considered most important," argued Worthington, "he avoided any reference to polygamy whatsoever."[29] The implication was, of course, that if polygamy was no longer important to the protestants, it should not be to the committee.

By frustrating any proof of large numbers of new polygamists and obtaining the resignations of Taylor and Cowley, Smoot had fulfilled his part of the bargain with the Roosevelt administration. It was now up to his Republican friends to deliver the vote to keep him in the Senate. The first vote would take place within the committee on the evidence it had heard during the hearing. The committee's decision would be cast in the form of a recommendation to the full Senate, which would then vote whether or not to accept the committee's findings. On 6 June 1906 the committee recommended that Smoot be expelled. All five Democrats on the committee were joined by Republicans Burrows and Dolliver to form the majority in opposition and deny Smoot the tie he had hoped for. A favorite of Iowa's powerful women's groups, Dolliver did not want to face their opposition in his reelection campaign. Moreover, on the morning the committee voted, Iowa's Protestant ministers had sent Dolliver a threatening telegram that persuaded him that he would have to vote against Smoot to save his own seat. It was a hard decision that broke a promise to Roosevelt and earned him the disrespect of his colleagues. "Dolliver's face was a study, when he cast his vote in the committee," reported Badger, "and some of his Republican friends are making him feel the betterness [sic] of reproach. [Winthrop M.] Crane of Massachusetts said that when a man wanted office as bad as Dolliver, he had better get out of politics."[30] Of the six other Republicans on the committee, five voted to permit Smoot to retain his seat, and Senator Depew abstained. Sick at home in New York, Depew had agreed initially to give Burrows his proxy to vote in opposition to Smoot. Party leaders in the Senate intervened, however, and Depew telegraphed Burrows to withdraw his vote. Happily, Smoot wired Salt Lake City, "Burrows furious. We can give Sen. Proctor Thanks."[31] As a consequence, the seven-to-five recommendation to remove Smoot was so close and so defined by party affiliation that it was only a technical victory for the protestants. The Senate would be open to full debate on the merits of the question.

Two reports were issued by the committee, one for each side. The contradictory recommendations were submitted to the Republican-controlled Senate on party lines and with no consensus condemnation of the L.D.S. Church. Finally, after four years of protest, investigation, and debate, on 20 February 1907 the Senate voted on resolution number 142, which provided in the language of the committee majority, "that Reed Smoot is not entitled to a seat as a senator of the United States from the State of Utah." A tally of the final vote reveals that only nine Republicans broke ranks to vote against their colleague from Utah; three Democrats crossed party lines to vote for him.[32] The year's delay in bringing the matter to a floor vote in the Senate restored Dolliver's nerve, and he redeemed himself with his party by not only voting for Smoot but delivering a speech in his behalf.[33] In the end, Smoot held his seat; forty-two senators voted in opposition to the resolution to unseat him, and twenty-eight in favor.

Several reasons were given at the time for Smoot's victory. Some believed that Smoot's personal qualifications had overridden antagonism toward his church. Senator Bois Penrose of Pennsylvania is reputed to have said, "I think the Senate should prefer a polygamist who doesn't 'polyg' to a monogamist who doesn't 'monog.'"[34] Four years in the Senate had earned Smoot the personal respect and, in some cases, affection of his Washington colleagues. He gave God the credit when President Theodore Roosevelt "remarked in a jocular way to me today, that he did not know how it was, but that someway or other he rather loved me."[35] Smoot's ability to ingratiate himself with the president and some of the most powerful Republicans in the Senate was, without doubt, a boon to his case. Yet Smoot's likability could have only facilitated, not created, the result of the hearing. Just as important as friendship was the administration's self-interest and political acumen.

The day he expressed his affection to Smoot, Roosevelt informed the senator that he himself "and his cabinet [would be] active now not passive in favor of me. They with the Republican leaders are willing for the case to be made political issue. Secy [William Howard] Taft is willing to go on the stump on this issue."[36] With Mormon voters able to influence three seats in the House, six seats in the Senate, and nine electoral votes, it is understandable that Smoot's survival was interpreted by some as merely an exercise in party politics. An outraged Dubois, in his final speech in the Senate, accused Roosevelt and the Republicans of being the first to politicize the "Mormon question" and promised they would regret exchanging the "moral support of the Christian women and men of the United States" for "temporary political advantage."[37] More dispassionate critics also concluded that Smoot's "retention was a matter of political expediency rather than for constitutional reasons."[38] Such conclusions were oversimplifications, however, expressing more cynicism than insight. Political interests mattered greatly but not to the exclusion of other causes.

In particular, "constitutional reasons" had worked to Smoot's advantage at critical points in the process, especially prior to the hearing when he first presented his credentials to the Senate. Smoot was seated initially and his case was referred to committee because of concerns about the Senate's right to nullify a state's vote by rejecting a duly elected representative. In final debate, Senator Hopkins of Illinois devoted much of his time to whether the Senate could determine the eligibility of its members on other than constitutional grounds. In particular, he pointed to the danger of holding any member of Congress liable for religious belief. "If we are to charge a member of a Christian church with all the crimes that have been committed in its name," Hopkins asked rhetorically, "where is the Christian gentleman in this body who would be safe in his seat?"[39] Of course, questions of religious liberty, too, were on everyone's mind from the inception of the case. It is the more obvious for the protestors' failure to mention it in their complaint, except in the defensive assertion, "We wage no war against his [Smoot's] religious belief as such."[40] Of course, the pro-Smoot forces relied explicitly on the constitutionally protected status of religious belief when defending the nonpolygamous but believing Smoot.[41] As for Mormon political power, Hopkins went so far as to remind the Senate that there was no constitutional prohibition against a state-established religion.[42]

Personal relationships, political leverage, and constitutional rights went into the mix that allowed Senator Smoot to retain his seat. Yet these factors had been present in earlier confrontations with the nation and had not prevented the imposition of extraordinarily oppressive sanctions against the Latter-day Saints. Additional reasons are needed to explain why the Senate could and did vote to legitimize the L.D.S. Church by accepting one of its hierarchs in its midst. It has been suggested in previous chapters that the Senate had the option of accepting Smoot because Protestant political hegemony was beginning to wane. Significantly, during this period the nineteenth-century ideal of unifying American Protestantism was being replaced by an acknowledgment of difference and a new goal of federated cooperation. While the L.D.S. Church's differences were too extreme for church federation, they no longer justified, for the majority of Protestants, attempts to destroy Mormonism. Growing differences among the Protestants themselves made them less able to command from their churches and offer their government the unified political support needed to oust Smoot. Moreover, the coalition of social reform and women's purity movements, which had been so effective against the Mormons in the nineteenth century, was losing its power to affect government policy. Women's groups especially were targets of a new public criticism of the "club woman" and were dismissed as having acted hysterically against the monogamist Smoot.[43]

One can take this argument too far, however. A weakened Protestantism was still formidable. Protestant relocation off-center merely cracked open the door to social acceptance; it did not pave the way or lend a hand to actual entry. The former had to be done by the church itself; the latter, by the Senate. No solution to the Mormon question could have been attempted, much less obtained, if the Latter-day Saints had not abandoned finally and convincingly their most socially offensive and politically rebellious behavior: plural marriage. By publicly disciplining two apostles and reconstituting their quorum with monogamous men, church leaders convinced the necessary Senate majority that the Mormons would subject themselves to the laws of the land, even at the expense of the law of their god. While the end of Mormon polygamy paved the way for Senate acceptance of Smoot, it did not address directly concerns about the church's institutional power, however. The church's dismissal of Taylor and Cowley, though traumatic to its own organization, was largely a symbolic response that left intact Mormon control over the West and facilitated extension of church influence to the seat of national power. Why this gesture satisfied the Senate that Mormon power was not a threat to the nation can only be fully understood in terms of the Senate's own evolution during this period. Weakened Protestant hegemony and Latter-day Saint abandonment of polygamy were only two parts of the equation that solved the nation's Mormon Problem. The final component of the solution was the Senate's new confidence in managing private concentrations of power.

The L.D.S. Church was only one of a number of large institutions investigated by the federal government at the turn of the century. Typically the scrutinized institutions were commercial enterprises that dominated the commodities, transportation, and financial markets of the time. After the excesses and conflicts of the Gilded Age, Americans were convinced that some activities and institutions had to be regulated in order to preserve not only the free market but also a free society. In 1890, the same year the Latter-day Saints issued the Manifesto on polygamy, Congress declared that the market needed to be made less free so that all Americans could compete freely. When he moved for passage of the Sherman Antitrust Act, Senator Hoar admitted, "This is entering upon a new and untrodden field of legislation. It is undertaking to curb by national authority an evil which, under the opinions which have prevailed of old under all our legislative precedents and policies, has been left to be dealt with either by the ordinary laws of trade or to be dealt with by the States." But, Hoar said, this means was no longer sufficient to curb the "evil" of monopoly. Congress was required to respond to "the complaint which has come from all parts and all classes of the country of these great monopolies, which are becoming not only in some cases an actual injury to the comfort of ordinary life, but are a menace to republican institutions themselves."[44]

Fourteen years later, when Senator Hoar was a member of the Smoot hearing panel, he considered these same dangers in the context of the free exercise of religion. He was joined by several other Progressives who had confidence in the power of federal regulation to control corporate power. As they sat in judgment on the Mormon economic, political, and social systems, Beveridge was imposing federal controls on the meatpacking industry and Dillingham was drafting legislation against the railroads. Philander Knox, too, as Roosevelt's former attorney general, had experience enforcing antitrust statutes against such giants as the Northern Securities Company. Each had reason to be confident in the government's capacity to balance public and private power.

Not only was the Smoot panel steeped in monopoly law, but the case as brought to them by the protestants lent itself to analysis in these terms.[45] Americans had long believed Mormonism was a conspiracy, both perfectly organized and secret, to restrain political liberty, social relations, and economic trade. Church leaders were commonly portrayed in the press as having absolute power over every facet of believers' lives and the intent to control all elements of the environment in which the church existed. Inevitably, then, protestants' counsel elicited from friendly and hostile witnesses alike examples of church power and employed the same categories muckraker Ida Tarbell used when she defined Standard Oil as the "ideal trust": the rule of one man over the many, secrecy of operations, and apparent invincibility. The overall effect of a monopoly was, she said, to bring people "by slow degrees and easy stages . . . into a condition of bondage and serfdom."[46] Tarbell could have written the script for the Smoot hearing.

Orlando W. Powers, former judge and longtime resident of Utah, was only one of many witnesses who described the church in terms of a monopoly. "Church organization is the most complete and perfect organization that I am cognizant of," he said.[47] As for secrecy and control, "You have asked me for instances of church interference. They are hard to give, because the church is a secret organization. We see the result; we can not tell always just how that result was attained."[48] Contemporary publications, too, characterized the church's power as complete: "The church never lets go its people even in their leisure hours . . . pursuing the policy of answering all the demands of rational life," concluded one investigative journalist.[49] Throughout the hearing the church was portrayed as a monopoly that threatened, in Senator Hoar's terms, "ordinary life" and "republican institutions." Thus in its twentieth-century incarnation, the Mormon Problem was susceptible to analysis in the same terms as a variety of monopolist enterprises that the nation had been thinking about for twenty years. Reporting on Powers's testimony, the *Washington Times* chose as its headline "Mormon Church Called a Trust by Utah Jurist."[50] Though

Mormon Octopus, in Alfred Henry Lewis, "The Viper on the Hearth,"
Cosmopolitan, March 1911, 445. Fear that the Mormons exercised monopolistic
power over private and public domains had long dominated negative perceptions
of the church. They would not stop with the end of the Smoot hearings, as
demonstrated in this 1911 illustration for a series of anti-Mormon articles in
Cosmopolitan. Here the octopus church is depicted with tentacles locked around
the U.S. Congress and "The Home" as well as mining, farming, school, and
railroads, by which means a temple cult is supported by amassed wealth.
Courtesy of LDS Family and Church History Library.

couched in contemporary muckraking terms, these arguments had been heard before. As Gordon has shown, nineteenth-century fears of Mormon economic power joined convictions that monogamy was the foundation of a free market to rationalize legislation that stripped the L.D.S. Church of both property and corporate standing.[51] This time, however, charges of monopoly did not galvanize either the administration or the legislature to action.

By the time Smoot arrived in Washington, the government's stance on industrial trusts had become more of a compromise position than it was popularly understood to be. Although he had a reputation as a trustbuster, Roosevelt was not so much against monopoly power as he was for regulating it. In his first address to Congress on 3 December 1901, Roosevelt advocated legislation to abolish abuses without destroying the combinations themselves. In this as in many things, Roosevelt's position was pragmatic. He did not attempt to dissolve large aggregations of economic power because he did not think dissolution was possible. He did, however, intend to police them. Roosevelt said one might as well try to reverse the Mississippi River as try to stop the growth of large industry in America. But, he added, one could "regulate and control them by levees."[52] Beveridge, too, serving as Roosevelt's point man on the Smoot hearing panel, "was not antagonistic to combinations of capital . . . [but] tried to walk along the uncharted line of distinction between good and bad trusts."[53]

Thus evidence at the hearing that the Mormon church was a monopoly could not, by itself, win the protestors' case. The Senate had become accustomed to concentrations of private power, even confident in its ability to control monopolies. The question was not whether Mormonism was a monopoly but whether it was a "bad" monopoly. Smoot was told as much by Senator Dolliver, who did "not care a snap of his finger about the Church being in business or in politics, for he admits frankly that the Mormon Church is no more in control of politics in Utah . . . than the Methodist Church is in control in Iowa. The only thing troubling him he said, was the impression . . . that the Church is . . . only waiting for an opportune time to restore polygamy."[54]

Polygamy made Mormonism a bad monopoly because it threatened republican institutions and ordinary life. To the general public, polygamy was primarily an embarrassment to civilized people and a vice corrosive of the moral fabric of democracy. But to those who had thought more about it, polygamy evidenced the greater problem of Mormonism's monopolistic powers. Josiah Strong, one of America's most read and quoted commentators, wrote in his agenda for America at the turn of the century, "Polygamy might be utterly destroyed, without seriously weakening Mormonism. . . . What, then, is the real strength of Mormonism? It is ecclesiastical despotism which holds it together, unifies it and makes it strong. The Mormon Church is probably the most complete organization in the world."[55]

The completeness of the church organization's power was, in antitrust terms, both horizontal and vertical. Polygamy exemplified the depth and breadth, the private and public extent of the church's power and its pretensions to self-government at the expense of statutory law. The threat of the church to "republican intuitions" lay in its power to command the obedience of the faithful to a principle so contrary to human decency. Once entrapped in polygamous unions, believers, especially women, were ostracized from civilized society. Thus imprisoned, the individual's life was forfeit, and the church's future control was ensured and complete. The polygamist was not free to choose another society and, therefore, had to do the church's will within the society created by polygamy. So said the popular literature of the day.[56] The church's power over "ordinary life" was manifest in the intricate kinship attachments created by polygamy. These attachments gave the church a definitive influence on such personal matters as romantic love and parental nurture, the most intimate aspects of human feeling and experience. Thus, to all America, polygamy was the proof that and means by which the church's power extended into every sphere and over every level of the believer's life.

This nexus between polygamy and the extent of control over the believer's life was not lost on the Senate. Though the senators expressed outrage at the immorality of Mormonism, their primary concern was the significance of polygamy as the marker of the church's power to contravene federal law. Consequently, by publicly sanctioning post-Manifesto polygamists who had resisted Senate subpoenas, the church demonstrated persuasively that it would obey the law of the land. The church may be a monopoly, but it was not a bad one and, therefore, was eligible for constitutional protection. While a larger claim could be made regarding the evolution of antitrust law during the Progressive Era and the rise of the administrative state, I will leave that to others whose focus is legal history. From the perspective of religious history, it is sufficient here to note that the government's antitrust experience facilitated the solution of the Mormon Problem. The preceding twenty years had given Progressive Era lawmakers sufficient confidence in managing private concentrations of power that compromise with the L.D.S. Church was finally possible. Though, in Tarbell's terms, the church retained its "perfect organization," kept its secrets and influential personalities, and held more political and economic power in the mountain West than any other single institution, the church was subordinated to the state.

Armed with this conception of permissible concentrations of power and the benefit that Latter-day Saint power offered his party, the trustbuster himself let it be known that Apostle Smoot was welcome in Washington. On two social occasions immediately prior to the Senate floor vote, President Roosevelt publicly displayed his support of Smoot. In early January 1907 at a Diplomatic Corps reception, as he retired with his cabinet in tow, Roosevelt walked across the room and past several rows of people to the much maligned Mrs. Smoot and announced "very pleasantly, loud enough for all to hear: 'Good night, Mrs. Smoot.'" A few days later, when Utah's representative entered a reception, "the President reached out his hand in front of a group of people, and said: 'How is Utah?'" signaling to all that "he wanted Senator and Mrs. Smoot treated well."[57] The message was received, and the vote for Smoot split on strict party lines. Nevertheless, a rationale for the party's support of the apostle-senator had to be given to the public. Though the Mormons were willing to be controlled by the Senate, the senators themselves were controlled by their voting constituencies. The role of convincing the American public that Smoot should retain his seat was assigned to the most able of the president's men: Senators Beveridge, Foraker, Hopkins, and Knox, who spoke on Smoot's behalf during the Senate vote.

Senate floor debate began on 6 February 1907, with galleries packed and overflow crowds in the halls straining to hear. One thirty-year veteran observer of the Senate told Badger "he could not recall when before this time the Sergeant at Arms of the Senate had allowed people to stand around the wall at the back of the galleries." Not wanting to miss the drama, members of the House of Representatives "stood behind the seats of the Senators, or sat on the leather seats along the wall—when they could find seats."[58] The debate alternated in an orderly fashion between those for and against the committee recommendation that Senator Smoot be expelled.

The Republicans who spoke in favor of keeping the apostle-senator in his seat presented a unified argument and only differed in their assigned emphasis. They addressed immediately and at length the question of polygamy, reassuring their colleagues that the problem had been solved. The arguments were a recapitulation of the church's own statements in the hearing. Not only was "polygamy . . . as dead as slavery," but "time would banish" cohabitation.[59] The young generation of the church did not believe in polygamy and would fight it if an attempt were made to bring it back. Smoot was not to blame for its slow demise any more than "the Presidents of the United States [who] time and time again in appointing to office Mormons, including governors . . . have maintained the polygamous relationships."[60] Pragmatically speaking, the leading wrongdoers had been punished. They had been "deposed from their official positions, expelled from the church, driven from the country, and are now fugitives from justice."[61] It was not appropriate for the Senate to ask for more, especially since Smoot himself had always been a champion of monogamy. Pennsylvania senator Knox made this case most succinctly: "Mr. President, polygamy is dying out. . . . As practical men, should we not be content with that?"[62]

Having disposed of the negative question, the committee minority built a positive case. First, they argued that the church had recently shown loyalty to the government and contributed to the nation's social welfare. Smoot had taken no apostolic oath in opposition to his country, only "some sort of archaic obligation."[63] His co-religionists also were loyal, having been "taught love of country and devotion to Republic."[64] Former attorney general Knox carried the bulk of this argument, rehearsing Latter-day Saint doctrine and actions that displayed patriotism in hymn and creed. The junior senator from Utah, George Sutherland, added that the citizens of his state were among the first to volunteer in the war with Spain and were led by a Latter-day Saint major "as brave and loyal and splendid a gentleman as ever wore the uniform of a soldier."[65] Beveridge elaborated by including in the record the name of every Utah volunteer wounded or killed in the war in the Philippines. "The Filipino bullets found no 'treason' in these Utah hearts," he said. "How better can men prove their loyalty than by their lives?"[66]

Smoot's defenders argued further that the L.D.S. Church had come to the nation's aid during other domestic crises. It had protected the government's property during a recent cyclone in the Society Islands and had sent disaster aid immediately after the San Francisco earthquake; such acts showed a commitment to the common good.[67] Evidence to the contrary could be mustered by only Senator James Berry of Arkansas, who remembered the slaughter of his neighbors who left for California and never made it out of Utah's Mountain Meadows alive. That was in 1857, however, five years before Smoot and many others in the chamber were born. No other recent examples of Latter-day Saint violence could be found.[68]

The third theme of Smoot's defenders was that the L.D.S. Church was, after all, just a church. Even Latter-day Saint belief in revelation and obedience to prophetic leaders was not so different from the creeds of other churches, argued Senator Dillingham. The church just had "a very peculiar method of using that term [revelation] . . . in connection with minor affairs of the church." Revelation to the Latter-day Saints was nothing more than a "prayer for guidance and in whatever follows they believe they have that guidance."[69] Moreover, Smoot had sworn that he was not required to obey his leaders, thus demonstrating that "members of his church are free agents, and that any one of them has the right to disobey any divine revelation given to the head of the church."[70] Mormonism was a voluntary organization.

Thinking of Mormons as a church like other churches was, however, a stretch of the imagination for many in the chamber. Therefore the speakers drew analogies to specific mainstream churches and selected points of comparison to define American denominationalism. Having shown that agreement with Mormon leaders was voluntary, the defenders pointed out that any church was clannish when engaged in politics and that many were so engaged. Do not "two Baptists—other things being equal—feel a little more kindly toward each other than they do toward two Presbyterians or two Congregationalists?"[71] Knox reminded his colleagues that Latter-day Saints "are not the only sect whose priesthood meddles with worldly affairs without members being for that reason excluded from Federal offices."[72] Besides, he continued, creedal positions were largely irrelevant to personal belief, were they not? Senator Nathan B. Scott of West Virginia interrupted to ask if the Presbyterian members of the Senate were "accountable . . . when many of them do not believe" in their church's doctrine of infant damnation? If not, then how could Smoot be held responsible for polygamy? Thus, Senator Scott concluded, when taken too seriously, creeds were a problem for all churches, not unlike the problem the Latter-day Saints *had*—in the past, that is.[73] Next, Senator Hopkins marginalized Latter-day Saint practitioners of polygamy as "fanatics in this, precisely as Sydney Smith, a hundred years ago, found fanatics in the Methodist Church."[74] In sum, argued Utah's other senator and lapsed Latter-day Saint, George Sutherland, Mormonism is simply a belief system and no crazier than others. "The melancholy fact runs through all history that nothing has been too absurd, nothing too cruel, to be believed and taught and done in the name of religion. . . . You can not reason with a false religious belief any more than you can argue with a case of typhoid fever. It simply runs its course and mental health returns, . . . when the false belief no longer appeals to [the intellect]."[75] It was a low standard, but one the Mormons could meet.

Having shaped Mormonism into a form that "satisfies the American ideas of a church, and a system of religious faith," Smoot's advocates made the next logical argument.[76] Both constitutional law and the principle of religious tolerance forbade excluding Smoot on the basis of his religious belief. To do otherwise was unlawful and un-American. Indeed, to Smoot's supporters the hearing itself read "like a chapter from the Spanish inquisition."[77] Beveridge offered a final denominational comparison by inviting the Senate to remember the history of religious intolerance against his own Methodists in England and "the terrible, but true tale of the burning of the witches in New England."[78]

There was, of course, another side to the debate. Many in the Senate, at least the twenty-eight who voted against Smoot, believed Mormonism was "an organization . . . so un-American, so lawbreaking, and law defying that he, on account of his position in it, is not fit to represent . . . the people of the United States in this Chamber."[79] The failure to describe here the anti-Smoot argument is not a reflection on its competence. Neither does the restatement of the pro-Smoot argument mean that it is a correct assessment of the facts of the case. It is fairly apparent that it was not. For example, the advocates' characterization of church doctrine differed considerably from the Latter-day Saints' own representations, especially regarding the significance of revelation. It is, however, these very disparities that illuminate what the church had to become in order to receive constitutional protection for its doctrines and practices. The value of the advocates' argument is not that it described the L.D.S. Church, but that it described what the state wanted this and all churches to be—or at least act like.

Beveridge summarized the terms for granting religious liberty to the L.D.S. Church: "Obedience to law, tolerance of opinion, loyalty to country —these are the principles which make the flag a sacred thing and this Republic immortal. These are the principles that make all Americans brothers and constitute this Nation God's highest method of human enlightenment and living liberty. By these principles let us live and vote and die, so that 'this Government of the people, for the people, and by the people may not perish from the earth.'"[80] The Senate galleries burst into applause as he finished his prescription for ending the Mormon Problem. Satisfying the first two criteria—obedience and loyalty—was a fairly straightforward proposition, though by no means easy. The Latter-day Saints had demonstrated obedience by subordinating their church to the state, through such means as Smith's 1903 address redefining the "Kingdom of God" and the 1906 punishment of Taylor and Cowley. Loyalty had been demonstrated by Mormons volunteering to fight the nation's battles and openly contributing to the nation's common welfare through relief efforts.

The requirement of religious tolerance was a more subtle undertaking. For the Senate, it was sufficient that the church expressed tolerance politically or, stated negatively, no longer imposed its beliefs on the citizens within its sphere of political influence. During the trial, non-Mormon witnesses had convincingly depicted Utah as tolerant of non-Mormon candidates for public office. Latter-day Saint witnesses had provided a reasonable explanation for the church's pre-approval of its officers who ran for public office, defining the process as a precaution against conflict of interests and resources, not an exercise of political control. Most convincingly, Salt Lake City's volatile electorate, which even Apostle-senator Smoot could not control for his party, evidenced the fact of an open society. These signs of political diversity, coupled with the demise of polygamy, were enough to assure a slim majority of senators that the L.D.S. Church did not cause "actual injury to the comfort of ordinary life, . . . [and neither was it] a menace to republican institutions."[81] The Senate's vote to retain Smoot marked the beginning of the nation's acceptance of the Latter-day Saints on the same denominational terms as other American religions: obedience, loyalty, and tolerance defined in political, not religious, terms.

As shown in Beveridge's speech, American "civil religion" served more purposes than endowing the state with religious authority.[82] It served also to define the criteria for standing in America's political economy and protection under its laws. Martin Marty's definition of the essence of civil religion is an apt description of what the Mormons were being measured against in the Smoot hearing: "the faith of the whole . . . an American tradition that is coextensive with the culture or society, in which apparently competing [religious] signals could be integrated or from whose viewpoint they could be dismissed."[83] The ultimate purpose of the Senate hearing was to determine whether Mormonism was to be "integrated" or "dismissed," and Smoot knew it: "I do hope I will be successful in retaining my seat, for if I am, I am very sure that in a short time the country will take it as a vindication of the Church, because the fight has been made entirely on the Church."[84]

When it came, vindication was civil, not religious, of course. Sutherland of Utah cautioned his fellow senators to distinguish between their political responsibilities and personal morality, reminding them that the Mormon Problem "was one which must be approached from the standpoint of practical statesmanship rather than from the standpoint of the religious reformer."[85] Not primarily concerned with inculcating virtue in citizens, the "practical statesman" would not press for moral conformity but would find obedience to law sufficient in the political sphere. A direct appeal to restraint in matters of substantive morality, Sutherland's statement suggests that, while the Smoot hearing began as an exercise in nineteenth-century moral reform, Smoot was accepted by the Senate on terms more compatible with twentieth-century procedural fairness and substantive neutrality. During the Progressive Era, as described most notably by Michael Sandel, "the notion that government should shape the moral and civic character of its citizens gave way to the notion that government should be neutral toward the values its citizens espouse, and respect each person's capacity to choose his or her own ends."[86]

Though it demanded the cessation of polygamy, the Senate did so on grounds that monogamy was the "law of the land." Moral censure was left to "the religious reformer." Thus the Senate demanded no more of the Mormons than what was politically practical, leaving it to them to punish instances of new polygamy and giving them considerable latitude and time to do so, as will be discussed in the Epilogue. In sum, it can be said that the Mormon Problem was solved finally because the Mormons had figured out how to act more like an American church, a civil religion; the Senate, less like one.

Perhaps, in the near future we may have

headquarters . . . in other mission fields, where

we can advertise our name and our principles,

and where we can have a permanent foothold

and exhibit our works to those who are inquiring

after the truth, and not leave the people, as in

years gone by, under the impression that we are

constantly on the wing in these distant lands.

—Joseph F. Smith (1903)

EPILOGUE

Given its long history, the Mormon Problem faded relatively quickly from the nation's consciousness after the 1907 decision to seat Apostle Smoot in the U.S. Senate. Subsequent efforts to attract attention to the evils of Mormonism were wasted on the larger public and appealed only to churches that found in Mormonism a useful foil against which to shape their own sectarian identities. The rest of America moved on, happy to forget about the Latter-day Saints and, if reminded, to consider them merely peculiar, not dangerous. "Some of the facts brought out of the Smoot investigation were surprising and disappointing, and it need scarcely be said disgusting," reported the *Washington Post*, "but they did not alarm the country. The statesmen and the people of the United States do not regard this sect as a menace to the republic."[1]

The *Boston Transcript* may have come closest to explaining how the Senate vote was understood by most Americans. Enumerating the senators who deviated from their party's position and reasoning that each was responding to pressures characteristic of his local electorate, the paper concluded, "The East [with only one senator voting against Smoot] thus holds religious tolerance in high regard. Moving westward [seven senators] . . . voted against Smoot's retaining a seat in the Senate, showing in the Northwest a considerable hostility to the Mormon Church, of which Mr. Smoot is an apostle. West of the Dakota line both parties usually like to stand well with the Mormons, except Idaho, where, under Mr. Dubois's leadership, to attack them has become a Democratic cause. . . . The issue is at last well settled. The next move of the MORMON Church will be awaited with interest."[2] Though suspicious of Mormonism's intentions, Americans were prepared to give the benefit of the doubt to the Senate's political solution to the Mormon Problem.

Latter-day Saints responded to Smoot's victory in a variety of ways. Some mixed relief and disappointment, as did young Badger: "Well, we are through with the agony. There were not as many votes for the Senator as I had expected."[3] On the other hand, Smoot's political cronies in Utah "jubilated so long last evening, over the good news from Washington, D.C., that," one reported, "I am almost unhorsed today."[4] Many believers felt that righteousness had triumphed over evil. The citizens of Smoot's hometown celebrated with a mock funeral procession for the *Salt Lake Tribune*. Led by a horned satan, honorary pallbearers gave comic orations and dressed in imitation of the senator's various antagonists, among them Rev. W. M. Paden of the Salt Lake Ministerial Association and editorialist Frank J. Cannon.[5]

Joseph F. Smith's response was more sedate and far more significant. He asked Smoot to

> kindly say to the President in my behalf, that God alone knows our heartfelt appreciation of his absolutely fair and kindly consideration of your case; and please say to him also that all we have to offer in return is the absolute assurance of the righteousness of our cause, and the loyalty of our hearts. . . . We are able to appreciate, and do appreciate, the strong and fair-minded statesmen of the nation who have the courage of their convictions in face of the opposition wrought up by unprincipled politicians, through and by organized women, and the religious element of the nation; and I say from the bottom of my heart, God bless them and theirs now and forever.[6]

The practical substance of his letter may have been more clearly stated by a more worldly colleague of Smoot's on the same occasion: "Politically you have assured the State to the grand old party of progress for at least the life of your generation."[7] History shows this to have been a conservative estimate, and Smith's "forever" was a more accurate forecast of Utah's twentieth-century party politics.

The protestants suffered the greatest immediate disappointment. Their hopes of eradicating Mormonism were not only dashed but crushed by the church's obtaining a seat in the Senate. Still, the legal supremacy of monogamous marriage had been secured, and most protestants could be satisfied with this victory. Like the *Boston Transcript*, the majority were willing to wait for and watch the church's next move "with interest." On the other side of the country, the *Northwestern Christian Advocate* consoled its readers that "the results of the investigation, while not crowned with success as measured by the actual fulfilment of its avowed purpose, still accomplished much in the great cause which underlay it all. Polygamy received a staggering blow from which it never recovered."[8] Those who had borne the burden of prosecuting the case against Smoot and his church were understandably not as sanguine, however.

Like the Latter-day Saints, but to opposite effect, the moral reform agencies promised never to forget the supporters of the apostle-senator. Some of Smoot's colleagues raised the issue jokingly with him, as did Senator Knox, who "laughingly remarked that the only thing that stood in the way of his receiving the nomination for President of the United States was the attitude taken by him in my case."[9] For supporters standing for election in 1908, the threat was more immediate. President Roosevelt tried to help Illinois senator Hopkins, who had taken the lead role in Smoot's defense on the Senate floor, notwithstanding his state's strong anti-Mormon bias.[10] In a widely published congratulatory letter, the president praised Hopkins for "courage, ability and sense of right," but to no avail. Hopkins was defeated by the previous incumbent.[11] The electoral fates of the members of the hearing committee were mixed. Anti-Smoot senators Bailey and Overman were reelected, while Burrows, Frazier, and Depew were defeated. Of the pro-Smoot senators on the committee, Foraker, who had drafted the minority report, was defeated, but Dolliver, who signed the report in opposition to Smoot but sided with him and gave a speech on his behalf on the Senate floor, was reelected. Dillingham was likewise successful. Senator Knox did not stand for popular election, having been appointed U.S. secretary of state in 1909.[12]

The significance of these election results is further complicated by the variety of issues at stake in any given campaign. For example, Republican senator Henry C. Hansbrough from North Dakota broke party ranks to oppose Smoot in hopes of strengthening his chances for reelection. Smoot was "glad to report" that "one of the Scandinavian representatives told me that Hansbrough went into the Scandinavian districts for the purpose of creating a sentiment in favor of him on the ground that he voted against me, and as soon as the Scandinavian people learned that my mother was a

Norwegian, they almost to a man denounced Hansbrough."[13] In addition to the effect of collateral issues, delay also makes it difficult to measure the backlash from the Smoot hearing on state senate elections, some of which occurred as long as two years after Smoot was seated. From the mixed election results among Smoot's defenders and detractors it appears that the fallout from Smoot's victory was marginal, at best.

In national politics, too, little notice was taken of Smoot's acceptance by the Senate. Democrat William Jennings Bryan was encouraged to make the vote for Smoot an issue in the next presidential campaign, but he apparently declined.[14] Nevertheless, organizations such as the National Congress of Mothers, the Woman's Christian Temperance Union, and the Daughters of the American Revolution maintained their distrust of Smoot and his church. For another fifteen years they lobbied for an antipolygamy amendment and confronted the Utah senator with reports of new plural marriages in his state. Ultimately, however, the reformers were unsuccessful in their bid to amend the Constitution. Smoot was partially responsible because he effectively badgered his apostolic brethren to do something about the reports. But more significant to the failure of the women reformers was a dramatic shift in gender politics.

In the nineteenth century, women's public authority had been based on the notion that their inherent purity gave them a civilizing effect on society and, therefore, a duty to engage in social reform. In the early twentieth century, a new consensus was forming that made women's reform activities suspect. The signs appeared even in a press generally unsympathetic to Smoot. Some editorialists dismissed the protest as comprised of "every known society from the Young Men's Sewing Circle of Cranberry, Wis., to the Heavyset Ladies' Glee Club of New York."[15] Others accused women generally of having "gone daft in their determination to strike obsolescent polygamy through unpolygamous Smoot."[16] Such gender slurs and accusations of hysteria by the press both manifested and enabled a change in American sexual politics that privileged a new masculine primitive over the feminine civilized "club woman" and even inspired limited admiration for Mormon patriarchy.[17] Smoot's patron Roosevelt embodied the spirit of the times and did not hesitate to articulate it as well. "Woman has lost her sense of duty," he warned the assembled National Congress of Mothers in 1905 as it led the Smoot protest, "if she is sunk in vapid self-indulgence or has let her nature be twisted so that she prefers a sterile pseudo-intellectuality to that great and beautiful development of character which comes only to those whose lives know the full self-sacrifice undergone."[18]

"De-Lighted." Roosevelt's campaign against "race suicide" made him a supporter
of Joseph F. Smith, according to *Salt Lake Herald* cartoonist Alan L. Lovey.
Implicit in this undated caricature is the country's shift to the masculine in
politics, which contributed to the nation's ambiguous response to Smoot hearing
testimony from Mormon patriarchs. Used by permission, Utah State Historical
Society, all rights reserved.

The effect of gender politics on the antipolygamy campaign was deci-
sive. "The new concepts of masculinity operated to shape a revised view
of the Mormons and antipolygamy, ultimately creating a backlash to antipolygamy," according to Joan Smyth Iversen. "It was a masculine backlash," she concluded, that found its "ultimate expression . . . with the en-
trance of Theodore Roosevelt into the Mormon controversy during the
battle to remove Mormon apostle Reed Smoot from the United States Senate."[19] The second blow to the women's reform effort came from women
themselves. As Nancy Cott has shown, during these years modern feminism abandoned purity and domesticity as the source of women's power
and the proper object of their efforts. Caught in a backlash against women
in politics, weakened by diminished numbers of adherents, and frustrated
by Senator Smoot's continuing defense of his church, the antipolygamy

movement ceased to be a force in American politics within a decade of the Smoot hearing. Though the coalition of Protestant ministers and women reformers continued to press Congress for an amendment as late as 1924, the Smoot hearing proved to be their last hurrah.[20]

The concerns of the moral reform agencies at the close of the Smoot hearing in 1907 were not baseless, however. There had been no disciplinary action against post-Manifesto polygamists other than the resignations of Taylor and Cowley. Even for some Latter-day Saints the action against the two apostles had been too mild a rebuke and done for the wrong reason. "I know that the resignations of these Apostles were given to shield the Church, not to punish their wrong," Badger fumed to his wife. "That in itself is not bad," he conceded, "but there is something so darkly dishonorable about claiming *Now* that they were given to punish the new cases of polygamy, that I should think impossible that a church could put forth any such false claim."[21] The most damning comment came from Senator Smoot himself. In an uncharacteristic indiscretion, on his way back to Utah eight weeks after the Senate vote, Smoot revealed to Badger that some church leaders intended to continue performing new plural marriages. Flabbergasted, Badger wrote his wife, "I must confess that the situation is beyond me. The Senator has just said that he intends to tell the brethren when he gets home that if they want to continue this 'polygamy business' they must leave the United States. I asked if he meant unlawful cohabitation, and he said no. Well, I am dumbfounded."[22]

The church's difficulty in ending polygamy was practical, not merely political, in terms of resistance from within. The quorum was, with the recent replacements of Cowley, Taylor, Merrill, and Teasdale, comprised predominantly of monogamous men committed to keeping Smith's promise to the Senate. But the authority to perform plural marriages had been disbursed broadly among subordinate officers of the church during the preceding twenty years of surreptitious practice. As a result, the church's presidency was probably not in sufficient administrative control to stop the practice immediately. Even where it had control, it did not have support. General ambivalence about both the 1890 and 1904 manifestos and specific family ties meant that little was done privately and nothing was done publicly until 1910. Other factors, too, played a part in the church's slow enforcement of its new policy. Included was, no doubt, sensitivity to accusations of political motivation and a desire to give believers time to realize the church meant its latest prohibition.

Smoot's correspondence and entries in his diary between 1908 and 1911 describe an ongoing struggle within the church's hierarchy over what should be done and to whom in response to reports of continuing criticism in Washington.[23] While church discipline was the obvious way of regaining control over new plural marriages, leadership disagreed over who and what should be punished. Should all parties or just those who performed the marriage be punished? Should all marriages after 1890, 1904, or even some later date be subject to scrutiny? In September 1910, concerned about rumors of new plural marriages and under pressure in Washington, Smoot attended a quorum meeting in Salt Lake City to recommend that "every person taking a plural wife since the [1890] manifesto should not be sustained in prominent positions in the Church." Moreover, he "strongly demand[ed] that cases at least since . . . 1904, be excommunicated and vigorous action commenced at once."[24] His fellow apostles did not, however, desire a "wholesale slaughter" of members who married plurally after 1890, preferring to "drop them as fast as conditions will permit without making a great stir about it." The next day Smoot reported to President Joseph F. Smith what he had said to the apostles and told Smith that "some public statement should be made by him at the coming Conference." Smoot asked also that midlevel church officers be granted authority "to handle all new cases" of plural marriage. His personal lobbying was successful. In a letter dated 5 October 1910, Smith instructed officers of the church to begin enforcing the Second Manifesto by excommunicating or disfellowshipping, at their discretion, all members in violation of the 1904 prohibition of plural marriage. Marriages solemnized between 1890 and 1904 were not actionable, unless they were a source of public embarrassment to the church.[25]

As people began to believe Joseph F. Smith's repeated statements that he "was in earnest in having it [plural marriage] stopped and any statement to the contrary was untrue," the issue of Smith's prophetic role was raised formally within the church.[26] Those who continued to practice plural marriage were deemed in apostasy for not accepting Smith as a prophet and were excommunicated. This made the issue a matter of modern revelation, not plural marriage per se. In other words, "Mormon fundamentalists," as they are popularly called to the discomfort of both groups, are viewed as in schism over the legitimacy of authority claimed by church leaders to suspend the practice of plural marriage.[27] Hence, when questioned recently about the enduring presence of polygamists in Utah, current church president Gordon B. Hinckley protested adamantly, "People mistakenly assume that this Church has something to do with that. It has nothing whatever to do with it. It has had nothing to do with it for a very long time. It's outside the realm of our responsibility. These people are not members."

Pilgrimage to the Joseph Smith Monument. The Smith monument quickly became a site of pilgrimage for twentieth-century Latter-day Saints. Here an unidentified group of L.D.S. missionaries are pictured with the monument and rebuilt Smith family home in the background. Used by permission, Utah State Historical Society, all rights reserved.

Or, in terms more appropriate to the categories used in this analysis of the church's adaptation through collective memory, Hinckley said, "It's behind us."[28]

While Latter-day Saints know their history and respect their forebears, they have successfully written out of their history the religious significance of plural marriage and its role in the restoration of their "Church of Jesus Christ in its fullness and perfection."[29] The numbers who left the church in the early decades of the twentieth century for the sake of plural marriage were relatively few, and their departure no doubt contributed to the church's successful reformulation of its reputation. As described, for those who remained with the main body of the church, use of Joseph Smith's autobiography helped to jettison plural marriage without destroying the necessary sense of identity with nineteenth-century tradition, much less confidence in Joseph Smith as founding prophet and Joseph F. Smith as his successor. To this was added the church's increasingly sophisticated exercises in collective memory that mapped the American landscape with Latter-day Saint significance and allowed the forgetting of the now doctrinally meaningless history of plural marriage.

Latter-day Saint use of their past, in general, and the Joseph Smith story, in particular, to create a future did not end with the commemorative trip to Vermont. Subsequent initiatives also reoriented the Latter-day Saints' identity by inscribing their history onto the American terrain and directing their attention beyond the Rocky Mountains to where they now believed their future lay. Joseph F. Smith oversaw the purchase not only of the Smith family farm in New York but of various plots of land in Missouri associated with the church's attempt to build Zion and with expectations of Jesus Christ's second coming; of the jail in Carthage, Illinois, where Joseph and Hyrum Smith died; and of a cemetery near Omaha at Winter Quarters, Nebraska, dedicated to those who did not survive the forced exodus from Illinois. Each of these places was a rich mine of Latter-day Saint history and, as such, has been a uniquely powerful resource for the constructive maintenance of Latter-day Saint identity under stress. These historical sites constitute the focus of Latter-day Saint monument building and pilgrimage to this day. Each has been developed with visitor centers and other historical restorations that invite tourism. Most recently, several of these sites have been sacralized by the building of temples, culminating in the 2002 dedication of the rebuilt Nauvoo temple on the anniversary of Joseph Smith's death.[30]

Joseph F. Smith's constructive use of the church's history was facilitated by the variety of centennials that occurred in the early twentieth century, beginning, as we have seen, with the commemoration of Joseph Smith's birth. Where centennial anniversaries did not provide the occasion, Joseph F. Smith developed his own. For example, paramount among identity markers for the Latter-day Saints was the heroic arrival of the pioneers to the Salt Lake Valley on 24 July 1847. Individual communities sometimes had held celebrations on this date to honor their aging settlers, and Joseph F. Smith's predecessor was known for planning the Pioneer Jubilee in 1897.[31] Smith was the first, however, to incorporate a ritual celebration of the event into the church calendar. Typically, he did so with an eye to the future, not the past; on resourcefulness and triumph, not privations and travail; and on rights, not wrongs. He personally instructed his people, "The leading purpose of the celebration is to provide an object lesson to our young people and create within their hearts feelings of patriotism and loyalty for those who pioneered the way to our western homes. . . . It is not the intention to make every Twenty-fourth of July an

Pioneer Day in Eureka, Utah, n.d. This photograph from the early twentieth century shows how the citizens of Eureka reenacted their forebears' march across the plains. Used by permission, Utah State Historical Society, all rights reserved.

occasion for so elaborate a celebration, but it is hoped that it may be sufficiently frequent to keep alive in the hearts and the memories of our youth the instructive lessons of our pioneer life."[32]

These lessons have not been lost on subsequent church or state leadership. Pioneer Day is a state holiday complete with a public parade in most Utah communities and even Salt Lake City, where Latter-day Saints are now a minority. The exportation of this event to the international church was evidenced during the 1997 sesquicentennial observance of the pioneer exodus. In addition to recapitulating the journey from Illinois to Utah, complete with wagons and handcarts as well as daily news coverage and real-time commentary on the internet by participants, the church invited its international members to stage processions in their own countries. Comprised as it was of 60,000 multiethnic Americans and immigrant Europeans who came by wagon and handcart to their Rocky Mountain Zion, the pioneering history of the Latter-day Saints is easily identified with the church's present international constituency. Today the annual memorial to the nineteenth-century pioneering church has become "the story of . . . an international church in the process of consolidating its resources and establishing a homeland from which to become solidly international again later."[33] Thus the collective memorials that stabilized the church during the Smoot hearing continue to anchor it during the current period of explosive international growth.[34]

This is not to say that Smith invented consciously or planned the solutions that hindsight has shown to be so effective. Like most historical actors, Smith was subject to his share of ironic results and unintended consequences. Certainly, he intended neither a four-year Senate investigation nor his own five-day grilling on the witness stand at "the seat of war" in Washington.[35] Indeed, it is by no means certain that he intended to abolish plural marriage. Nevertheless and notwithstanding the variety of intentions and opportunities competing for causal power in the years during which Mormonism was transformed, events during the administration of Joseph F. Smith, including the Smoot hearing, remain key to understanding the present shape and success of the L.D.S. Church.

The present prosperity of the L.D.S. Church is due also to Senator Smoot's more pragmatic interventions in national and international politics. Once seated, Smoot remained in the national legislature for thirty years, all the while an apostle of the L.D.S. Church. Reelected to the Senate four times, Smoot served from 4 March 1903 to 3 March 1933, rising quickly and staying long in positions of power. A year after his second election, Smoot was given a seat on the Senate Appropriations Committee. Two years later he joined the Senate Finance Committee and became its chair in 1923. He was known for his "great devotion" to the Republican Party and played a major role in securing Warren G. Harding's presidential nomination in 1920, as well as drafting the party's platform.[36] Smoot also had a significant part in the development of national land policy.[37] Today Smoot is best remembered for his cosponsorship of the highly protectionist Smoot-Hawley Tariff Act of 1930, which many believe precipitated the Great Depression.[38] As Smoot continued to impress his colleagues with his party loyalty, personal productivity, and business acumen, he was given increasingly greater power in the Senate and access to several presidents. After a private meeting with the newly elected President Harding, Smoot recorded in his journal that they "talked over the situation and discussed men for his cabinet. . . . He wanted me to consider myself as one of his advisers. . . . I was to come to the Whitehouse [sic] at any time and at any hour."[39]

Throughout his tenure Senator Smoot employed both his power and po-

Harding and Smoot in the Provo tabernacle, 26 June 1923. A week before he left to negotiate the recognition of his church in several European countries, Smoot hosted President Harding's visit to Salt Lake City. Smoot conducted an evening meeting in the Mormon Tabernacle in honor of the president's visit, as well as arranging an afternoon round of golf between his two presidents. Courtesy of LDS Family and Church History Library.

litical access in service of his church. On numerous occasions he cured the church's immigration, missionary, and public relations problems. "Bro. Reed Smoot . . . came in time to get our emigrants released who were detained at Boston," reported a member of the church's presidency in 1908. "It shows that it is good to have a man with influence at headquarters."[40] While these interventions were of great import to his co-religionists, they were unimportant to the nation. The protestants' fears that he would rule at the expense of the nation were never realized.

Ultimately, however, Smoot's lack of conflict with the nation's agenda was "not because Smoot would not accept dictation [from his church leaders]," wrote Smoot's biographer, "but because he received none. The Mormon leaders . . . were entirely acquiescent in the political and economic course pursued by the Senator. They received no revelations which required beliefs or practices contrary to the established mores of the country." From this Merrill concluded that "Mormonism was a completely Americanized religion."[41] This is probably too simple an explanation, however. At least, it does not account for Mormonism's continuing difference within American society or its adaptability to foreign cultures. Another possible explanation for the L.D.S. Church's lack of domestic political initiative during Smoot's tenure is disinterest. As in the nineteenth century, the church was intent in the twentieth century on building its own kingdom, not reforming American society. Having achieved the peace and obtained the power it needed to pursue its own ends, the L.D.S. Church had the luxury of ignoring the nation. The apostle-senator's role was to ensure that the peace achieved by the Smoot hearing was preserved so that the nation, too, could ignore the church.[42]

Smoot was the public voice of Mormonism for several years, and many came to understand its beliefs as he modeled them from Washington, D.C. He was, for example, a notorious advocate of book and film censorship. The issue was raised in debate over the Smoot-Hawley tariff bill's continuation of the authority of the Customs Service to interdict the importation of immoral books. Smoot's vehement battle against works by such figures as D. H. Lawrence and Rabelais earned him a reputation for prudery and intolerance.[43] Having been present during the Smoot hearing, Alice Roosevelt Longworth did not miss the irony. Calling the protestors against Smoot "the witch-burning element," she observed that they were "amusingly enough, precisely the same element of pruriency and intolerance that Smoot in turn represented twenty-three years later in his advocacy of a censorship on literature."[44] Whether Mormonism's sexual conservatism was aggravated by the years in which it was accused of sexual license, another study will have to determine. Regardless of its origin, the conservative morality Smoot represented on the floor of the Senate communicated a radically different and, for the L.D.S. Church, more comfortable stereotype of Mormonism.

In addition, and no doubt to the dismay of some church leaders who thought "him poorly grounded in his faith and unlearned in his doctrines," Smoot was often asked to define Latter-day Saint belief.[45] In 1926, for example, *Forum* magazine invited the senator to explain his religion in print. After describing the church's beliefs, he said, "These doctrines look reasonable to me. They are scriptural and consistent. . . . They measure up to the eternal fitness of things."[46] Americans were unpersuaded. As Shipps demonstrated in her statistical analysis of 1920s and 1930s publications, the public shifted its distrust of Mormons as a people to Mormonism as a belief system.[47] This represented progress for the church politically, however, just as Smoot's diatribe in favor of literary censorship had for the church morally. The change in public opinion from a distrust of the Latter-day Saints to a suspicion of their beliefs fit the permissible limits of American religious difference. Mormonism was no longer perceived as a political threat, merely an ethnic peculiarity. The Latter-day Saints had succeeded in becoming merely odd. Like the Amish pietists of the Midwest and Orthodox Jews of the East, the Mormons in the West became part of America's cultural diversity, a reassuring reminder of its capacity for religious liberty.

Gradually, national press coverage of Latter-day Saints emphasized their pioneer virtues, especially industriousness, cooperation, and self-reliance. This is not to say that the church was accepted in full fellowship with the rest of religious America. As Shipps's analysis of the more positive press from the 1920s and 1930s has shown, Mormonism was considered "ridiculous, and if anything, even more un-Christian than it had been in the past." While "the people were inherently good," their church was "still . . . an un-American system."[48] This may be why Senator Smoot's 1926 explanation of his faith still included the assurance that "the Latter-day Saints believe that they must be loyal to their country, honoring its laws, upholding its institutions, its constituted authorities, and doing all things that American citizens ought to do."[49] Nevertheless, the increasingly neutral and sometimes even positive press coverage of the church and the aggressively middle-class values represented by Smoot in the national legislature erased any lingering concerns that the Mormons were a problem.

The ultimate benefit to the church of Smoot's senatorial office became apparent in the summer of 1923. On 4 July, Smoot boarded the ship *Leviathan* bound for Europe. His church was sending him on a special mission to lobby several European governments that had banned its missionaries and forbade its members to assemble. At the time, Smoot was both chairman of the powerful Senate Finance Committee and a member of the War Debt Funding Commission. He traveled with a special passport signed by U.S. Secretary of State Charles Hughes and visited the capitals of Great Britain, Denmark, Sweden, and Norway to convince these nations, as he had his own, that Latter-day Saints were loyal and virtuous and that their church should receive official recognition. Although the church's European missions had been in crisis for several decades due to its inability to obtain visas for missionaries and permission to organize congregations, the end of World War I and the extension of Smoot's senatorial power over international affairs provided the church both the opportunity and the power to address directly the awful state of its missions in Europe.

The preceding May, Smoot had been invited to sail on *Leviathan*'s maiden voyage and to address the prestigious British Pilgrim's Society's "mammoth dinner to celebrate," in the company of the British ambassador, the mammoth ship's arrival.[50] When Smoot's wife's health did not permit her to accompany him, Smoot offered the opportunity to his apostolic brethren. At their weekly meeting in the Salt Lake temple, the quorum assigned fellow apostle, Norwegian-born convert, and Göttingen-educated scientist John A. Widtsoe to accompany Smoot on a mission "to Norway, Sweden and Denmark and try and secure the repeal of the law in each one . . . prohibiting Mormon missionaries from entering those countries."[51] Three weeks later, having "obtained special letters from Pres Harding and Secy of State" as well as a briefing from the secretary of state on "the difficulty he was having with foreign countries," Smoot left to catch his boat in New York. The new ship's Independence Day departure was celebrated with thousands at the pier, a flotilla of smaller craft in the water, and several "aeroplanes" hovering overhead. After not so patiently "stand[ing] for moving picture machines and cameras of all kinds," Smoot boarded *Leviathan* for Great Britain, with his missionary companion in tow.

Because of his status in the Senate and his personal relationship with President Harding, Smoot was granted direct access to high officials and introduced to opinion makers, including heads of the state churches, in each of the countries he visited. In London he met with Prime Minister Stanley Baldwin, was guest of honor at a luncheon hosted by the governor of the Bank of England, and was invited to make his case in the homes of both Lord Beaverbrook, owner of the *London Express*, and Sir Edward Hutton, owner of the *London News* and the *London Mail*. Of his meeting with Beaverbrook, Smoot recorded, "The question of the *Express* publishing bitter attacks on the Mormon church came up and he told me he had become convinced that the attacks were unjust and upon my assuring him they were he told me they would not occur again."[52]

In Denmark four days later, Smoot was introduced to the director general and the minister of foreign affairs by the American minister, who "spoke in the highest terms of our people . . . and introduced me as the most power[ful] U S Senator and a dear friend of President Harding." Smoot and the director general "talked over American politics, conditions in the Ruhr and World affairs and finally reached the troubles we were having in getting our Missionaries into Denmark and I told the Count [that] I had come all the way to have conditions changed." After Smoot explained "a history of Polygamy in the church and conditions today," the count "saw no reason why we should not be treated as all other church organizations and would do what he could to help to that end."[53] The scenario was repeated in Sweden and Norway. Smoot met with prime ministers who listened to his argument and promised to lift the injunction against Mormon proselytizing. American diplomats, too, showed him every courtesy. As the senator was assured by the U.S. representative to Norway, had he known of the church's problem, "he would have done anything in his power to assist us and will continue to do so." The reason was obvious. "He knew of my work in the Senate," Smoot wrote in his journal, "and always had a great admiration for me. He did everything in his power to show his appreciation."[54]

In each country, Smoot was not only entertained by his own and foreign governments but interviewed by the press. Both the *London Daily Express* and *London Daily Mail* give him a forum to explain the church to a public that had heard only ill of it.[55] The Danish paper *Politiken* published an extended interview that was reprinted throughout the Scandinavian countries and was considered "worth all the time and expense of the trip."[56] In Stockholm the four leading newspapers covered the senator's visit and discussed his religious purposes. Widtsoe's report of the mission to church authorities rejoiced that the "*Social-demkraten* had the interview on the first page, with a big headline covering several columns, 'Polygamy no longer practiced in Utah.' In Christiana, Norway, the two leading dailies printed interviews with Brother Smoot and," he noted, "a great number of minor notices appeared in papers." Widtsoe rightly concluded that "it is probable that the Church has never before had such extensive favorable newspaper publicity in Europe."[57] Within one month, Smoot succeeded in reopening northern Europe to L.D.S. proselytizing by ameliorating foreign regulation of missionaries, restraining an adverse press, attracting positive news coverage, and securing the assistance of U.S. diplomats. In his final report of their journey, Widtsoe informed church leaders that "no other man in the Church could have done such work in our behalf."[58] This was an understatement.

No one in the L.D.S. Church and few in the country possessed the power that Smoot had in 1923 as senior member of the Senate Appropriations Committee and chair of the Senate Finance Committee. He also wielded great power through his personal association with Presidents

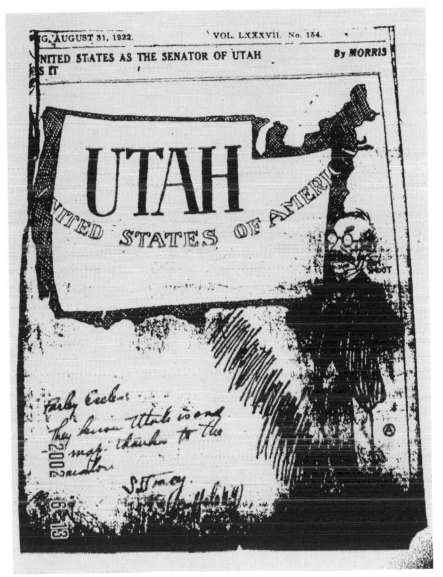

"United States as the Senator from Utah Sees It," 31 August 1922. This cartoon published in an unidentified newspaper and preserved in the senator's clipping files indicates the extent of Smoot's authority when he embarked on his mission to Europe. Courtesy of L. Tom Perry Special Collections, Harold B. Lee Library, Brigham Young University, Provo, Utah.

Roosevelt, Taft, and Harding and his senior position within the Republican Party. These offices and relationships gave Smoot access to heads of state and front-page coverage in the European press. Twenty years in the Senate had prepared Smoot to exploit his access to both audiences. He was an experienced political chief, meeting European cabinet officers as peers and obtaining the service of American diplomats as his subordinates. Smoot doubtless disarmed his European audience by contradicting its stereotypes of Mormonism, much as he did his American audience during his first years in the Senate. In 1923 the senior senator showed even less of Utah's frontier ruggedness and displayed none of his church's reputed religious fanaticism and sexual license. Neither could he be described any longer as "a retiring, unobtrusive, and friendly man."[59] The apostle-senator was a sophisticated and seasoned politician. He displayed the confidence of one who counseled presidents, dominated party politics, and managed the Senate purse strings. When he informed European governments that the L.D.S. Church no longer practiced polygamy and dismissed allegations of Latter-day Saint exploitation of local citizens, Smoot spoke with authority.

At home, however, Smoot's authority was slipping, as it was for Republicans throughout the nation in the early 1930s. Weakened not only by the dismal economy but by his opponents' charges that he cared for the nation more than the state of Utah, Smoot was a casualty of Franklin D. Roosevelt's landslide victory in 1932. It was a cruel defeat for Smoot. Joseph F. Smith, who had understood best Smoot's importance and could control his detractors, had died sixteen years earlier in 1918, after expressing to Smoot his hope that the church "shall never be without a friend in Congress capable of representing and taking care of our affairs."[60] Smith's successor Heber J. Grant, who had spent the Smoot hearing years in exile in England and only as church president had grown to appreciate Smoot's position in the Senate, did not or could not marshal the votes to exempt Smoot from the general Republican rout. As one who knew from experience, John A. Widtsoe expressed his condolences not just for Smoot but for the church: "When you retire from the Senate the cause of the Lord in these days will have lost its most effective missionary."[61]

Yet Smoot had done his job so well that by the time he lost it, his church had no more need for an apostle in the Senate. Americans had been convinced of the Latter-day Saints' tolerance, obedience, and loyalty and had bestowed upon them denominational citizenship with its constitutional privileges and protections. At the 1935 dedication of another monument to the church's past, President Heber J. Grant gave thanks to God "that the spirit of opposition has disappeared. We are thankful that the reputation of thy people has changed. That today from New York to San Francisco, from Canada to Mexico to be known as a Latter-day Saint living the gospel is of great value."[62] Though it may exaggerate the "value" ascribed to Mormonism, this statement made thirty years after the Smoot hearing at yet another dedication of a memorial to Joseph Smith accurately measures a truly "great" change in the public's attitude toward the Mormons while Smoot represented them in the U.S. Senate.

Today it is apparent that the Latter-day Saints have found a way to embrace multiple loyalties and publicly display a willingness to subordinate themselves to the state by obeying the law of the land. This is true both in the United States and in any state that allows the church to establish itself. Indeed, the church will not proselytize or organize congregations without the formal license by the local authorities. Thus it can be said that the denominational form imposed on the Latter-day Saints by the Senate not only solved the church's problems in the United States but taught it how to thrive in other nations, even nondemocratic ones, to which it has sent its missionaries. An international source says it best: "Nothing in the material and temporal order is of more important concern, daily and constantly, than the simple statement that the L.D.S. Church and its people intensely desire to be known as a law-abiding group. Anyone familiar with their writing or anyone who has had any little contact with them is acutely aware of this positive attitude on the part of the Mormon Church to demonstrate that they are dedicated to upholding the law of the land in which they find themselves."[63] Regardless of its host's governmental system, the twenty-first-century church has applied successfully Senator Beveridge's formula—obedience to law, political tolerance, and loyalty to country—to any country that will allow it to build its version of a kingdom of God. Doing so enabled the church to grow from 290,000 Rocky Mountain exiles into a global institution of more than 11 million members by the end of the twentieth century. Joseph F. Smith was right: "'Mormon-ism,' as it is called, has come to the world to stay."[64]

NOTES

Abbreviations

CABP
> Carlos Ashby Badger Papers, L. Tom Perry Special Collections, Harold B. Lee Library, Brigham Young University, Provo, Utah

Clawson, *Diary*
> Stan Larson, ed., *A Ministry of Meetings: The Apostolic Diaries of Rudger Clawson* (Salt Lake City: Signature Books in association with Smith Research Associates, 1993)

CR
> *Official Report of the Semi-Annual Conference of The Church of Jesus Christ of Latter-day Saints* (Salt Lake City: Deseret News, 1897–1964; The Church of Jesus Christ of Latter-day Saints, 1965–present)

JD
> *Journal of Discourses*, 26 vols. (Liverpool: F. D. Richards, 1855–86)

Journal History
> Journal History of The Church of Jesus Christ of Latter-day Saints (microfilm) (Church History Library, The Church of Jesus Christ of Latter-day Saints, Salt Lake City, Utah). The Journal History is also available as volume 2 of *Selected Collections from the Archives of the Church of Jesus Christ of Latter-day Saints* (Provo, Utah: Brigham Young University Press, 2002).

JWML
> Special Collections and Manuscripts, J. Willard Marriott Library, University of Utah, Salt Lake City

KJV
> King James Version of the Bible

LDSCA
> L.D.S. Church Archives, The Church of Jesus Christ of Latter-day Saints, Salt Lake City, Utah

NA
> National Archives and Records Administration, Washington, D.C.

Proceedings
> U.S. Senate, Committee on Privileges and Elections, *Proceedings before the Committee on Privileges and Elections of the United States Senate in the Matter of the Protests against the Right of Hon. Reed Smoot, a Senator from the State of Utah, to Hold His Seat*, 4 vols., 59th Cong., 1st sess., S. Rept. No. 486 (Washington, D.C.: Government Printing Office, 1904–6)

RSC
> Reed Smoot Collection, L. Tom Perry Special Collections, Harold B. Lee Library, Brigham Young University, Provo, Utah

SC
Selected Collections from the Archives of the Church of Jesus Christ of Latter-day Saints, 2 vols. (Provo, Utah: Brigham Young University Press, 2002)

SGKC
Scott G. Kenney Collection, Special Collections and Manuscripts, J. Willard Marriott Library, University of Utah, Salt Lake City

USHS
Utah State Historical Society, Salt Lake City

WMPC
Wiley M. Paden Collection, Special Collections, Giovale Library, Westminster College, Salt Lake City, Utah

Introduction

1. Shipps, *Sojourner*, 69.

2. Carl Badger to Rose Badger, 17 Feb. 1907, CABP.

3. For an analysis of the origins and limits of the trope of center and margin in American religious history, see Moore, *Religious Outsiders*, 3–21.

4. Of course, nativist stereotypes of Roman Catholic popery and urban violence against Catholic immigrants also reveal the project to have been a more narrowly Protestant endeavor. The classic discussion of this phenomenon is in Handy, *Christian America*. See also Foster's more recent *Moral Reconstruction*.

5. Quoted in Graham, *Cosmos*, 225.

6. Hill and Allen, introduction to *Mormonism and American Culture*, 1.

7. *New York American*, 4 Apr. 1904.

8. For the church's guidelines on use of its name, see *Style Guide: The Name of the Church* at <http://www.lds.org/> (5 July 2002).

9. For a general history of Mormonism, see Arrington and Bitton, *Mormon Experience*.

10. The secondary literature on each of these topics is voluminous. The most complete guide is Allen, Walker, and Whittaker, *Studies in Mormon History*. For aid in finding primary materials, see Whittaker, *Mormon Americana*. A particularly helpful source for primary documents related to the church's history of conflict with the U.S. government is Fales and Flake, *Mormons and Mormonism in U.S. Government Documents*. In December 2002 the church published a DVD collection containing 487,000 pages from its history archives; see *SC*. Both primary and secondary materials are available on CD-ROM from several sources, the most scholarly of which is *New Mormon Studies CD-ROM*. The L.D.S. Church's canon, as well as other official statements on church beliefs and practices, are available at the church's official website, <http://www.lds.org>.

11. Cullom, "Menace of Mormonism."

12. See, for example, Lyford, *Mormon Problem*, and Lum, *Utah and Its People*.

13. For an analysis of three examples of the conflict between minority religion and U.S. law, see Mazur, *Americanization of Religious Minorities*. Mazur's analysis of the Latter-day Saints accepts the traditional view that the church "capitulated" to U.S.

authority and became "one bureaucratized denomination among many" (ibid., 91). The present study differs from this interpretive tradition by arguing that the Mormon Problem was solved not by legal force but by political negotiation that satisfied the principal interests of both the nation and the L.D.S. Church.

14. See, for example, the *Religious Freedom Restoration Act of 1993*, 42 U.S.C.S. 2000, section 2(b)(2). Held unconstitutional in *City of Boerne v. Flores*, 117 S.Ct. 2157 (1997).

15. For a discussion of the changing circumstances of the Protestant establishment during this period, see Hutchison, "Protestantism as Establishment."

16. See Sandel, *Democracy's Discontent*.

17. Brogan, *American Political System*, 354. Quoted in Milton R. Merrill, *Apostle in Politics*, 96.

18. For the sole exception, see Alexander, *Mormonism in Transition*, 16–27.

Chapter One

1. Not until ratification of the Seventeenth Amendment would senators be elected by popular majorities and Senate elections be conformed gradually to even-numbered years. See, generally, Moore, Preimesberger, and Tarr, *Congressional Quarterly's Guide to U.S. Elections*, 1:1229–33.

2. The nearest analogy to a Latter-day Saint apostle is probably found in the office of Catholic cardinal, though the comparison can fail to express the extent of an apostle's plenary authority over L.D.S. Church affairs at all levels of administration. Technically, apostle is a priesthood office and lifetime appointment given members of the church's leading hierarchy of fifteen men, three of whom comprise the "First Presidency," and the remainder, the "Quorum of the Twelve Apostles." Upon the death of the church's president, his successor is chosen from among the apostolic quorum, another source of concern to the protestors.

3. *Salt Lake Tribune*, 9 Jan. 1903, as quoted in Malmquist, *First One Hundred Years*, 219.

4. *Proceedings*, 1:592; Lund, Diary, 23 Jan. 1901, LDSCA.

5. Quoted in Roberts, *Defense of the Faith*, 1:123–24.

6. From an associated press report, "Mormon Out for Senator: Reed Smoot Wants to Succeed Senator Rawlins," Provo, Utah, 15 May, enclosed in a 20 May 1902 letter, Ben E. Rich to John Henry Smith, George A. Smith Family Papers.

7. *Proceedings*, 1:1, 25. An additional complaint, accusing Smoot of being a polygamist, was filed on 26 Feb. 1903 by Rev. John Luther Leilich, superintendent of the Utah Methodist missions and a signatory on the original protest. Because this was patently false, Leilich's brethren in the Salt Lake Ministerial Association tried to distance themselves from the accusation initially. See *Proceedings*, 1:26–30.

8. Halstead, foreword to Beadle, *Polygamy*, xvi.

9. Mead, *Lively Experiment*, 36–37.

10. Not until 1947, when the Supreme Court decided *Everson v. Board of Education*, 330 U.S. 1 (1947), was the Constitution interpreted to prohibit state establishment of religion.

11. Curry, *First Freedoms*, 177.

12. The importance of space in the development of American religion is a common theme. An uncommonly good analysis is found in Mead's essay "The American People: Their Space, Time, and Religion," in *Lively Experiment*, 1–15. For the contemporary discussion of the felt sense of "centripetal tendencies" and disappearing frontier, see Strong, *New Era*, and of course, Turner, "Significance of the Frontier."

13. For a discussion of Protestantism's schismatic tendencies and diminishing cultural authority during the early twentieth century, see Handy, "American Religious Depression"; Hutchison, "Protestantism as Establishment"; and Szasz, *Divided Mind*.

14. *Congressional Globe*, 36th Cong., 2d sess., 1860, 20, pt. 2.

15. See, generally, Cross, *Burned-Over District*. For a book-length treatment devoted to the impact of the seeker movement on Mormonism, see Vogel, *Religious Seekers*.

16. Joseph Smith, "The Temple," 776.

17. As naive as this appears today, the constitutionality of the Mormon proposal had yet to be determined, as evidenced by President Millard Fillmore's appointment of President Brigham Young as governor of the Utah Territory. Nevertheless, Utah petitioned unsuccessfully for admission to the Union six times: 1849, 1856, 1862, 1872, 1882, and 1887, finally succeeding in 1896.

18. *Congressional Record*, 59th Cong., 2d sess., 1906, 41, pt. 1:333.

19. Mead, *Lively Experiment*, 116.

20. "The Smoot Case," *Kalamazoo Telegraph*, 22 Apr. 1904.

21. Williams, "Multitude of Denominations."

22. It should be remembered that Latter-day Saint marriage customs included monogamy. There is, however, scholarly debate about the relative legitimacy (within the nineteenth-century L.D.S. Church) of monogamy versus polygamy. See, for example, the extended note in Daynes, *More Wives Than One*, 225 n. 19.

23. *Congressional Record*, 58th Cong., Spec. Sess., 1903, 37, pt. 2:96.

24. Mead, *Lively Experiment*, 103–33. Note, however, that Russell Richey has argued that the definition of denomination is "period specific"; see Richey, "Denominations and Denominationalism." This conclusion results, however, from his emphasis on the role that shared purpose plays in the definition of denomination. My emphasis here is on the function of tolerance in the definition of denomination and what that function implies about claims to authority in both church and state.

25. Mead, *Lively Experiment*, 116.

26. Ibid.

27. See Gordon, "Blasphemy" and *Mormon Question*, 71–77. Note especially Gordon's discussion of the manner in which the antipolygamy cases demonstrate "the problem of language and the relationship of religious expression to political legitimacy" ("Blasphemy," 708).

28. McLoughlin, "Nation Born Again," 190.

29. Mead, *Lively Experiment*, 11; Handy, *Christian America*.

30. *Congressional Record*, 59th Cong., 2d sess., 1906, 41, pt. 1:333.

31. A. S. Bailey, "Anti-American Influences in Utah," 17–23.

32. McLoughlin, "Nation Born Again," 190.

33. In addition to the records of the U.S. Senate in the National Archives, see also "Petitions against the Seating of Reed Smoot," *Congressional Record*, 58th Cong., 3d sess., 1904–5, 39, pts. 1–4.

34. Citizens of Southeast, New York, to the United States Senate, 5 Nov. 1903, SEN58A-J68, NA.

35. Josiah Leeds (Rocouncy, PA) to Senator Philander C. Knox, 18 May 1906, SEN59A-J97, NA.

36. Petition from the First Presbyterian Church, Austin, Chicago [Ill.], SEN58A-J68, NA.

37. Mrs. H. K. Schoff to Frank B. Braudegee, 22 Jan. 1907, SEN58A-J6A, NA.

38. Edward Berger to Philander Knox, 14 May 1906, SEN59A-J97, NA.

39. G. A. Barrett to Philander Knox, 12 Jan. 1905, SEN58A-J68, NA.

40. Citizens of the town of Pembina, North Dakota, to the Senator from North Dakota, 19 Nov. 1903, SEN58A-J68, NA.

41. Johnson and Porter, *National Party Platforms*, 27, 133.

42. Handy, *Christian America*, 159; Wilson, *Church and State*, xviii–xix.

43. Given that the Smoot hearing concerns, inter alia, a contest over the Latter-day Saint concept of the kingdom of God, Handy's observation is worth noting: "The new social Christianity had a vision of a vastly better human society, but it was essentially the old vision of a religious nation socialized" (*Christian America*, 139).

44. *Abbreviated Minutes of the Synod of Utah*, WMPC. Utah's population figures are from Alexander, *Utah*, 186.

45. George W. Martin to George E. Davies, 28 May 1915, WMPC.

46. Journal History, 26 Oct. 1899, 13, citing the *Deseret News*, presumably of the same date.

47. Beggs, "Mormon Problem in the West," 755–56.

48. Charles L. Thompson, "Resistance and Aggression," *Assembly Herald*, Oct. 1905, quoted in Brackenridge, "Presbyterians and Latter-day Saints," 221.

49. Banker, *Presbyterian Missions*, 153.

50. *Abbreviated Minutes of the Synod of Utah*, WMPC, 8. "Gentile" was a term used by Latter-day Saints to refer to persons not of their faith. The term originates in L.D.S. doctrines that identify the church with the House of Israel. As indicated by the quoted text, "Gentile" was appropriated by non-Mormon residents of Utah to distinguish themselves from the Mormons. At times, even the national press used the term.

51. The referral of Roberts's case is found at "Representative-elect from Utah," *Congressional Record*, 56th Cong., 1st sess., 1899, 33, pt. 1:5–6, 38–53. The debate on whether to seat Roberts is found at *Congressional Record*, 56th Cong., 1st sess., 1900, 33, pt. 2:1012–13, 1072–1116, 1123–49, 1175–82, 1184–1217. For a discussion of Roberts's rejection, see Bitton, *Ritualization*, 150–70.

52. Quoted in Roberts, *Comprehensive History*, 7:515.

53. "Regulating the Mormonites," *New York Observer*, 24 Aug. 1833, 135.

54. The historiography of antipolygamy law is voluminous. One of the most complete treatments is Linford, "Mormons and the Law." The most recent contributions

are Sears, "Punishing the Saints," and Gordon, *Mormon Question*. The effect of anti-polygamy law in Utah is discussed in Firmage and Mangrum, *Zion in the Courts*, 129–260.

55. For a summary of fictional and other popular accounts of the Latter-day Saints, see Arrington, "Mormonism," 144. The classic treatments of anti-Mormon fiction are Charles A. Cannon, "Awesome Power of Sex," and Arrington and Haupt, "Intolerable Zion." For a more recent study, see Gordon, "'Our National Hearthstone.'" A book-length interpretation of the literature, taking for its title a phrase used in *Cosmopolitan* magazine in 1911, is Givens, *Viper on the Hearth*.

56. Carl Badger to Rose Badger, 4 Dec. 1906, CABP.

57. Twain, *Roughing It*, 108.

58. For further data and analysis of the subject, see Evans, "Judicial Prosecution," which concludes that sentences given to and served by polygamists were in many cases longer than terms given to those guilty of crimes against person and property.

59. See Van Wagoner, *Mormon Polygamy*, 108–43, or Hardy, *Solemn Covenant*, 39–83.

60. Quotations are from *Davis v. Beason*, 133 U.S. 333 at 341–42 (1890), and *Late Corporation of the Church of Jesus Christ of Latter-day Saints v. United States*, 136 U.S. 1 at 1, 49 (1890). Analysis of Supreme Court antipolygamy cases is found in a number of sources, of course. See, for example, Firmage and Mangrum, *Zion in the Courts*, and Linford, "Mormons and the Law." Gordon's *Mormon Question* broadens existing analyses to document the effect of the antipolygamy campaign on American law itself.

61. Quinn, "New Plural Marriages," 42.

62. As will be discussed in Chapter 5, the 1890 Manifesto was titled "Official Declaration—1" when placed at the back of the *Doctrine and Covenants*. The *Doctrine and Covenants* is one of four "standard works" or canon of the L.D.S. Church and is largely comprised of revelations to Joseph Smith on church order and doctrine. "Official Declaration—1" reads as follows:

To Whom It May Concern:

Press dispatches having been sent for political purposes, from Salt Lake City, which have been widely published, to the effect that the Utah Commission, in their recent report to the Secretary of the Interior, allege that plural marriages are still being solemnized and that forty or more such marriages have been contracted in Utah since last June or during the past year, also that in public discourses the leaders of the Church have taught, encouraged and urged the continuance of the practice of polygamy—

I, therefore, as President of the Church of Jesus Christ of Latter-day Saints, do hereby, in the most solemn manner, declare that these charges are false. . . . Inasmuch as laws have been enacted by Congress forbidding plural marriages, which laws have been pronounced constitutional by the court of last resort, I hereby declare my intention to submit to those laws, and to use my influence with the members of the Church over which I preside to have them do likewise.

There is nothing in my teachings to the Church or in those of my associates, during the time specified, which can be reasonably construed to inculcate or encourage polygamy; and when any Elder of the Church has used language which appeared to convey any such teaching, he has been promptly reproved. And I now publicly declare that my advice to the Latter-day Saints is to refrain from contracting any marriage forbidden by the law of the land.

WILFORD WOODRUFF,
President of the Church of Jesus Christ
of Latter-day Saints.

63. Merrill, Diary, 6 Oct. 1890, quoted in Melvin Clarence Merrill, *Utah Pioneer*.

64. Smith's initial reticence over Smoot's candidacy is recorded in Lund, Diary, 8 Nov. 1900, LDSCA. As indicated supra, Smith's papers are not public. Such papers as are published contain few materials relevant to the Smoot hearing, and none refer to Smith's reversal. See *SC*, 1:26–30.

65. Charles W. Nibley, "Reminiscences," 195.

66. Joseph F. Smith, Sermon, in *CR*, Nov. 1901, 70.

67. The reference is found in KJV Isaiah 5:26 ("And he will lift up an ensign to the nations from far, and will hiss unto them from the end of the earth: and, behold, they shall come with speed swiftly") and 11:12 ("And he shall set up an ensign for the nations, and shall assemble the outcasts of Israel, and gather together the dispersed of Judah from the four corners of the earth"), repeated verbatim in the Book of Mormon at 2 Nephi 15:26 and 21:12. For a discussion of the sign function of the Book of Mormon, see Givens, *By the Hand of Mormon*, 62–88.

68. Journal History, 22 Mar., 6 Nov. 1900, 5, 6; James G. Duffin to L.D.S. First Presidency, 13 June 1902, SGKC. See also Hatch, *There Is No Law*.

69. Journal History, 22 June 1901, 3.

70. First Presidency to Francis M. Lyman, 20 May 1903, in Clark, *Messages of the First Presidency*, 4:52.

71. Joseph F. Smith, Sermon, in *CR*, Nov. 1901, 70.

72. A. S. Bailey, "Anti-American Influences in Utah," 17–23.

Chapter Two

1. "The Sentiment against Mormons as Senators," *Harper's Weekly*, 24 Jan. 1903, 136 37; *Proceedings*, 1:25

2. Senator George Frisbie Hoar speaking on behalf of Senator J. C. Burrows, in *Congressional Record*, 58th Cong., Spec. sess., 1903, 35, pt. 7:1.

3. Reed Smoot to Joseph F. Smith, 10 Nov. 1903, RSC. Nelson W. Aldrich (R-Rhode Island), Redfield Proctor (R-Vermont), and Marcus A. Hanna (R-Ohio) were senior members of the Senate and influential within the Republican Party. Aldrich had been in the Senate more than twenty years by the time Smoot arrived. Proctor was a former secretary of war under President Benjamin Harrison and had served in the Senate since 1891. Hanna was a former chair of the Republican Party and intended to be its next nominee for president.

4. "Men We Are Watching," *Independent*, Jan.–Mar. 1907, 494–95.

5. "Women Giggle at the Smoot Testimony," *New York World*, 10 Mar. 1904.

6. Abraham O. Smoot (1815–95) had six wives. His first marriage was in 1838 to widow Margaret Thompson McMeans Adkinson, who was six years his senior. In 1846, on the eve of captaining a wagon train to the Rockies, Smoot entered "the Principle" by marrying two more women: forty-five-year-old Sarah Gibbons and thirty-nine-year-old Emily Hill Harris. Sarah did not make the 1847 exodus to Utah and divorced Smoot in 1852. Two other wives joined the family in Utah: Diana Tanner Eldredge, born 28 Mar. 1837, and, in 1855, the woman who would become Reed's mother, Anne Kirstine Morrison (1833–94). Abraham Smoot had twenty-seven children, including three adopted children. See Nixon and Smoot, *Abraham Owen Smoot*, 147–212.

7. Clawson, *Diary*, 7 Jan. 1902.

8. Daynes, *More Wives Than One*, 173–87. For additional analysis of post-Manifesto polygamy, see Hardy, *Solemn Covenant*, 206–44; Quinn, "New Plural Marriages"; Kenneth L. Cannon II, "After the Manifesto"; and Jorgenson and Hardy, "Taylor-Cowley Affair."

9. A biography of Smoot's life has yet to be written. Milton R. Merrill's *Apostle in Politics* is limited to Smoot's senatorial career. This work has the advantage, however, of reference to the author's personal interviews with Smoot and certain of his contemporaries. Other biographical treatments include Vernon, "Public Career of Reed Smoot," and Maud E. Smith, "Reed Smoot." A brief but insightful biographical essay appears in Heath, *Diaries of Reed Smoot*, xxviii–xxxiv. See also introduction to Heath, "First Modern Mormon," 1–197.

10. Milton R. Merrill, *Apostle in Politics*, 7; Jenson, *Biographical Encyclopedia*, 1:179.

11. Jenson, *Biographical Encyclopedia*, 1:178–81. *Deseret News*, 9 Apr. 1900. See also Heath, *Diaries of Reed Smoot*, xxix.

12. Clawson, *Diary*, 12 Feb. 1903. Five years later, Smoot was again set apart for a mission related to his senatorship. See Lund, Diary, 11 July 1908, LDSCA. After successfully defending his seat the preceding year, Smoot was appointed by President Roosevelt to a forestry delegation to Europe. "The council [of the twelve apostles] . . . felt that this is an honor . . . and that it will allay prejudice abroad and help Bro. Smoot at home. It will show that he has the confidence of the administration. . . . The council voted to give him a leave" (Anthon H. Lund to Joseph F. Smith, 1 July 1908, SGKC).

13. Milton R. Merrill, *Apostle in Politics*, 5.

14. *Proceedings*, 3:207.

15. Ibid., 1:164.

16. B. H. Roberts to Richard R. Lyman, 30 Mar. 1908, RSC.

17. Shipps, "Public Image," 389.

18. Nels Anderson, "Pontifex Babbitt," 181. The title combines a reference to Smoot's high position in a priestly structure with an allusion to Sinclair Lewis's middle-class hero of the same name.

19. James Howell to W. W. Salmon, 9 Mar. 1905, SC, 1:30.

20. Clawson, *Diary*, 2 Apr. 1903.

21. Telegram from George F. Gibbs, secretary to the First Presidency, to Reed Smoot, 27 Feb. 1903, RSC.

22. Carl Badger to Rose Badger, 10 Dec. 1906, CABP.

23. *Proceedings*, 2:302, 320.

24. A number of dates could be chosen to mark the beginning and end of L.D.S. polygamous practices. Because the emphasis here is not on Joseph Smith's own conviction but on the larger church's adherence to polygamy, I have chosen a more limited period. These dates represent the years between Joseph Smith's extension of the practice to others within the church and Joseph F. Smith's first disciplining of members for the practice, discussed infra. The broadest definition of the L.D.S. practice of plural marriage would circumscribe events occurring between 1833 and 1911. Joseph Smith himself appears to have practiced polygamy as early as 1833. See Compton, *In Sacred Loneliness*, 2–10. Church discipline for unlawful polygamous marriage was not applied to the church at large until 1911, when the first excommunications occurred. For a history of the L.D.S. Church's practice of polygamy, see Hardy, *Solemn Covenant*, and Van Wagoner, *Mormon Polygamy*. For comprehensive treatment of L.D.S. marital customs, using data on individuals who practiced plural marriage, and the effects of the campaign on those customs, see Daynes, *More Wives Than One*, and Embry, *Mormon Polygamous Families*.

25. Hardy, *Solemn Covenant*, 363–80.

26. *Doctrine and Covenants*, sec. 131:11–12 and sec. 132:4, 6. Those who did not accept plural marriage as originating with Joseph Smith formed their own churches emphasizing other principles. Most notably, the Reorganized Church of Jesus Christ of Latter-day Saints (R.L.D.S.) ordered themselves on the contrary principle that Smith had never practiced polygamy and that his sons, who had stayed in Illinois with their widowed and antipolygamous mother, had sole authority to lead the church their father had founded. For the history of the R.L.D.S. (now Community of Christ) movement, see Inez Smith Davis, *Story of the Church*. For a description of the many groups organized out of Smith's Nauvoo church after his death in 1844, see Shields, *Divergent Paths*.

27. Orson Pratt, Sermon, in *JD*, 29 Aug. 1852, 1:53–66. This sermon was delivered in the Salt Lake Tabernacle on 29 Aug. 1852. Technically, Joseph Smith's revelation regarding plural marriage was not his last. As indicated, Joseph Smith appears to have practiced the principle as early as 1833 but did not reduce it to writing until 1843. Hence, the 1852 sermon inaugurating churchwide practice of plural marriage in the Utah Territory is not correct when it states that the doctrine had been "given" to Joseph Smith in the last year of his life. This sermon is correct, however, to the extent that church members did not learn of this principle, if at all, until the last months of Joseph Smith's life. Thus, the Latter-day Saints experienced plural marriage as Joseph Smith's last revelation. Since it is their experience and the meaning ascribed to it that matters for the purposes of this work, I, too, will refer to plural marriage as Joseph Smith's "last" vision.

28. "Minute Book of the School of the Prophets," [30] Mar. 1870, SGKC.

29. Joseph F. Smith, Sermon, in *JD*, 7 Sept. 1879, 21:9–13. This sermon was deliv-

ered at the funeral services of pioneer settler William Clayton, Salt Lake City, 7 Dec. 1879.

30. *Doctrine and Covenants*, 131:11–12.

31. Section 131 included the bracketed material when first published in the 1876 edition of the *Doctrine and Covenants*. See Woodford, "Historical Development of the Doctrine and Covenants," 3:1724.

32. At the time of the Smoot hearing, four living apostles were known to have taken additional wives after the Manifesto and, as will be discussed, became subjects of the Smoot hearing: Matthias F. Cowley, Marriner W. Merrill, John W. Taylor, and George Teasdale. The post-Manifesto marriages of two other, deceased apostles, Abraham H. Cannon (d. 1896) and Abraham O. Woodruff (d. 1904), were also put at issue in the hearing.

33. As will be discussed, federal law proscribed also cohabitation between plural wives and their husbands, and evidence of such was much easier to obtain than that of polygamy. During the Smoot hearing, the panel noted that Joseph F. Smith had eleven children after the Manifesto, and the last one was born on the date Reed Smoot was called to the office of apostle in 1900. See *Proceedings*, 1:197, 3:184. As a result of publicity from the hearing, Smith was indicted for cohabitation in November 1906 and fined $300. See Joseph F. Smith to Willard R. Smith, 20 Nov. 1906, and Joseph F. Smith to Heber Chase Smith, 24 Nov. 1906, SC, 1:30.

34. Unsigned (Taylorsville, Utah) to Heber J. Grant, 19 July 1929, SGKC.

35. Johnson, *Mormonism*, 30.

36. Lewis, "Great Mormon Conspiracy," 11.

37. Not until the ratification of the Seventeenth Amendment in 1913 would U.S. senators be elected by popular vote.

38. Reed Smoot to Joseph F. Smith, 5 Feb. 1904, SGKC.

39. James H. Anderson to Joseph F. Smith, 3 Mar. 1903, SGKC.

40. Reed Smoot to Joseph F. Smith, 14 Nov. 1903, RSC.

41. Ibid., 4 Jan. 1903[4].

42. Edward Callister to Carl Badger, 9 Mar. 1904, CABP.

43. Orcutt, *Burrows of Michigan*, 2:193. For Burrows's family connection to Mormonism, see Reed Smoot to Joseph F. Smith, 12 Mar. 1903, RSC. It appears that Senator Burrows was the nephew of Sylvester Smith, an early leader in the L.D.S. Church who, disaffected from Joseph Smith, left the church by 1838. Regarding any bias this may have created in Burrows, see Milton R. Merrill, *Apostle in Politics*, 61.

44. Quoted in Lowe, "Fred T. Dubois," 9. To his political detriment, Dubois pinned his hopes for reelection on fomenting anti-Mormon sentiment and devoted himself exclusively to the hearing and anti-Smoot rallies. See Cook, "Political Suicide of Senator Fred T. Dubois," and Graff, *Senatorial Career of Fred T. Dubois*.

45. *Congressional Record*, 58th Cong., Spec. Sess., 1903, 37, pt. 2:96.

46. *Proceedings*, 1:604.

47. Joseph F. Smith, Sermon, in *CR*, Nov. 1901, 1.

48. A. S. Bailey, "Anti-American Influences in Utah," 18.

49. Reed Smoot to James H. Anderson, 6 Jan. 1904, RSC.

50. Reed Smoot to C. E. Loose, 26 Jan. 1904, RSC.

51. "Senator Smoot's Answer," *Salt Lake Herald*, 12 Jan. 1904.

52. *Deseret Evening News*, 25 Feb. 1904.

53. "Says Smoot Case Made Him a Mormon," *Pittsburgh Inquirer*, 15 Mar. 1904.

54. "Senate Shocked by Smoot Trial," *Chicago Tribune*, 4 Mar. 1904.

55. *Deseret Evening News*, 25 Feb. 1904.

56. John Henry Smith and Marriner W. Merrill produced doctors' certificates to excuse their absences. Smith recovered sufficiently to appear at the hearing the following December. Merrill never recovered fully and died two years later. For the background to the unavailability of Teasdale, Taylor, and Cowley, see Teasdale, Diary, 3 Apr. 1902, 25 Aug. 1906, Teasdale Papers, JWML. When asked about Teasdale, Smith testified that he had "an attack of grip, and asked for permission to go away from home and from duties for a little while to recuperate" (*Proceedings*, 1:386).

57. Reed Smoot to Joseph F. Smith, 8 Jan. 1904, RSC. Grant succeeded Smith as church president in 1918.

58. Smith later protested to Smoot that he was unaware that Grant was "wanted as a witness" (Joseph F. Smith to Reed Smoot, 20 Apr. 1904, SC, 1:28). Nevertheless, Grant was told by fellow apostle John Henry Smith that he "could not come home until the Smoot case was out of the way" (Confidential Unsigned [probably Benjamin F. Grant] to Heber J. Grant, 7 July 1905, SGKC). Teasdale remained banished in Mexico until Aug. 1906, and Grant stayed in Europe until the following November, several months after the committee issued its findings to the full Senate.

59. *Deseret Evening News*, 25 Feb. 1904.

60. James Clove to Reed Smoot, 16 Jan. 1903, RSC. "Alrota" was a code name applied to Smith. Correspondence between Smoot and Utah leadership was often coded, especially telegrams. As late as 1917, Smith and Smoot were still corresponding in code. See Heinerman, "Reed Smoot's 'Secret Code.'" For information on Smoot's Utah correspondents, see *Biographical Record of Salt Lake City*. Badger gives evidence of the need for a code when he reports, "Dillingham tells the Senator that some of the members of the Committee believe him to be a polygamist, and he traces the suspicion to the telegram he [Smoot] sent McRae in Denver—'Have visitor leave for a few days'—notifying Cowley that his whereabouts was known" (Badger, Diary, 27 Apr. 1904, CABP). Espionage was not limited to the antipolygamy forces, however. Smoot admitted that "Brother Henry Peterson is secretary to Rep. French of Idaho . . . [and is] passing on information" (Reed Smoot to Joseph F. Smith, 11 June 1904, SGKC).

61. Joseph F. Smith to Reed Smoot, 28 Jan. 1904, SC, 1:30.

62. *Argus*, 9 Feb. 1904.

63. Charles W. Nibley, "Reminiscences."

64. Smith set the "general policy being pursued" during the hearing, though Smoot was "entirely free in the use of [his] own discretion as to the details," according to instructions he received from Smith in 1905. The letter was careful to admit "we wish you to know that we recognize *you* as the central figure in this fight, notwithstanding the fact that our enemies are warring against the Church through you; and that you are therefore entitled to know for yourself what to do, and what not to do" (Joseph F. Smith to Reed Smoot, 18 May 1905, SC, 1:30).

65. Clark, *Messages of the First Presidency*, 4:79.

66. Ibid., 82. For a discussion of the political dimensions of the Latter-day Saint concept of the kingdom of God, see Hansen, *Quest for Empire*; Ehat, "'It Seems Like Heaven Began on Earth.'"

67. *Proceedings*, 4:79.

68. See Thatcher's testimony and accompanying documents in ibid., 1:936–1050. See also Smoot's testimony in ibid., 3:187.

69. Several of Smoot's witnesses were devoted to proving this argument. See, for example, ibid., 2:784 (William Hatfield), 2:796 (John Meakin), 2:857 (William P. O'Meara), 3:145 (Glen Miller), 3:162 (John Hughes), and 3:335 (J. U. Eldridge).

Chapter Three

1. *Proceedings*, 1:80.

2. Joseph F. Smith Journal, quoted in Preston Nibley, *Presidents of the Church*, 147. There is no scholarly biography available on the life of Joseph F. Smith. Devotional treatments include Gibbons, *Joseph F. Smith*, and Joseph Fielding Smith Jr., *Life of Joseph F. Smith*. See also Kenney, "Joseph F. Smith," 178–209.

3. Preston Nibley, "Friendship of Charles W. Nibley and President Joseph F. Smith," 352.

4. Joseph F. Smith to Levira Annette Clark Smith, 28 June 1860, SC, 1:27 (emphasis original).

5. The miniature was on a "souvenir button" made for the observance of Smith's father's 104th birthday anniversary. Smith evidently had a "supply" of them. See Joseph F. Smith to Edith A. Smith, 22 Mar. 1904, SC, 1:30. See also "Reed Smoot's Case," *Washington Star*, 4 Mar. 1904.

6. Gibbons, *Joseph F. Smith*, 26–27. Throughout his life, Smith struggled with rage, often evoked by events triggering past associations with his own powerlessness. The following is an account from a colleague's journal (Lund, Diary, 8 Nov. 1902, LDSCA):

> Pres. Smith . . . warned against yielding to impulses. Related how he at one time felt when a man in Iowa told him that he lived near Carthage where his father and the Prophet were murdered. This man said he was present. Joseph said when he heard this everything turned black and, when he [the speaker] further stated his opinion concerning that act had not changed, but was the same today, the President said he could only think of that dastardly crime and that here was one of the perpetrators before him. What a relief to have the man say that he thought it was one of the most wicked crimes ever committed. . . . The President said I woke up as of a trance and found my knife open in my hand. Had he boasted of being one of the murderers I would have killed him. How thankful I was that I was preserved against such a fate. The Lord says "Revenge is mine." Men must not take it themselves.

7. Joseph F. Smith, "My Missions," *Deseret Evening News*, 21 Dec. 1901. Notwithstanding such preparations on both sides, the battle between the L.D.S. Church

and the U.S. Army was bloodless. A compromise deposed Brigham Young as territorial governor and installed a garrison of federal troops in the foothills above Salt Lake City but otherwise left church rule unchanged. The conflict is chronicled in Furniss, *Mormon Conflict*.

8. Edwin H. Anderson, "Lives of Our Leaders," 70.

9. "Women Giggle at the Smoot Testimony," *New York World*, 10 Mar. 1904.

10. The comparison of Mormonism to a viper was frequent and overt. See, for example, Lewis, "Viper on the Hearth." For an extended analysis of the theme and its literature, see Givens, *Viper on the Hearth*.

11. *Salt Lake Tribune*, 3 Mar. 1904.

12. *Deseret Evening News*, 3 Mar. 1904.

13. *Washington Evening Star*, 3 Mar. 1904.

14. Accompanying Smith were Francis M. Lyman, president of the apostolic quorum; Hyrum M. Smith, apostle and son of Joseph F. Smith; several sons of the ailing apostle Marriner W. Merrill; Moses Thatcher, former apostle; and B. H. Roberts, who had been denied admission to the House five years earlier.

15. "Smoot Trial Begins with Brief Meeting," *New York Times*, 1 Mar. 1904.

16. *Baltimore Sun*, 2 Mar. 1904.

17. Quoted in Unsigned [probably Franklin S. Richards, the L.D.S. Church's attorney] to L.D.S. First Presidency, 18 Jan. 1904, RSC.

18. *Proceedings*, 2:375.

19. Ibid., 1:81–83, 86.

20. Alexander, *Mormonism in Transition*.

21. *Proceedings*, 1:796–97.

22. As noted in Chapter 2, apostles Abraham H. Cannon, John W. Taylor, George Teasdale, and Abraham Owen Woodruff married polygamously after the Manifesto. Having died prematurely from illness in July 1896 and June 1904, respectively, neither Cannon nor Woodruff testified. Their marriages became an issue during the hearing, however.

23. James H. Howell to Ed Callister, 18 Jan. 1906, SGKC.

24. "The Mormon Investigation," *Independent*, 22 Dec. 1904, 1463.

25. *Harper's Weekly*, quoted in "A Doubtful Question," *Deseret Evening News*, 19 Mar. 1904.

26. *Daily Eagle*, 28 Dec. 1904; *Poughkeepsie Press*, 30 Nov. 1904, CABP.

27. Unsigned [Franklin S. Richards] to L.D.S. First Presidency, 18 Jan. 1904, RSC.

28. Congress eventually enacted three more statutes regarding Latter-day Saint marriage practices. In addition to the Morrill Act (1862) outlawing polygamy, Congress passed the Poland Act (1874), placing the territorial courts under federal jurisdiction in order to enforce the Morrill Act; the Edmunds Act (1882), imposing civil penalties such as disfranchisement and simplifying the evidentiary burden for polygamy convictions; and finally, the Edmunds-Tucker Act of 1887, dissolving the corporate status of the L.D.S. Church and providing for confiscation of its property. The historiography of antipolygamy law is voluminous. One of the most complete treatments is Linford, "Mormons and the Law." The most recent contributions are Sears,

"Punishing the Saints," and Gordon, *Mormon Question*. For an in-depth treatment of the effect of antipolygamy law in Utah, see Firmage and Mangrum, *Zion in the Courts*, 129–260.

29. *Proceedings*, 2:898, citing from the record of 6th Judicial District Court of Utah, 21 Oct. 1899.

30. Ibid., 736.

31. Ibid., 1:131.

32. Ibid., 197.

33. "Mormon Smith Defies Country," *Chicago Daily Tribune*, 6 Mar. 1904.

34. "Priceless Golden Wedding," 371.

35. Joseph F. Smith to Reed Smoot, 9 Apr. 1904, SC, 1:30.

36. Bashore, "Life behind Bars," 24.

37. Alexander, *Utah*, 188–89. Alexander continues with the following specifics: "Using 1880 census data, geographer Lowell C. 'Ben' Bennion found the lowest percentage of polygamous families—5 percent—in Davis County's south Weber and the highest—67 percent—in Orderville. He found 15 percent in Springville. In a study of St. George, historian Larry Logue found nearly 30 percent of the families polygamous in 1870 and 33 percent in 1880" (ibid.).

38. *Proceedings*, 1:200, 208. On the decline of plural marriage, see Daynes, *More Wives Than One*, 173–87.

39. Badger, Diary, 18 June 1904, CABP.

40. Van Wagoner, *Mormon Polygamy*, 138. See also Franklin D. Richards, Sermon, in *JD*, 6 Oct. 1879, 20:313.

41. Tanner, *Mormon Mother*, 75–76. See also Firmage and Mangrum, *Zion in the Courts*, 194–209.

42. Quoted in Embry, *Mormon Polygamous Families*, 22.

43. *Proceedings*, 2:679.

44. Ibid., 732–33.

45. Ibid., 1:844.

46. Unsigned [Franklin S. Richards] to L.D.S. First Presidency, 18 Jan. 1904, RSC.

47. *Proceedings*, 2:741.

48. For an example of the debate regarding the difficulty of statehood revocation, see Cannon and O'Higgins, *Under the Prophet in Utah*, 278.

49. "Brigham Roberts Again," *Buffalo Express*, 21 Apr. 1904. See also E. H. Callister to Reed Smoot, 29 Feb. 904, RSC.

50. Joseph H. Anderson to Reed Smoot, Jan. 1904, RSC.

51. Edward H. Callister to Reed Smoot, 29 Feb. 1904, RSC.

52. *Goodwin's Weekly*, 14 Feb. 1903, quoted in Milton R. Merrill, *Apostle in Politics*, 32–33. The anxiety over dual allegiances also was a key element in anti-Catholicism in this same period. See David Brion Davis, "Some Themes of Counter-Subversion." This did not, however, prevent the Catholics from contributing to anti-Mormon sentiment with their own antagonistic writings, though more as a matter of deflecting attention from their own differences with American religious ideals. See, for example, five articles that ran in the nineteenth-century *American Catholic Quar-*

terly Review, esp. "Forty Years in the American Wilderness," Jan. 1890, 123–50, as noted by Shipps, *Sojourner*, 78.

53. *New York Times*, 4 Mar. 1904.

54. "Mormon Smith Defies Country," *Chicago Daily Tribune*, 6 Mar. 1904.

55. Badger, Diary, 17 Jan. 1904, CABP.

56. Roberts, *Comprehensive History*, 2:99.

57. Ibid., 99–100.

58. For a history of Smith's personal practice of plural marriage, see Compton, *In Sacred Loneliness*. Smith's institutionalization of the practice is detailed in Van Wagoner, *Mormon Polygamy*, 17–88.

59. *Deseret Evening News*, 11 Oct. 1890.

60. Lund, Diary, 9 Jan. 1899, LDSCA.

61. Clawson, *Diary*, 1 Oct. 1903.

62. Joseph Eckersley, Diary, 9 Nov. 1903, LDSCA. For a discussion of the authorization of post-Manifesto marriages by Joseph F. Smith, see Quinn, "New Plural Marriages," 85–95. See also Stanley S. Ivins, Diary, 29 Nov. 1944, USHS.

63. Clawson, *Diary*, 5 Jan. 1904.

64. Samuel Woolley Taylor, *Family Kingdom*, 201.

65. Franklin S. Richards to Reed Smoot, 16 Apr. 1904, RSC.

66. This strategy, too, can be traced to the early practice of polygamy when the 1835 article on marriage was drafted in Joseph Smith's absence, but with his approval. For its continuance during Joseph F. Smith's administration, see Cowley, "Family History," JWML.

67. L.D.S. First Presidency to Reed Smoot, 20 Jan. 1904, RSC.

68. Reed Smoot, Journal, 14 Mar. 1911, RSC. In the next sentence, Smoot added, "Many of them were authorized by President [George Q.] Cannon." Cannon was a former territorial representative to Congress and counselor in the church's presidency at the time the Manifesto was issued. Until his death in 1901, he appears to have had the responsibility of authorizing plural marriages, while enabling church presidents Woodruff and Snow to deny their occurrence. For Cannon's role, see Jorgenson and Hardy, "Taylor-Cowley Affair," 16. Examples of Cannon's authorization to Mexican church authorities to perform plural marriages are in the Anthony W. Ivins Collection, USHS.

69. *Proceedings*, 1:34.

70. Ibid., 411, 415.

71. Carl Badger to Franklin S. Richards, 23 Mar. 1904, CABP.

72. Ludwig, *Importance of Lying*, ix.

73. Ray Stannard Baker, "Vitality of Mormonism."

74. Cannon and O'Higgins, *Under the Prophet in Utah*, 268.

75. George A. Smith to Reed Smoot, 27 Feb. 1904, RSC.

76. "The Trial of Apostle Matthias F. Cowley [10 May 1911]," in *New Mormon Studies CD-ROM*.

77. Bok, *Lying*, 144.

78. "Mormon's Ordeal," *Washington Post*, 5 Mar. 1904.

79. *Proceedings*, 1:585–623.

80. "Secretary" to E. H. Callister, 12 Mar. 1904, SGKC.

81. Carl Badger to Rose Badger, 15 Feb. 1906, CABP.

82. "Polygamy Revealed by God to Mormon Prophet: To Reject It Would Be Equivalent to Rejecting the Deity," *Salt Lake Herald*, 5 Mar. 1904.

83. Carl Badger to Rose Badger, 24 Feb. 1905, quoted in Badger, *Liahona*, 257.

84. For a description of Joseph F. Smith's role in Abraham H. Cannon's marriage, see Quinn, "New Plural Marriages," 85. In discussing Smith's testimony during the Smoot hearing, Quinn omits the nuances to the exchange that serve as the basis for my conclusion that Smith engaged in sophistry but did not lie. I agree, however, with Quinn's ultimate conclusion: "Joseph F. Smith set a pattern for all other witnesses in the Smoot investigation by exposing himself to public ridicule and to criminal prosecution for unlawful cohabitation by telling the truth about his personal marital relations, but at the same time risking a perjury indictment by concealing any evidence detrimental to the Church as an institution or to any individual (including himself) who acted in his capacity as a Church official in promoting post-Manifesto polygamy" (ibid., 97–98).

85. *Proceedings*, 1:328; Joseph F. Smith to Anthony W. Ivins, 6 Feb. 1900, as quoted in Quinn, "New Plural Marriages," 86.

86. *Proceedings*, 1:130.

87. Ibid., 77.

88. Ibid., 143.

89. Ibid., 612. See also Richard R. Young's answer on the same subject: "My explanation of both those notices [denying the practice of polygamy by Joseph Smith] would be this, that possibly the effect of each of them would be that they would be construed in the public mind to be a denial of the existence of polygamy. Technically, I think, they may escape that construction. But I think some justification for those announcements might be found in the exigency of the times and the circumstances" (ibid., 2:966).

90. Ibid., 1:1.

91. Ibid., 99.

92. Williams, "Multitude of Denominations," 30. For the historical origins of the tension between autocracy and democracy at work in Latter-day Saint conceptions of priesthood, see Wood, "Evangelical America and Early Mormonism."

93. "M'Gurrin on the Smoot Case," *Deseret News*, 18 Mar. 1904, quoting a Grand Rapids, Michigan, newspaper of 6 Mar. 1904.

94. *Proceedings*, 1:99. Compare David Brion Davis's argument that aggression against Catholics, Masons, and Mormons "evinced an underlying tension over the meaning of intellectual and moral diversity in a land without ultimate authorities . . . [and] the role of organization in an individualistic society" ("Some Ideological Functions of Prejudice," 120).

95. *Proceedings*, 1:96.

96. Ibid., 95–96, 135.

97. Ibid., 312–13.

98. Belva Lockwood to the Interdenominational Council of Women, published in

"Senator Smoot's Case: Belva Lockwood Writes in His Defense, Demands Toleration and Light," *New York Tribune*, 5 Feb. 1904.

99. *Proceedings*, 1:728.

100. Ibid., 313.

101. Ibid.

102. *Doctrine and Covenants*, 58:21.

103. Joseph F. Smith, Sermon, in *JD*, 9 Apr. 1882, 23:70–71.

104. *Proceedings*, 1:107.

105. Ibid., 196.

106. Ibid., 390, 447, 504, 417, 691.

107. For Dubois's concerns about his campaign and its relation to the Smoot hearing, see Lowe, "Fred T. Dubois," 35.

Chapter Four

1. See *Washington Times*, 14 Dec. 1904; *New York Herald*, 14 Dec. 1904; and *World Today*, Feb. 1905. See also *Proceedings*, 2:426.

2. Quoted in *Proceedings*, 1:79, 147. For a brief account of the oath as it relates to the Smoot hearing, see Buerger, *Mysteries of Godliness*, 133–36.

3. The protestants believed that an 1857 massacre of a wagon train as it passed through southern Utah on its way to California was an act of retribution. No more recent example of Mormon antipathy could be found. Consequently, the "Mountain Meadows Massacre," as it was called, was grist for the newspaper campaign, not the hearing itself. To date, the most unbiased analysis of this much-contested episode in Latter-day Saint history is Brooks, *Mountain Meadows Massacre*.

4. Carl Badger to Rose Badger, 24 Dec. 1904, CABP.

5. *Philadelphia Inquirer*, 16 Dec. 1904.

6. Ibid.

7. These generalizations have become commonplace in the analysis of American religion. Designed to bring order to the complexity of American religious history, they necessarily omit much that happened from 1900 to 1920. Social historians have yet to capture the complexity of the period, though a significant contribution was recently made by Foster, *Moral Reconstruction*. Sidney Mead's work remains the standard interpretive paradigm for American denominationalism during this as well as all other eras; see *Lively Experiment*, 115–21. For Protestant identification with the state at the turn of the twentieth century, see Handy, *Christian America*, 101–58. See also Richey, "Denominations and Denominationalism," 82–87, for a brief discussion of the institutional effect of the changes from "missionary denominationalism" to "corporate organization."

8. Hendrix, "Ideal State," 587. Hendrix was reverend bishop of the Methodist Episcopal Church, South, Kansas City, Missouri.

9. Foster, *Moral Reconstruction*, 3.

10. Rice, *Ambassador to the Saints*, 105, 230.

11. J. Cleveland Cady, "The Letter Missive," in Sanford, *Church Federation*, 30. Cady was president of the National Federation of Churches and Christian Workers.

12. Not until 1913 did the church begin to dismantle its regional academies and local congregationally sponsored schools. For a discussion of the relationship between Protestant and Latter-day Saint educational programs in Utah, see Buchanan, *Culture Clash and Accommodation*. See also Brackenridge, "Presbyterians and Latter-day Saints."

13. Russell, "Mr. Roosevelt to the Mormons."

14. *Proceedings*, 1:1–29. Much has been written about the L.D.S. Church's aspirations for political dominion and how the Latter-Day Saints achieved it in the West. All agree that, to a remarkable degree, the church constituted a separate nation-state that competed effectively with the U.S. government and negotiated with foreign powers. Why the church did so is a source of disagreement, however, as evidenced conveniently in the titles of two histories: Hansen, *Quest for Empire*, and Hill, *Quest for Refuge*. It should be noted, however, that the Latter-day Saints' reasons were theological as well. Their Zion was to fill the American continent, broadly defined by geographical, not political, boundaries. In 1842, in response to the request of the editor of the *Chicago Democrat*, Joseph Smith listed his church's key beliefs, including, "We believe . . . Zion will be built upon this [the American] continent" (Clark, *Messages of the First Presidency*, 1:142). Based on Book of Mormon prophecy, this teaching was carried forward by Brigham Young and subsequent leaders of the church. A summary of the relevant historiography is found in Hansen, "Metamorphosis of the Kingdom of God," 239 n. 1.

15. Quinn, *Mormon Hierarchy*, 263. See also Parker, "Deseret," which provides an etymology of the term the Latter-day Saints applied to their temporal kingdom and still attach to many of their institutions, such as the *Deseret News*.

16. Mead, *Lively Experiment*, 179. Note, however, Foster's contrary conclusion that "few" Protestant reformers during this period were intent on "expanding human freedom; instead they exploited what might best be called an antislavery precedent to outlaw sin, not to promote justice or equality" (*Moral Reconstruction*, 3). Mead's attention to the social gospel and Foster's to social reform may account for the difference in their points of view. Ultimately, for evangelical Christian theology, sin was bondage, and therefore human freedom was based on reform as repentance, or the act of turning away from sin. Note, for example, the biblical injunction, from KJV Galatians 5:1, to "stand fast therefore in the liberty wherewith Christ hath made us free, and be not entangled again with the yoke of bondage."

17. Mangum and Blumell, *Mormons' War on Poverty*, 75–92.

18. W. J. McConnell to Joseph F. Smith, 24 Jan. 1904, RSC.

19. *Proceedings*, 3:233.

20. Nels Anderson, "Pontifex Babbitt," 178.

21. *Proceedings*, 2:184.

22. Carl Badger to "Wells," 16 June 1903, CABP.

23. "Reed Smoot Inquiry to be Resumed," *Brooklyn Eagle*, 10 Jan. 1905.

24. *Proceedings*, 2:678 (J. W. N. Whitecotten), 801 (John P. Meakin), 590 (F. H. Holzheimer).

25. Ibid., 953, 959.

26. Ibid., 3:248–54, 304, 189, 306.

27. Russell, "Mr. Roosevelt to the Mormons," 6.

28. *Proceedings*, 3:213, 115, 224–25.

29. Reed Smoot to Joseph F. Smith, 10 Feb. 1905, RSC.

30. *Proceedings*, 1:178.

31. Clark, *Messages of the First Presidency*, 4:84.

32. Lund, Diary, 16 May 1904, LDSCA. See also Badger, Diary, 18 Apr. 1904, CABP.

33. It is known that John W. Taylor married his fourth and fifth wives, Eliza Roxey Welling and Rhoda Welling, in 1901 and his sixth wife, Ellen Sandberg, in 1909. Matthias F. Cowley took a third wife, Harriet Bennion, in 1899 and a fourth, Lenora Taylor, in 1905. Only the 1899 marriage came to the attention of the Senate committee. In addition, Cowley performed the wedding of apostle Marriner W. Merrill to his eighth wife, Hilda M. Erickson, in 1901. Supporting documentation and historical interpretation of these and other post-Manifesto plural marriages by lesser-known members of the church can be found in Quinn, *Mormon Hierarchy*, 705; Alexander, *Mormonism in Transition*, 11–12, 62–66; Hardy, *Solemn Covenant*, 206–44; Jorgenson and Hardy, "Taylor-Cowley Affair"; Kenneth L. Cannon II, "After the Manifesto"; and Quinn, "New Plural Marriages."

34. George Teasdale married his fifth wife, Marion E. Scholes, and sixth wife, Letita Thomas, in 1897 and 1900, respectively. His last marriage was officiated by Anthon Lund, member of the church's First Presidency. The senators knew of both these marriages, but not their officiators. While Apostle Rudger Clawson and Pearl Udall married plurally in Aug. 1904, it was not known to the Senate committee.

35. *Proceedings*, 1:386, 487, 456, 491. Both Taylor and Cowley were born in 1858 and were forty-six years old when the Smoot hearing began. In contrast, Merrill was nearly seventy when first subpoenaed, and he died in February 1906. Born in 1831, George Teasdale was in his mid-seventies at the time of the hearing and died in the summer of 1907, four months after the Senate voted to retain Smoot. Heber J. Grant was two years younger than Taylor and Cowley and would become president of the L.D.S. Church in 1918.

36. Lund, Diary, 2, 18 Jan. 1905, LDSCA.

37. Clawson, *Diary*, 7 July 1904.

38. Badger, Diary, 22 Mar. 1904, CABP.

39. Carl Badger to Rose Badger, 20 Jan. 1905, CABP.

40. Heber J. Grant to Joseph F. Smith, 5 Jan. 1906, SGKC.

41. Ben E. Rich to Joseph F. Smith, 15 Nov. 1905, SGKC.

42. Badger, Diary, 16 Mar. 1904, CABP.

43. Carl Badger to Rose Badger, 11 Jan. 1905, quoted in Badger, *Liahona*, 298.

44. Reed Smoot to L.D.S. First Presidency, 8 Dec. 1905, RSC.

45. Smith had testified during the first phase of the hearing, which was adjourned on 24 April 1904. The committee reconvened the hearing on 12 December 1904 to hear the remainder of the protestants' case. Smoot began his defense on 11 January 1905, presenting forty-two witnesses over a three-week period. What were thought

to be closing arguments were heard on 28 January. Realizing they had not made their case, however, the protestants convinced the committee chairman to reopen the hearings on 8 February 1906 for promised new evidence.

46. *Proceedings*, 1:99. This appears to have been, as Smith would later insist in an interview with the Pittsburgh press, "the exact truth" (*Pittsburgh Times*, 4 Apr. 1905). See, for example, the manner in which he made a promise regarding blessings associated with church tithe six months prior to becoming church president: "You may call it a prophecy if you will" (Joseph F. Smith, Sermon, in *CR*, Apr. 1901, 70).

47. Joseph F. Smith to D. C. Wixom, 25 Mar. 1904, *SC*, 1:30.

48. "The Church Disavows Itself," *Salt Lake Tribune*, 30 Mar. 1905.

49. Cannon's representations of Smith are in *Salt Lake Tribune*, 1 Feb., 16 Apr. 1905. Smith's caricature of Cannon is in Joseph F. Smith to Heber J. Grant, 26 Oct. 1905; Joseph F. Smith to Isaac Smith, 11 Oct. 1906; and Joseph F. Smith to George C. Smith, 27 Oct. 1906, *SC*, 1:30.

50. Journal History, 19 Mar. 1905. For Smith's personal response to someone who found his testimony "'very strange,'" see Joseph F. Smith to Elder C. Hermansen, 13 Nov. 1905, *SC*, 1:30.

51. *Salt Lake Tribune*, 20 Mar. 1905.

52. David John, Diary, 7 Apr. 1905, David John Papers.

53. Carl Badger to Rose Badger, 15 Mar. 1905, CABP.

54. Lund, Diary, 16 Apr. 1905, LDSCA.

55. George Albert Smith to Carl Badger, 31 Mar. 1905, quoted in Badger, *Liahona*, 264.

56. David K. Udall to Joseph F. Smith, 8 May 1905, and Andrew Kimball to Joseph F. Smith, 15 May 1905, SGKC.

57. "Smoot and the Conference," *Salt Lake Tribune*, 1 Apr. 1905.

58. Carl Badger to Rose Badger, 1 Jan. 1905, CABP.

59. Pearson, "Woman of Mormondom / Smoot Investigation," ca. 1905, LDSCA. Other than the reference to her membership in the church, Pearson's reflections on the Smoot hearing provide no personal information. According to her obituary, Pearson was born in Nevada in 1871 and died seventy-two years later in Duchesne, Utah. At the time of her death, she was the widow of John Pearson and was survived by five daughters and five sons. See *Salt Lake Tribune*, 19 Dec. 1943. For a rare example of Smith's private defense of his testimony regarding polygamy, see Joseph F. Smith to Elder C. Hermansen, 18 Nov. 1905, *SC*, 1:30.

60. Carl Badger to Rose Badger, 15 Apr. 1905, CABP.

61. Joseph Howell to W. W. Salmon, 9 Mar. 1905, *SC*, 1:30.

62. Quoted in Milton R. Merrill, *Apostle in Politics*, 69.

63. Badger, Diary, 8 Feb. 1905, CABP.

64. Ibid., 12 Feb. 1905.

65. For an extended analysis of the necessity of consensus among these two bodies, see Alexander, "'To Maintain Harmony.'"

66. Joseph F. Smith to Reed Smoot, 9 Apr. 1904, *SC*, 1:30.

67. Ibid., 20 Mar. 1904. For Smith's objections to Burrows, see ibid., 9, 20 Apr. 1904.

68. Joseph F. Smith to J. C. Burrows, 15 Apr. 1904, RSC. See also Joseph F. Smith to Reed Smoot, 9 Apr. 1904, SC, 1:30.

69. Badger, Diary, 26 Mar. 1904, quoted in Badger, *Liahona*, 215.

70. Quinn, "New Plural Marriages," 100-101. See John W. Taylor to Joseph F. Smith, 16 Mar. 1904, RSC, and Matthias F. Cowley to Joseph F. Smith, 22 Mar. 1904, SGKC.

71. John W. Taylor to Joseph F. Smith, 7 May 1904, SGKC.

72. Badger, Diary, 8 Sept. 1905, CABP; Matthias F. Cowley to Francis M. Lyman, 1 Aug. 1904, SGKC.

73. Quinn, "New Plural Marriages," 99.

74. It would take many years for church leaders to convince members that this time they meant the prohibition on plural marriage. See Hardy, *Solemn Covenant*, 310-35, and Bradley, *Kidnapped from That Land*, 6-17.

75. Access to Joseph F. Smith's papers and those of a majority of the church's apostles is highly restricted by the L.D.S. Church. Even the publication in December 2002 of nearly a half-million pages of archival material does not include Smith's journals for the years coinciding with the Smoot hearing. See SC, 1:26. Likewise, with very few exceptions, references to the hearing appear to have been removed from the published version of Smith's letterbooks. See SC, 1:27-30. Thus, analysis of Smith's personal response to the hearings, as well as that of many of his contemporaries in church leadership, must be based largely on its reflection in the records of others or from correspondents who retained copies of letters, such as Badger and Smoot, respectively. For notes taken on relevant church archival material prior to its withdrawal from circulation, I thank Scott G. Kenney.

76. Journal History, 4 Apr. 1904; Carl Badger to Rose Badger, 15 Apr. 1905, CABP.

77. Carl Badger to Rose Badger, 15 Apr. 1905, CABP.

78. Clark, *Messages of the First Presidency*, 4:84.

79. Joseph F. Smith, Sermon, in CR, Apr. 1904, 97.

80. Francis M. Lyman to George Teasdale, 9 July 1904, SGKC. Virtually identical instructions were given to the other members of the quorum. See Jorgenson and Hardy, "Taylor-Cowley Affair," 4-36, 26 n. 39.

81. Clawson, *Diary*, 29 Sept. 1904.

82. Joseph F. Smith to Reed Smoot, 9 Apr. 1904, SC, 1:30.

83. Lund, Diary, 2 June 1904, LDSCA.

84. Eckersley, Diary, 4 Apr. 1906, LDSCA.

85. Richards, "Record of Matters of Special Importance," 275. All quotations from the deliberations on Taylor's and Cowley's resignations come from Richards's notes. It appears that no official minutes were taken. The original manuscript of Richards's account is held in the L.D.S. Church Archives and is not available to the public. The only available account from Taylor's point of view is found in minutes taken during his 1911 excommunication hearing. See "The Trial of Apostle John W.

Taylor," *New Mormon Studies CD-ROM*. Cowley's perspective is likewise indicated in his 1911 hearing, which resulted in loss of priesthood privileges. See "The Trial of Apostle Matthias F. Cowley," *New Mormon Studies CD-ROM*. Additional detail is available in Cowley, "Family History."

86. Joseph F. Smith to Heber J. Grant, 14 Dec. 1905, SC, 1:30.

87. Richards, "Record of Matters of Special Importance," 276–77.

88. Ibid.

89. Cowley, "Family History."

90. Ibid. Eventually, Taylor and Cowley were dropped from the quorum but retained their memberships in the church and their office as apostles. It also appears the principals expected that both men would be restored to their positions as soon as possible. This proved impossible as church leadership was required to take increasingly harsher actions to convince its own membership that plural marriages were proscribed and to combat schismatic movements by those who objected to the new policy. In 1911 the church began excommunicating leaders at various levels who continued to espouse polygamy. Taylor and Cowley were excommunicated and disfellowshipped, respectively, at this time.

91. Lund, Diary, 19 Nov. 1905, LDSCA.

92. Reed Smoot to L.D.S. First Presidency, 8 Dec. 1905, RSC.

93. Ibid.

94. George F. Gibbs to Reed Smoot, 9 Dec. 1905, SGKC.

Chapter Five

1. Joseph F. Smith, Sermon, in *CR*, Nov. 1901, 1.

2. Halstead, foreword to Beadle, *Polygamy*, xvi.

3. Shipps, *Mormonism*, 148. The evolution of the Latter-day Saint theology of revelation is analyzed in Persons, "Analysis of Changes."

4. Shipps, "Principle Revoked," 67.

5. Senator Smoot was in Washington, D.C., preparing for the last round of his battle before the Committee on Privileges and Elections. Apostle Merrill was still sick and would die within a few months. Apostle Teasdale pined away in Mexico, where he and his wife "read aloud the Smoot investigation until we were tire[d] of it and glad to go to bed." In similar fashion, Apostle Heber J. Grant watched the centennial festivities from England, having been told he "could not return until the Smoot case was out of the way." Apostles Cowley and Taylor continued to travel in Mexico and Canada on church business, speaking at church conferences in out-of-the-way areas and avoiding the Senate subpoena power, with Smoot's help. See Teasdale, Diary, 17 Feb. 1905, Teasdale Papers, JWML; B. F. Grant to Heber J. Grant, 7 July 1905, SGKC. For Smoot's assistance to Taylor and Cowley, see Reed Smoot to A. J. McRae, 16, 18 Apr. 1904, RSC; Carl Badger to E. H. Callister, 6 Feb. 1905, CABP; and Badger, Journal, 27 Apr. 1904, CABP. For the circumstances of Grant's return from England, see Joseph F. Smith to Heber J. Grant, 19 Oct. 1906, SC, 1:30.

6. *Proceedings at the Dedication*, 1–14.

7. Accompanying Smith were

Anthon H. Lund of the First Presidency; President Francis M. Lyman of the quorum of Apostles and Elders John Henry Smith, Hyrum M. Smith, George A. Smith and Charles W. Penrose of that quorum; Presiding Patriarch John Smith; Elders Seymour B. Young and Rulon S. Wells of the first council of Seventy; Patriarchs Lorin Farr and Angus M. Cannon; Elders Lewis W. Shurtliff, President of the Weber stake, Frank Y. Taylor, President of the Granite stake, Jesse M. Smith of the Davis stake presidency, and George F. Richards of the Tooele stake; Bishop George Romney; Elders Elias A. Smith, John McDonald, Benjamin F. Grant, Arthur Winter, Benjamin Goddard, Ashby Snow and Joseph F. Smith Jr.; Sisters Susa Y. Gates, Edith A. Smith, Julina C. Smith, Ida B. Smith and Alice Richards and her son Oliver L., aged 19 months, a total of thirty souls. (*Proceedings at the Dedication*, 5)

See also Erekson, "American Prophet, New England Town," 314. For Smith's description of the party and the dedication journey, see Joseph F. Smith to Alvin F. Smith, 4 Jan. 1906, *SC*, 1:30.

8. Another "55 Utah people" living in the East joined the Salt Lake City travelers for the dedication, including "John G. McQuarrie (president of the Eastern States mission), his wife Maggie S. McQuarrie, Hyrum K. Porter (secretary of the Eastern States mission), Murray K. Jacobs, Fred J. Pack, Sadie G. Pack, Gene G. Pack, Emma Lucy Gates, Cecil Gates, Robert C. Easton, Jennette Y. Easton, Henry Peterson, Frederick J. Jackson, Orestes U. Bean, Hyrum Homer, Joseph J. Larsen, M. S. Gudmansen, Fred J. Clark, Ellen Thomas and Eva Y. Davis" (from the entry for 23 Dec. 1905, in Jenson, *Church Chronology*).

9. *Proceedings at the Dedication*, 6. Local antagonism toward the memorial project is described in Erekson, "American Prophet, New England Town," 107–12.

10. *Proceedings at the Dedication*, 13, 15.

11. Joseph F. Smith, Sermon, in *CR*, Oct. 1905, 97.

12. Halstead, foreword to Beadle, *Polygamy*, xvi.

13. Statues of Joseph Smith and his co-martyr brother, Hyrum Smith, were erected in Salt Lake City in 1907. For a brief discussion of this and other monuments built by the church at the turn of the century, see Bitton, *Ritualization*, 178, and his conclusion that "the 1930s and 1940s were a time of almost feverish activity in the erection of monuments and historical markers" (ibid.). Earlier efforts to commemorate Smith's birth and death are discussed in Erekson, "American Prophet, New England Town," 46–49.

14. *Proceedings at the Dedication*, 17. For a discussion of the construction of the Joseph Smith monument that catalogs Latter-day Saint roots in Vermont and analyzes the effect of the construction and subsequent use of the monument on the twentieth-century relationship of Vermonters to the L.D.S. Church, see Erekson, "American Prophet, New England Town."

15. *Proceedings at the Dedication*, 73.

16. Ibid., 54.

17. Ibid., 17.

18. Ibid., 29.

19. Ibid., 30–31.

20. For Halbwachs's foundational studies, see *Les Cadres Sociaux de la Mémoire* and *La Mémoire Collective*. More recent studies include Hobsbawm and Ranger, *Invention of Tradition*; Lowenthal, *Past Is a Foreign Country*; and Connerton, *How Societies Remember*. For the critical adaptation of the theory of collective memory to the American context, see McConkey, *Anatomy of Memory*; Bodner, *Remaking America*; Kammen, *Mystic Chords of Memory*; and Linenthal, *Sacred Ground*. Davis Bitton may have been the first to note the ritual aspects of Latter-day Saint memorial activity in an article first published in the 1975 *Utah Historical Quarterly* and reprinted in *Ritualization*, 171–87.

21. Thelan, "Memory and American History," 1123 (emphasis added).

22. Nora, "Between Memory and History."

23. Of course, public curiosity periodically requires the church to dispose of the subject anew by commenting on its present relationship to plural marriage. See, for example, the 8 September 1998 CNN interview of current church president Gordon B. Hinckley. "When our people came West, they permitted it on a restricted scale," he explained, but "that's 118 years ago. It's behind us." A transcript of the interview is available at <http://www.lds.org/en/4_News_Update/19980908_CNN_Transcript.html> (29 Sept. 1998), or see CNN Transcript 98090800V22.

24. *Proceedings at the Dedication*, 22.

25. Ibid., 26.

26. All relevant references that follow are to the canonized account published as "Joseph Smith—History" in *The Pearl of Great Price*. For an analysis of other versions, see Jesse, "Early Accounts."

27. "Joseph Smith—History," 1:19.

28. Alexander, "Reconstruction of Mormon Doctrine"; Allen, "Significance of Joseph Smith's 'First Vision'"; Allen, "Emergence of a Fundamental"; Richard Lloyd Anderson, "Circumstantial Confirmation"; Paulsen, "Doctrine of Divine Embodiment"; and Vogel, "Earliest Mormon Concept of God."

29. Allen, "Emergence of a Fundamental," 53. The debate is summarized in Paulsen, "Doctrine of Divine Embodiment," 7–94. From Smith's failure to write an account of this story until 1832 or to use it as an explicit basis for doctrinal exposition, it appears that he considered his First Vision a personal experience, unrelated to later theophanies that led him to organize his own church and direct its development. Allen hypothesizes that the relative lack of importance of the First Vision in the nineteenth-century missionary efforts can be explained by the fact that, unlike so much else of Mormonism, it was not capable of biblical proof-texting as a fulfillment of biblical prophecy. Arguably, Allen's hypothesis explains the First Vision's limited use within the church as well. Nineteenth-century Latter-day Saints did not lose their convictions about the Bible by becoming Mormons. Consistent with their initial response to Latter-day Saint primitivist claims, they would continue to focus their convictions and identity on, for example, the Book of Mormon's claim to restore those "plain and precious things" and on their own pentecostal experiences and priestly ordinations. In sum, the First Vision was not a necessary basis of faith for members, though it was by no means unknown.

30. Allen, "Emergence of a Fundamental," 55.

31. Backman, "First Vision."

32. Lucy Mack Smith, *Biographical Sketches*, 146.

33. Joseph F. Smith, *Two Sermons*.

34. Joseph F. Smith, Sermon, in *CR*, Apr. 1909, 4.

35. *Reynolds v. U.S.*, 98 US 145, 166 (1878).

36. Shipps, *Mormonism*, 33.

37. For the appropriateness of designating plural marriage Joseph Smith's "last" vision, see Chapter 2, n. 27.

38. McKay, *Gospel Ideals*, 85.

39. At least eight accounts of the First Vision were produced during Joseph Smith's life. The one chosen by the L.D.S. Church as the official version was dictated by Smith to a scribe in 1838 and published originally in a Latter-day Saint newspaper in 1842. The texts of all eight accounts are in Jesse, *Papers of Joseph Smith*, 1:3–7, 127–28, 267–75, 389–91, 405–9, 429–30, 444, 448–49, 461.

40. Ricoeur, *From Text to Action*, 124.

41. *Doctrine and Covenants*, 1:30.

42. "Joseph Smith—History," 1:1.

43. Ibid., 23–26.

44. Lund, Sermon, in *CR*, Apr. 1920, 19, 21.

45. Allen, Embry, and Mehr, *Hearts Turned to the Fathers*, 59–90. Though Smith had introduced baptism for the dead in 1840, it was not the primary focus of his own discourses on temple. Instead, the role of the temple in relation to doctrines of deification and celestial marriage, or its sanctifying import for the living, had dominated Smith's instruction to the Latter-day Saints during his own life. For reports of Smith's sermons during the Nauvoo period, see Ehat and Cook, *Words of Joseph Smith*.

46. "Joseph Smith—History," 1:65.

47. *Proceedings at the Dedication*, 67. Joseph Smith's identification of Anthon with the "learned man" of Isaiah 29 is discussed in Bushman, *Joseph Smith*, 86–89.

48. "Joseph Smith—History," 1:69. Compare KJV Malachi 3:3.

49. Ricoeur, *Symbolism of Evil*, 262.

50. Ibid., 6.

51. The entire history of the L.D.S. Church can be written as a crisis of authority. See, for example, Hill, *Quest for Refuge*. The particular crisis that came to a head during the Smoot hearing may have originated as early as the Saints' disappointed expectations of a Second Coming after the Civil War and the increasing dominance of their kingdom by the federal government during the 1870s and 1880s. Certainly by the early twentieth century, however, when the Smoot hearing precipitated the dismissal of Taylor and Cowley, the Saints needed reassurance that their church was truly capable of fulfilling its millennial mission or, for that matter, simply true.

52. "Joseph Smith—History," 1:69.

53. Bushman, *Joseph Smith*, 188–89. See also Shipps's related point that "in replicating sacred story—Mormon history itself took on a sacred character" (*Mormonism*, 64).

54. Lund, Sermon, in *CR*, Apr. 1920, 19.

55. Widtsoe, *Evidences and Reconciliations*, 46.

56. *Proceedings at the Dedication*, 68.

57. A historical study of Joseph Smith's theology during this period is found in Esplin, "Significance of Nauvoo," and Lyon, "Doctrinal Development." See also Shipps, *Mormonism*, 67–86, for a discussion of the increasingly esoteric nature of Joseph Smith's teachings.

58. *Proceedings at the Dedication*, 86.

59. Ibid., 42.

60. Ibid., 57–58.

61. Shipps, *Mormonism*, 145.

62. Shepherd and Shepherd, *Kingdom Transformed*, 229–59.

63. Hughes, "Why Restorationists Don't Fit."

64. *Deseret Evening News*, 18 Dec. 1908, 4. The other three referenced "standard" or canonized works are the Bible, the Book of Mormon, and *The Pearl of Great Price*, which contains "Joseph Smith—History" as well as other of Smith's revelations.

65. Charles W. Penrose to Joseph F. Smith, 31 Mar. 1908, SGKC.

66. Clark, *Messages of the First Presidency*, 1:224.

67. Stanley S. Ivins, Diary, 29 Nov. 1944, USHS.

68. For an analysis of the effects of *Reynolds* on Latter-day Saint belief by means of regulating Latter-day Saint action, see Harmer-Dionne, "Once a Peculiar People."

69. See Hardy, *Solemn Covenant*, 297–99, and Alexander, *Mormonism in Transition*, 60.

70. Phelps, "Praise to the Man."

71. *Deseret Evening News*, 23 Dec. 1905.

72. Quoted in Roberts, *Comprehensive History*, 7:515.

73. Joseph F. Smith, Sermon, in *CR*, Oct. 1902, 86–87. For a sense of the conflict and loss experienced in local communities, see Geary, "Mormondom's Lost Generation."

74. *Proceedings at the Dedication*, 88.

75. Van Orden, *Building Zion*, 114.

76. Francis M. Lyman to Reed Smoot, 15 Dec. 1905, RSC.

Chapter Six

1. *Congressional Record*, 59th Cong., 2d sess., 1906, 41, pt. 1:241.

2. Carl Badger to Rose Badger, 7 Jan. 1906, CABP.

3. Reed Smoot to Joseph F. Smith, 9 Jan. 1906, RSC.

4. See Edward H. Callister to Reed Smoot, 24 Jan. 1906, RSC, for the cause of Washington rumors that the church wanted Smoot removed from the Senate. See also Joseph F. Smith to Alvin F. Smith, 18 Mar. 1906, SC, 1:10.

5. Frank I. Sefrit to Thomas Shipps, 16 Nov. 1905, Beveridge Collection.

6. Charles Penrose to Reed Smoot, 9 Mar. 1906, RSC.

7. Heber J. Grant to Reed Smoot, 7 Mar. 1906, RSC.

8. Reed Smoot to Joseph F. Smith, 21 Jan. 1906, RSC.

9. Reed Smoot to L.D.S. First Presidency, 31 Mar. 1906, RSC.

10. *Proceedings*, 4:4.

11. Carl Badger to Rose Badger, 18 Jan. 1906, CABP. The Nephites are the protagonists in the Book of Mormon.

12. Reed Smoot to Joseph F. Smith, 12 Mar. 1906, RSC.

13. See "Polygamy B. F. Johnson Letter," Stanley Snow Ivins Collection, USHS. See also Hardy, *Solemn Covenant*, 389, for an annotated list of 220 plural marriages performed after 1890, largely in Mexico. During the hearing, Anthony Ivins was, like Teasdale and sometimes Taylor and Cowley, in Mexico. Unlike the other three, however, no effort was made by protestants' counsel to obtain Ivins's testimony.

14. Carl Badger to Rose Badger, 10 Feb. 1906, CABP.

15. *Proceedings*, 4:502.

16. Ibid., 478–81.

17. Reed Smoot to Joseph F. Smith, 8 Jan. 1906, RSC.

18. *Proceedings*, 4:7.

19. KJV Revelation 6:9–10.

20. *Proceedings*, 4:72 (William Jones Thomas).

21. Joshua Stansfield to Albert J. Beveridge, 1 Feb. 1905, Beveridge Collection.

22. *Proceedings*, 2:799. For a discussion of the role of such societies, see Carnes, *Secret Ritual*. Note, however, Carnes's treatment of the Latter-day Saint temple ritual does not consider that it was jointly enacted by women and men.

23. According to Dolliver, Roosevelt confronted Burrows at a dinner attended by several senators. He asked Burrows "how much longer he was going to keep me [Smoot] in suspense, and why he did not bring my case to a close and get the matter settled. Before Burrows could answer, the President took a hand in the conversation, and Senator Dolliver said that for nearly an hour the President told Burrows just what he thought of him, and everybody else engaged in this unwarranted fight against me" (Reed Smoot to Joseph F. Smith, 9 Mar. 1906, RSC). For Dubois's reputation, see ibid., 12 Mar. 1906.

24. Ibid., 12 Feb. 1906. The leaders of the two churches were literally cousins. Joseph F. Smith of the L.D.S. Church and Joseph Smith III, president of the Reorganized Church, were sons of the two martyred brothers, Hyrum and Joseph Smith, respectively.

25. Lund, Diary, 5 Apr. 1906, LDSCA.

26. Francis M. Lyman, Sermon, in *CR*, Apr. 1906, 93. The vagueness of the charge made against Taylor and Cowley may have been employed to facilitate their return at a later date. Events overtook intentions, however. There was no way to bring Taylor and Cowley back into the quorum without reversing the signal that their dismissal had given.

27. Orson F. Whitney, David O. McKay, and George F. Richards were selected to fill the vacancies. The next year, George Teasdale, the fourth culprit, passed away and was replaced by monogamist Anthony W. Ivins.

28. Carl Badger to Rose Badger, 29 Apr. 1906, CABP.

29. *Proceedings*, 4:410–34, 441. Instead, Carlisle addressed the issue of revelation, arguing that the L.D.S. theology necessarily contradicted civil authority and made Smoot ineligible to serve in the senate.

30. Carl Badger to Rose Badger, 6 June 1906, CABP.

31. Telegram, Reed Smoot to George Gibbs, 30 May 1906, RSC.

32. Republican senators Burrows, Moses E. Clapp, Henry A. Du Pont, Eugene Hale, Henry C. Hansbrough, James A. Hemenway, Alfred B. Kittredge, Robert M. La Follette, and William A. Smith and Democrats William A. Clark, Joseph C. S. Blackburn, and John W. Daniel were the dissenters from their respective parties. Smoot never ceased to attempt to change the minds of those who voted against him. In some cases he succeeded. In 1909 Smoot reported,

> After I had taken the oath of office [for a second term] most of the senators heartily congratulated me and wished me every success in the world. Even Hale expressed himself as being pleased with the result and stated that he was glad they would have my assistance for the next six years. After adjournment Senator Clapp came to me and congratulated me from the bottom of his heart. He said that during his whole service in the Senate there was only one vote which he had cast that he would like to recall, and that was his vote against me. He stated that he made a mistake and was ready and willing to acknowledge it. He also said that he had learned to love me and admired me for not showing any resentment toward him for his voting against me. (Reed Smoot to Ed Callister, 8 Mar. 1909, RSC)

33. The delay was, as the previous ones had been, inspired by political considerations. This time the Republicans had electoral concerns. Whatever confidence they had in persuading the majority of their colleagues that it was good for the party to accept the apostle-senator, Republican confidence was not strong enough to face the voting public in the fall of 1906. To avoid more defections like Dolliver's, the vote was scheduled after national elections. Smoot's chances of retaining his seat were strengthened when Idaho Democratic senator Fred Dubois lost his reelection campaign. Analysts of his career credit the defeat to Dubois's miscalculation of anti-Mormon sentiment in his home state and to a resurgence of the Republican Party in Idaho. See Graff, *Senatorial Career of Fred T. Dubois*, ix, and Cook, "Political Suicide of Senator Fred T. Dubois." Roosevelt facilitated this result by sending Secretary of War Taft to campaign for the Idaho Republican ticket. The lesson could not have been lost on Smoot's supporters, especially nervous ones like Senator Dolliver, who decided to vote for Smoot after all when the matter was brought to the floor for a vote.

34. Malmquist, *First One Hundred Years*, 229.

35. Reed Smoot to Joseph F. Smith, 8 June 1906, RSC.

36. Ibid.; telegram, Reed Smoot to George Gibbs, 7 June 1906, RSC.

37. *Congressional Record*, 59th Cong., 2d sess., 1907, 41, pt. 4:3408. Foraker considered Dubois's speech "the dying wail of a dishonest politician" (Reed Smoot to Joseph F. Smith, 15 June 1906, RSC).

38. Gibbs, *Lights and Shadows of Mormonism*, 518.

39. *Congressional Record*, 59th Cong., 2d sess., 1907, 41, pt. 1:938.

40. *Proceedings*, 1:25.

41. Ibid., 4:500.

42. *Congressional Record*, 59th Cong., 2d sess., 1907, 41, pt. 1:942.

43. See, for example, "Reed Smoot," *Independent*, Jan.–Mar. 1907, 46. For an analysis of the backlash against women's organizations after the Smoot hearing, see Iversen, *Anti-Polygamy Controversy*, 222–48.

44. *Congressional Record*, 51st Cong., 1st sess., 1890, 21, pt. 4:3146.

45. I am not the first to comment on this theme in the hearing. See Samuel Woolley Taylor, *Family Kingdom*, 199. Taylor, however, limits his conclusion to the ways in which the church's economic and political activities were characterized as monopolistic.

46. Tarbell, *History of the Standard Oil Company*, vii, 165–66, 238, 189–99, 259.

47. *Proceedings*, 1:797.

48. Ibid., 886.

49. Ray Stannard Baker, "Vitality of Mormonism," 176–77.

50. *Washington Times*, 23 Apr. 1904.

51. Gordon, *Mormon Question*, 187–98, 200–208.

52. *New York Times*, 5 July 1902, quoted in Mowry, *Era of Theodore Roosevelt*, 132. For a more recent discussion of the Progressives' "masterful compromise" on the monopoly question, see Dawley, *Struggles for Justice*, 148–59.

53. Clarke, "Andrew Hoover Comes to Indiana," 264.

54. Reed Smoot to Joseph F. Smith, 26 June 1906, RSC. The following September, Dolliver visited Salt Lake City, where his hosts convinced him otherwise.

55. Strong, *Our Country*, 112.

56. See, for example, Lewis, "Great Mormon Conspiracy."

57. Carl Badger to Rose Badger, 4, 8 Jan. 1907, CABP.

58. Ibid., 17 Feb. 1907.

59. *Congressional Record*, 59th Cong., 2d sess., 1907, 41, pt. 4:3280, 3278, and pt. 2:1492.

60. Ibid., pt. 3:3280, 2938.

61. Ibid., pt. 4:3277.

62. Ibid., pt. 3:2939.

63. Ibid., pt. 2:1490.

64. Ibid., pt. 4:3411–12.

65. Ibid., pt. 2:1500.

66. Ibid.

67. Ibid.

68. Ibid., pt. 3:2681–88.

69. Ibid., pt. 4:3273.

70. Ibid., pt. 3:2937–38.

71. Ibid., pt. 1:941.

72. Ibid., pt. 3:2939.

73. Ibid., pt. 1:937.

74. Ibid., 939.

75. Ibid., pt. 2:1492.

76. A. S. Bailey, "Anti-American Influences in Utah," 18.

77. *Congressional Record*, 59th Cong., 2d sess., 1907, 41, pt. 3:2937.

78. Ibid., pt. 4:3412.

79. Ibid., 3405.

80. Ibid., 3412.

81. *Congressional Record*, 51st Cong., 1st sess., 1890, 21, pt. 4:3146.

82. Use of the term "civil religion" is notoriously problematic. Marty offers five definitions in his treatment of American religious identity, *Nation of Behavors*. The religio-political discourse of the Smoot hearings manifests elements of all five: "folk religion," "religious nationalism," "democratic faith," "Protestant civic piety," and "transcendent universal religion of the nation" (ibid., 185–86). See also Marty, *Religion and Republic*, 77–94.

83. Marty, *Nation of Behavors*, 180.

84. Reed Smoot to Joseph F. Smith, 8 Jan. 1906, as quoted in Milton R. Merrill, *Apostle in Politics*, 70.

85. *Congressional Record*, 59th Cong., 2d sess., 1907, 41, pt. 2:1494 (22 Jan. 1907).

86. Sandel, *Democracy's Discontent*, 200.

Epilogue

1. "The Latter-day Saints," *Washington Post*, 26 Aug. 1907.

2. "East and West on Smoot," *Boston Transcript*, 20 Feb. 1907.

3. Carl Badger to Rose Badger, 17 Feb. 1907, CABP.

4. James Clove to Reed Smoot, 21 Feb. 1907, RSC.

5. Sam D. Thurman to Reed Smoot, 26 Feb. 1907, RSC.

6. Joseph F. Smith to Reed Smoot, 23 Feb. 1907, SC, 1:30.

7. James Clove to Reed Smoot, 21 Feb. 1907, RSC. See also Joseph F. Smith to Willard R. Smith, 25 Oct. 1906, SC, 1:30.

8. *Northwestern Christian Advocate*, 27 Feb. 1907, as quoted in Orcutt, *Burrows of Michigan*, 2:193.

9. Reed Smoot to Joseph F. Smith, 15 Dec. 1907, RSC.

10. The L.D.S. Church had been headquartered in Nauvoo, Illinois, between 1839 and 1846. Joseph Smith had been murdered in the adjacent town of Carthage, and mob action catalyzed the removal of the church to the Great Basin two years later.

11. Roosevelt's letter was printed in several newspapers nationally as well as in Illinois. See, for example, "Roosevelt Glad to See Smoot Seated," *Los Angeles Examiner*, 20 Aug. 1907. For some, the letter merely proved an unholy alliance between the Republicans and the Mormons and may have harmed Hopkins. See *Natchez Mississippi Democrat*, 23 Aug. 1907. The following year Hopkins introduced a joint resolution for an antipolygamy amendment to the Constitution, but he was defeated nonetheless. See Reed Smoot to Joseph F. Smith, 1 Feb. 1908, RSC.

12. James, *Dictionary of American Biography*.

13. Reed Smoot to Joseph F. Smith, 1 Feb. 1908, RSC.

14. Ibid., 15 Dec. 1907.

15. "Harry Daniel's Minor Observations," *Youngstown Telegram*, 27 Feb. 1904. See also "Trying the Mormon Church," *New York Sun*, 13 Mar. 1904.

16. "Reed Smoot," *Independent*, Jan.–Mar. 1907, 494.

17. "A Gentleman Even If He Has Got Five Wives," *Detroit Journal*, 5 Mar. 1904.

18. *Address by President Roosevelt before the National Congress of Mothers*, 4.

19. Iversen, *Anti-Polygamy Controversy*, 146.

20. Ibid., 238–56. See also Cott, *Grounding of Modern Feminism*.

21. Carl Badger to Rose Badger, 29 Apr. 1906, CABP.

22. Ibid., 21 Feb. 1907.

23. For Smoot's account of quorum debates and actions during this period, see Heath, *Diaries of Reed Smoot*, beginning with the entry of 18 Aug. 1909. Smoot's last entry on the subject is made on 4 Apr. 1931 and contains another denunciation of "men still preaching polygamy and telling false statements." Smoot's journals for the years of the hearing through 1908 have not been found.

24. For a description of the situation in Washington, see Reed Smoot's typed, eight-page letter to Joseph F. Smith, 1 Feb. 1908, RSC.

25. See Clark, *Messages of the First Presidency*, 4:216. Regarding plural marriages after 1904, see Anthony W. Ivins, Diary, 7 Jan. [1911], USHS.

26. Quoted in Smoot, Diary, 25 Aug. 1909, RSC.

27. As with most internecine arguments, the literature on this subject is voluminous and heated. See, for example, Short, *Questions on Plural Marriage*. A more accessible and scholarly discussion of the "Monogamous Triumph" in Utah is Hardy, *Solemn Covenant*, 336–62. For a discussion of schismatic groups who do practice plural marriage, see Bradley, *Kidnapped from that Land*, and Quinn, "Plural Marriage and Mormon Fundamentalism."

28. Gordon B. Hinckley interview with Larry King, 8 Sept. 1998. A transcript of the interview is available at <http://www.lds.org/en/4_News_Update/19980908_CNN_Transcript.html> (29 Sept. 1998), or see CNN Transcript 98090800V22.

29. *Proceedings at the Dedication*, 26.

30. As the locus of Joseph Smith's most public practice of plural marriage and his doctrinal comments relating marriage to temple worship, the Nauvoo temple is a more complicated site for L.D.S. remembrance. Its reconstruction may signal a new confidence on the part of leadership. More likely, it indicates a sensitivity to placing Joseph Smith within the church's contemporary effort to make temples the primary indicia of Latter-day Saint identity. See, for example, Hunter, "Great Symbol of Our Membership," 5. Note in this regard that the late-twentieth-century equation of membership with temple worship coincided with the church's international growth; see Flake, "'Not to be Riten.'" The scope of this program and its implications for twenty-first-century Mormonism can be seen in the scale of temple building. In 1950 there were eight L.D.S. temples, and all were in the United States, except one at the northern end of the Mormon culture region in Alberta, Canada. By the end of the twentieth century, 103 L.D.S. temples had been built throughout the world; see *Deseret News 2001-2002 Church Almanac*, 453–54.

31. For an extended analysis of the church's public commemoration of "Pioneer Day," see Olsen, "Celebrating Cultural Identity" and "Community Celebrations," and Eliason, "Mormon Pioneer Nostalgia," 142–53.

32. Joseph F. Smith, "Celebration of the Twenty-Fourth of July by the Sunday Schools," 178–79.

33. Eliason, "Mormon Pioneer Nostalgia," 161. See also Eliason, "Pioneers and Recapitulation in Mormon Popular Historical Expression," 203.

34. Between 1970 and 2000 the church grew at a rate of 50 percent per decade. See Stark, "So Far, So Good," 175.

35. George A. Smith to Reed Smoot, 27 Feb. 1904, RSC.

36. Milton R. Merrill, "Reed Owen Smoot."

37. See Alexander, "Senator Reed Smoot and Western Land Policy."

38. See Milton R. Merrill, *Apostle in Politics*, 285–343; Alexander, "Reed Smoot, the LDS Church, and Progressive Legislation."

39. Smoot, Diary, 8 Dec. 1920, RSC.

40. Lund, Diary, 7 Sept. 1908, LDSCA.

41. Milton R. Merrill, *Apostle in Politics*, 398.

42. Only in the late twentieth century would the L.D.S. Church engage in overt political activity on issues of national concern. Ironically, the church was motivated by a socially conservative agenda on sexual politics defined in terms of sexual morality. In the nineteenth century, women's franchise was first exercised in Utah, creating an unusual alliance between women's rights activists and Latter-day Saint women, as well as their male church leadership, anxious to prove that plural marriage did not oppress women. See Van Wagenen, "In Their Own Behalf." A century later, the Latter-day Saints were accused of defeating the Equal Rights Amendment by effectively lobbying legislatures in key states needed for ratification, including the "Mormon states" of Arizona, Nevada, and Utah. See Mansbridge, *Why We Lost*, 13, 34. The basis for the church's opposition lay in its conviction that the amendment undermined the traditional marriage relationship and legitimized homosexuality. Consequently, it is no surprise that in the 1990s the church mobilized the votes and provided a major source of the funding necessary to defeat initiatives legalizing same-sex unions in Hawaii, California, and Alaska. See "Mormons Urged to Block Gay Marriages," *San Francisco Chronicle*, 13 Mar. 1996; "A Mormon Crusade in Hawaii: Church Aims to End Gay Union," *Salt Lake Tribune*, 9 June 1996; "LDS Cash Carries Gay-Marriage Fight: Mormon Church Has Spent $1.1 Million on Ballot Battles in Hawaii and Alaska," *Salt Lake Tribune*, 26 Oct. 1998; "Church Backing Helps Measures in 2 States," *Deseret News*, 8 Nov. 2000. Whether this signals the church's growing confidence in and willingness to exercise its political power, only time will tell. It is just as likely that the L.D.S. Church's interest in this type of question reflects its doctrinal conviction that marriage is "celestial," or the primary sacrament of the church, and therefore justifies political action and social disapproval in its defense, as in the nineteenth century.

43. The matter was settled by removing authority from the executive branch and giving it to the courts—but not before Ogden Nash satirized the senator in the following ditty:

Senator Smoot (Republican Ut.)

Is planning a ban on smut.

Oh rooti-ti-toot for Smoot of Ut.

And his reverent occiput.

Smite, Smoot, smite for Ut.,

Grit your molars and hold your dut.,

Gird up your l—ns,

Smite h-p and th-gh,

We'll all be Kansas

By and by. (Harmon, *American Light Verse*, 423–24)

44. Quoted in Milton R. Merrill, *Apostle in Politics*, 170.

45. Carl Badger to Rose Badger, 30 Dec. 1906, CABP.

46. Chesterton and Inge, *Twelve Modern Apostles*, 182. Smoot's essay appeared originally in "Why I Am a Mormon," *Forum*, Oct. 1926, 562–69.

47. Shipps, *Sojourner*, 67.

48. Ibid., 72.

49. Chesterton and Inge, *Twelve Modern Apostles*, 183.

50. Smoot, Diary, 7, 23 May 1923, RSC. The cause for transatlantic celebration was not only that USS *Leviathan* was the largest luxury liner in the American Merchant Marine, but it was also a symbol of Allied triumph in the Great War. *Leviathan* was a reconditioned version of the SS *Vaterland*, Germany's largest passenger ship, with a displacement power of 58,000 tons. Built in 1913 and seized while docked in the United States at the outbreak of World War I, the ship was commandeered as a troop carrier for the Allies and renamed *Leviathan*. It was decommissioned in 1919 and extensively refurbished for return to commercial status in 1923. See <http://www.greatoceanliners.net/vaterland.html> (6 June 2003).

51. Smoot, Diary, 7 June 1923, RSC. Smoot visited Switzerland also, but President Harding's unexpected death required the senator to return quickly to the United States. Nevertheless, his brief visit there, as well as in Germany and France, garnered the church much-needed positive publicity. An account of the journey from Widtsoe's point of view is in Parrish, *John A. Widtsoe*, 326–37. The church's difficulties in Europe and additional details on events leading up to Smoot's 1923 European mission are provided in Thomas, "Apostolic Diplomacy."

52. Smoot, Diary, 16 July 1923, RSC.

53. Ibid., 20 July 1923.

54. Ibid., 27 July 1923.

55. Britain's anti-Mormon press campaign and the violence it engendered is discussed in Thorp, "'Mormon Peril.'"

56. Smoot, Diary, 20 July 1923, RSC.

57. John A. Widtsoe Papers, George H. Durham, Salt Lake City, Utah.

58. John A. Widtsoe, "Report on European Mission," 8 Aug. 1923, George H. Durham, Salt Lake City, Utah. See also John A. Widtsoe, "Excelsior Entries," 10 Feb. 1941.

59. "Reed Smoot," *Independent*, Jan.–Mar. 1907, 494.

60. Joseph F. Smith to Reed Smoot, 7 Apr. 1917, RSC.

61. Quoted in Milton R. Merrill, *Apostle in Politics*, 144. Smoot was defeated by

another Latter-day Saint, Elbert D. Thomas (1883–1953), who served for eighteen years and distinguished himself as senior member of the Senate Foreign Relations Committee during World War II.

62. Dedication of the Hill Cumorah Monument, 21 July 1935, quoted in Reeve and Cowan, "Hill Called Cumorah," 79.

63. Milton R. Taylor, "Mormon Marriage and Its Canonical Consequences," 66.

64. Joseph F. Smith, Sermon, in *CR*, Oct. 1903, 4.

BIBLIOGRAPHY

Manuscripts, Personal Journals, and Papers

Badger, Carlos Ashby, Papers. L. Tom Perry Special Collections. Harold B. Lee Library. Brigham Young University, Provo, Utah.

Beveridge, Albert J., Collection. Manuscripts Collection, Library of Congress. Washington, D.C.

Cowley, Matthias F. "Family History: Sketch of the History of Matthias F. Cowley." Special Collections and Manuscripts. J. Willard Marriott Library. University of Utah, Salt Lake City.

———. Papers. Special Collections and Manuscripts. J. Willard Marriott Library. University of Utah, Salt Lake City.

Eckersley, Joseph, Diary. Joseph Eckersley Papers. L.D.S. Church Archives. The Church of Jesus Christ of Latter-day Saints. Salt Lake City, Utah.

Ivins, Anthony W., Collection. Utah State Historical Society, Salt Lake City.

Ivins, Stanley S., Collection. Utah State Historical Society, Salt Lake City.

John, David, Papers. L. Tom Perry Special Collections. Harold B. Lee Library. Brigham Young University, Provo, Utah.

Journal History of The Church of Jesus Christ of Latter-day Saints (microfilm). Church History Library. The Church of Jesus Christ of Latter-day Saints. Salt Lake City, Utah.

Kenney, Scott G., Collection. Special Collections and Manuscripts. J. Willard Marriott Library. University of Utah, Salt Lake City.

Lund, Anthon H., Diary. L.D.S. Church Archives. The Church of Jesus Christ of Latter-day Saints. Salt Lake City, Utah.

Paden, Wiley M., Collection. Special Collections. Giovale Library. Westminster College, Salt Lake City, Utah.

Pearson, Sarah E. "Woman of Mormondom, Smoot Investigation." L.D.S. Church Archives. The Church of Jesus Christ of Latter-day Saints. Salt Lake City, Utah.

Smith, George A., Family Papers. Special Collections and Manuscripts. J. Willard Marriott Library. University of Utah, Salt Lake City.

Smith, Joseph. "The Temple." *Times and Season*, 2 May 1842, 775–76.

Smoot, Reed, Collection. L. Tom Perry Special Collections. Harold B. Lee Library. Brigham Young University, Provo, Utah.

Teasdale, George, Papers. Special Collections and Manuscripts. J. Willard Marriott Library. University of Utah, Salt Lake City.

Widtsoe, John A. "Excelsior Entries, 1903–1949." Typescript in possession of George H. Durham, Salt Lake City, Utah.

Newspapers and Popular Periodicals

American Catholic Quarterly Review. Philadelphia, Pa.
American Mercury. Torrence, Calif.
Argus. Albany, N.Y.
Baltimore Sun. Baltimore, Md.
Boston Transcript. Boston, Mass.
Capital. Topeka, Kans.
Chicago Daily Tribune, Chicago, Ill.
Collier's. Springfield, Ohio
Cosmopolitan. New York, N.Y.
Deseret News. Salt Lake City, Utah
Eagle. Brooklyn, N.Y.
Evening Star. Washington, D.C.
Express. Buffalo, N.Y.
Goodwin's Weekly. Salt Lake City, Utah
Harper's Weekly. New York, N.Y.
Improvement Era. Salt Lake City, Utah
Independent. New York, N.Y.
Los Angeles Examiner. Los Angeles, Calif.
Natchez Mississippi Democrat. Natchez, Miss.
New York American. New York, N.Y.
New York Herald. New York, N.Y.
New York Observer. New York, N.Y.
New York Sun. New York, N.Y.
New York Times. New York, N.Y.
New York Tribune. New York, N.Y.
New York World. New York, N.Y.
Philadelphia Inquirer. Philadelphia, Pa.
Pittsburgh Times. Pittsburgh, Pa.
Poughkeepsie Press. Poughkeepsie, N.Y.
Relief Society Magazine. Salt Lake City, Utah
Salt Lake Herald. Salt Lake City, Utah
Salt Lake Tribune. Salt Lake City, Utah
Topeka Capital. Topeka, Kans.
Washington Evening Star. Washington, D.C.
Washington Post. Washington, D.C.
Washington Times. Washington, D.C.
World Today. Chicago, Ill.
Youngstown Telegram. Youngstown, Ohio

Public Documents

Abbreviated Minutes of the Synod of Utah in the Session in the First Presbyterian Church of Pocatello, Idaho, October 12–14, 1905. N.p.: Published by Direction of the Synod, n.d.

Address by President Roosevelt before the National Congress of Mothers, Washington, Mar. 13, 1905. Washington, D.C.: Government Printing Office, 1905.

Depew, Chauncey M. (New York). "Statehood Bill." *Congressional Record*, 57th Cong., 2d sess., 11, 13, 17 Feb. 1903, 36, pt. 3: appendix, pp. 87–114.

Kearns, Thomas (Utah). "Conditions in Utah: Speech of Hon. Thomas Kearns, of Utah, in the Senate of the United States, Tuesday, Feb. 28, 1905, Washington, 1905." *Congressional Record*, 58th Cong., 3d sess., 28 Feb. 1905, 39, pt. 4:3608.

"Petitions against the Seating of Reed Smoot." *Congressional Record*, 58th Cong., 3d sess., 7, 8, 12, 13, 14, 15, 16 Dec. 1904, 39, pt. 1:43–45, 63, 120, 186, 190, 253, 295, 340, 395.

"Petitions against the Seating of Reed Smoot." *Congressional Record*, 58th Cong., 3d sess., 4, 5, 6, 10, 11, 13 Jan. 1905, 39. pt. 1:434, 435, 456, 457, 510, 621, 674, 769.

"Petitions against the Seating of Reed Smoot." *Congressional Record*, 58th Cong., 3d sess., 20, 23, 25, 26, 27, 28, 30, 31 Jan., 1, 3, 4, 6, 8 Feb. 1905, 39, pt. 2:1116, 1121, 1218, 1326, 1382, 1440, 1441, 1442, 1502, 1572, 1573, 1622, 1667, 1814, 1815, 1860, 1910, 2057.

"Petitions against the Seating of Reed Smoot." *Congressional Record*, 58th Cong., 3d sess., 9, 10, 11, 13, 14, 16, 18, 20, 22 Feb. 1905, 39, pt. 3:2143, 2144, 2224, 2388, 2446, 2511, 2512, 2707, 2816, 2887, 2888, 3017.

"Petitions against the Seating of Reed Smoot." *Congressional Record*, 58th Cong., 3d sess., 25, 28 Feb., 1, 2, 3 Mar. 1905, 39, pt. 4:3361, 3598, 3599, 3600, 3718, 3821, 3927.

"Protest." 58th Cong., 2d sess. *Congressional Record* (6 Apr. 1904), vol. 38, pt. 5, p. 4345.

"Senator from Utah." *Congressional Record*, 59th Cong., 1st sess., 11 June 1906, 40, pt. 9:8218–38.

"Senator from Utah." *Congressional Record*, 59th Cong., 2d sess., 11, 13, 18 Dec. 1906, 41, pt. 1:241–55, 330–48, 498.

"Senator from Utah." *Congressional Record*, 59th Cong., 2d sess., 11 Jan. 1907, 41, pt. 1:933–45.

"Senator from Utah." *Congressional Record*, 59th Cong., 2d sess., 22, 30 Jan. 1907, 41, pt. 2:1486–1501, 1933–34.

"Senator from Utah." *Congressional Record*, 59th Cong., 2d sess., 11, 14 Feb. 1907, 41, pt. 3:2681–88, 2934–39.

"Senator from Utah." *Congressional Record*, 59th Cong., 2d sess., 19, 20 Feb. 1907, 41, pt. 4:3268–81, 3404–30.

U.S. House. *Joint Resolution Proposing an Amendment to the Constitution of the United States, January 3, 1924.* 68th Cong., 1st sess., H.J. Res. 114. Washington, D.C.: Government Printing Office, 1924.

U.S. Senate. Committee on Privileges and Elections. *Proceedings before the Committee on Privileges and Elections of the United States Senate in the Matter of the Protests against the Right of Hon. Reed Smoot, a Senator from the State of Utah, to Hold His Seat.* 59th Cong., 1st sess., S. Rept. No. 486. Washington, D.C.: Government Printing Office, 1904–6. 4 vols. [Serial Set 2932–35].

"Utah Senatorial Investigation." *Congressional Record*, 58th Cong., 2d sess., 25, 27 Jan. 1904, 38, pt. 2:1100, 1239.

Case Law

City of Boerne v. Flores, 521 U.S. 507 (1997).
Davis v. Beason, 133 U.S. 333 (1890).
Everson v. Board of Education, 330 U.S. 1 (1947).
The Late Corporation of the Church of Jesus Christ of Latter-Day Saints v. United States, 136 U.S. 1 (1890).
Reynolds v. U.S., 98 U.S. 145 (1878).

Secondary Sources

Ahlstrom, Sydney E. *A Religious History of the American People*. New Haven: Yale University Press, 1972.
Albanese, Catherine L. *America: Religions and Religion*. Belmont, Calif.: Wadsworth, 1992.
Alexander, Thomas. *Mormonism in Transition: A History of the Latter-day Saints, 1890-1930*. Urbana: University of Illinois Press, 1986.
———. "The Reconstruction of Mormon Doctrine: From Joseph Smith to Progressive Theology." *Sunstone* 5 (July/Aug. 1980): 24-33.
———. "Reed Smoot, the LDS Church, and Progressive Legislation, 1903-1933." *Dialogue: A Journal of Mormon Thought* 7 (Spring 1972): 47-52.
———. "Senator Reed Smoot and Western Land Policy, 1905-1920." *Arizona and the West* 13 (Autumn 1971): 245-64.
———. "'To Maintain Harmony': Adjusting to External and Internal Stress, 1890-1930." *Dialogue: A Journal of Mormon Thought* 15 (Winter 1982): 44-58.
———. *Utah, the Right Place: The Official Centennial History*. Salt Lake City: Gibbs Smith, 1995.
Allen, James. "Emergence of a Fundamental: The Expanding Role of Joseph Smith's First Vision in Mormon Religious Thought." *Journal of Mormon History* 7 (1980): 43-61.
———. "The Significance of Joseph Smith's 'First Vision' in Mormon Thought." *Dialogue: A Journal of Mormon Thought* 1 (Autumn 1966): 29-45.
Allen, James B., Jesse L. Embry, and Kahlile B. Mehr. *Hearts Turned to the Fathers: A History of the Genealogical Society of Utah, 1894-1994*. Provo: BYU Studies, 1994.
Allen, James B., Ronald W. Walker, and David J. Whittaker, eds. *Studies in Mormon History, 1830-1997: An Indexed Bibliography*. Urbana: University of Illinois Press, 2000.
Anderson, Edwin H. "Lives of Our Leaders—the Apostles: Joseph F. Smith." *Juvenile Instructor*, 1 Feb. 1900, 65-71.
Anderson, Nels. "Pontifex Babbitt." *American Mercury* 9 (1926): 177-82.

Anderson, Richard Lloyd. "Circumstantial Confirmation of the First Vision through Reminiscences." *BYU Studies* 9 (Spring 1969): 373–404.

Arrington, Leonard J. "Crisis in Identity: Mormon Responses in the Nineteenth and Twentieth Centuries." In *Mormonism and American Culture*, edited by Marvin S. Hill and James B. Allen, 168–89. New York: Harper and Row, 1972.

———. *Great Basin Kingdom: An Economic History of the Latter-Day Saints, 1830–1900*. Cambridge: Harvard University Press, 1958.

———. "Mormonism: Views from Without and Within." *BYU Studies* 14 (Winter 1974): 140–53.

———. "Religion and Economics in Mormon History." *BYU Studies* 3 (Spring and Summer 1961): 15–33.

Arrington, Leonard J., and Davis Bitton. *The Mormon Experience: A History of the Latter-day Saints*. New York: Knopf, 1979.

Arrington, Leonard J., and Jon Haupt. "Intolerable Zion: The Image of Mormonism in Nineteenth Century American Literature." *Western Humanities Review* 22 (Summer 1968): 243–60.

Atkins, Gaius Glenn. *Religion in Our Times*. New York: Round Table Press, 1932.

Backman, Milton V., Jr. "First Vision." In *Encyclopedia of Mormonism*, edited by Daniel H. Ludlow, 2:515–16. New York: Macmillan, 1992.

Badger, Rodney J. *Liahona and Iron Rod: The Biography of Carl A. and Rose J. Badger*. Salt Lake City: Family History Publishers, 1985.

Bailey, A. S. "Anti-American Influences in Utah." In *Christian Progress in Utah: The Discussions of the Christian Convention*, 17–23. Salt Lake City: Frank H. Nelden, 1888.

Bailey, F. G. *The Prevalence of Deceit*. Ithaca: Cornell University Press, 1991.

Baird, Robert. *Religion in America*. New York: Harper and Bros., 1844.

Baker, Ray Stannard. "The Vitality of Mormonism." *Century Magazine*, June 1904, 176–77.

Baker, Ward N. "Mishawaka and Its Volunteers through the Shiloh Campaign." *Indiana Magazine of History* 58 (June 1962): 101–16.

Banker, Mark T. *Presbyterian Missions and Cultural Interaction in the Far Southwest, 1850–1950*. Urbana: University of Illinois Press, 1993.

Bashore, Melvin L. "Life behind Bars: Mormon Cohabs of the 1880's." *Utah Historical Quarterly* 47 (Winter 1979): 22–41.

Beggs, F. S. "The Mormon Problem in the West." *Methodist Review*, Sept. 1896, 754–57.

Bellah, Robert N. "Civil Religion in America." *Daedalus* 96 (Winter 1967): 1–21.

Bennion, John. "Mary Bennion Powell: Polygamy and Silence." *Journal of Mormon History* 24 (1998): 85–128.

Berns, Walter. *The First Amendment and the Future of American Democracy*. New York: Basic Books, 1976.

Biographical Record of Salt Lake City and Vicinity Containing Biographies of Well-Known Citizens of the Past and Present. Chicago: National Historical Record, 1902.

Bitton, Davis. *The Ritualization of Mormon History and Other Essays*. Urbana: University of Illinois Press, 1994.

Bodner, John. *Remaking America: Public Memory, Commemoration, and Patriotism in the Twentieth Century*. Princeton: Princeton University Press, 1992.

Bok, Sissela. *Lying: Moral Choice in Public and Private Life*. New York: Pantheon, 1978.

Brackenridge, R. Douglas. "Presbyterians and Latter-day Saints in Utah: A Century of Conflict and Compromise, 1830–1930." *Journal of Presbyterian History* 80 (Winter 2002): 205–24.

Bradley, Martha Sonntag. *Kidnapped from That Land: The Government Raids on the Short Creek Polygamists*. Salt Lake City: University of Utah Press, 1993.

Brogan, Dennis W. *The American Political System*. London: Hamish-Hamilton, 1933.

Brooks, Juanita. *The Mountain Meadows Massacre*. 2d ed. Norman: University of Oklahoma Press, 1962.

Buchanan, Frederick S. *Culture Clash and Accommodation: Public Schooling in Salt Lake City, 1890–1994*. Salt Lake City: Signature Books in association with Smith Research Associates, 1996.

Buenker, John D., and Nicholas C. Burckel. *Progressive Reform: A Guide to Information Sources*. Detroit: Gale, 1980.

Buerger, David John. *The Mysteries of Godliness: A History of Mormon Temple Worship*. San Francisco: Smith Research Associates, 1994.

Bunker, Gary L., and Davis Bitton. *The Mormon Graphic Image, 1834–1914: Cartoons, Caricatures, and Illustrations*. Salt Lake City: University of Utah Press, 1983.

Burrows, Julius C. "Another Constitutional Amendment Necessary." *Independent*, 9 May 1907, 1074–78.

Bushman, Richard. *Joseph Smith and the Beginnings of Mormonism*. Urbana: University of Illinois Press, 1988.

Cady, J. Cleveland. "The Letter Missive." In *Church Federation: Inter-Church Conference on Federation, New York, Nov. 15–21, 1905*, edited by Elias B. Sanford, 29–31. New York: Fleming H. Revell, 1906.

Cannon, Frank, and Harvey J. O'Higgins. *Under the Prophet in Utah: The National Menace of Political Priestcraft*. Boston: C. M. Clark, 1911.

Cannon, Kenneth L., II. "After the Manifesto: Mormon Polygamy, 1890–1906." *Sunstone* 8 (Jan.–Apr. 1983): 27–35.

Cannon, Charles A. "The Awesome Power of Sex: The Polemical Campaign against Mormon Polygamy." *Pacific Historical Quarterly* 43 (Feb. 1974): 61–82.

Cappon, Lester J., ed. *The Adams-Jefferson Letters: The Complete Correspondence between Thomas Jefferson and Abigail and John Adams*. 2 vols. Chapel Hill: University of North Carolina Press, 1988.

Cardon, A. F. "Senator Reed Smoot and the Mexican Revolution." *Utah Historical Quarterly* 31 (Spring 1963): 151–63.

Carnes, Mark C. *Secret Ritual and Manhood in Victorian America*. New Haven: Yale University Press, 1989.

Cavert, Samuel McCrea. *Church Cooperation and Unity in America: A Historical Review, 1900-1970*. New York: Association, 1970.

Chambers, John Whiteclay, II. *The Tyranny of Change: America in the Progressive Era, 1900-1917*. New York: St. Martin's, 1980.

Chesterton, Gilbert K., and William R. Inge. *Twelve Modern Apostles and Their Creeds*. New York: Duffield, 1926.

Clark, James R., ed. *Messages of the First Presidency of the Church of Jesus Christ of Latter-day Saints*. 6 vols. Salt Lake City: Bookcraft, 1965-75.

Clarke, Grace Julian. "Andrew Hoover Comes to Indiana." *Indiana Magazine of History* 24 (Dec. 1928): 242-94.

Coleman, Neil K. "A Study of the Church of Jesus Christ of Latter-Day Saints as an Administrative System: Its Structure and Maintenance." Ph.D. diss., New York University, 1967.

Compton, Todd. *In Sacred Loneliness: The Plural Wives of Joseph Smith*. Salt Lake City: Signature Books, 1997.

Connerton, Paul. *How Societies Remember*. Cambridge: Cambridge University Press, 1989.

Cook, Rufus G. "The Political Suicide of Senator Fred T. Dubois of Idaho." *Pacific Northwest Quarterly* 60 (Oct. 1969): 193-98.

Cott, Nancy F. *The Grounding of Modern Feminism*. New Haven: Yale University Press, 1987.

Cross, Whitney R. *The Burned-Over District: The Social and Intellectual History of Enthusiastic Religion in Western New York, 1800-1850*. Ithaca: Cornell University Press, 1950.

Cullom, Shelby M. "The Menace of Mormonism." *North American Review*, July 1905, 379 85.

Curry, Thomas J. *The First Freedoms: Church and State in America to the Passage of the First Amendment*. New York: Oxford University Press, 1986.

Davis, David Brion. "Some Ideological Functions of Prejudice in Ante-Bellum America." *American Quarterly* 15 (Summer 1963): 115-25.

———. "Some Themes of Counter-Subversion: An Analysis of Anti-Masonic, Anti-Catholic, and Anti-Mormon Literature." *Mississippi Valley Historical Review* 47 (Sept. 1960): 205-24.

Davis, Inez Smith. *The Story of the Church*. Independence, Mo.: Herald House, 1977.

Dawley, Alan. *Struggles for Justice: Social Responsibility and the Liberal State*. Cambridge: Belknap Press of Harvard University Press, 1991.

Daynes, Kathryn M. *More Wives Than One: Transformation of the Mormon Marriage System, 1840-1910*. Urbana: University of Illinois Press, 2001.

Deseret News 1997-1998 Church Almanac. Salt Lake City: Deseret News, 1996.

Deseret News 2001-2002 Church Almanac. Salt Lake City: Deseret News, 2000.

The Doctrine and Covenants of the Church of Jesus Christ of Latter-day Saints. Salt Lake City: Church of Jesus Christ of Latter-day Saints, 1981.

Dreisbach, Daniel L., ed. *Religion and Politics in the Early Republic*. Lexington: University Press of Kentucky, 1989.

Ehat, Andrew F. "'It Seems Like Heaven Began on Earth': Joseph Smith and the Constitution of the Kingdom of God." *BYU Studies* 20 (Spring 1980): 253–79.

Ehat, Andrew F., and Lyndon W. Cook, eds. *Words of Joseph Smith: The Contemporary Accounts of the Nauvoo Discourses of the Prophet Joseph.* Orem, Utah: Grandin Book, 1991.

Eliason, Eric A. "The Cultural Dynamics of Historical Self-Fashioning: Mormon Pioneer Nostalgia, American Culture, and the International Church." *Journal of Mormon History* 28 (2002): 139–73.

———. "Pioneers and Recapitulation in Mormon Popular Historical Expression." In *Usable Pasts: Traditions and Group Expressions in North America*, edited by Tad Tuleja, 175–211. Logan: Utah State University Press, 1997.

Embry, Jessie L. *Mormon Polygamous Families: Life in the Principle.* Salt Lake City: University of Utah Press, 1987.

Erekson, Keith A. "American Prophet, New England Town: The Memory of Joseph Smith in Vermont." Master's thesis, Brigham Young University, 2002.

Esplin, Ronald K. "The Significance of Nauvoo for Latter-Day Saints." *Journal of Mormon History* 16 (1990): 71–86.

Evans, Rosa Mae McClellan. "Judicial Prosecution for L.D.S. Plural Marriage: Prison Sentences, 1884–1895." Master's thesis, Brigham Young University, 1986.

Fales, Susan L., and Chad J. Flake, comps. *Mormons and Mormonism in U.S. Government Documents: A Bibliography.* Salt Lake City: University of Utah Press, 1989.

Firmage, Edwin Brown, and Richard Collin Mangrum. *Zion in the Courts: A Legal History of the Church of Jesus Christ of Latter-day Saints, 1830–1900.* Urbana: University of Illinois Press, 1988.

Flake, Kathleen. "'Not to Be Riten': The Nature and Effects of the Mormon Temple Rite as Oral Canon." *Journal of Ritual Studies* 9 (Summer 1995): 1–21.

Foster, Gaines M. *Moral Reconstruction: Christian Lobbyists and the Federal Legislation of Morality, 1865–1920.* Chapel Hill: University of North Carolina Press, 2002.

Fry, C. Luther. *The U.S. Looks at Its Churches.* New York: Institute of Social and Religious Research, 1930.

Furniss, Norman F. *The Mormon Conflict, 1850–1859.* New Haven: Yale University Press, 1960.

Geary, Edward A. "Mormondom's Lost Generation: The Novelists of the 1940s." *BYU Studies* 18 (Fall 1977): 89–97.

Gibbons, Francis M. *Joseph F. Smith: Patriarch and Preacher, Prophet of God.* Salt Lake City: Deseret Book, 1984.

Gibbs, J. F. *Lights and Shadows of Mormonism.* Salt Lake City: Salt Lake Tribune, 1909.

Givens, Terryl L. *By the Hand of Mormon: The American Scripture That Launched a New World Religion.* New York: Oxford University Press, 2002.

———. *The Viper on the Hearth: Mormons, Myths, and Construction of Heresy.* New York: Oxford University Press, 1997.

Goldman, Eric F. *Rendezvous with Destiny: A History of Modern American Reform.* 1952. Reprint, New York: Vintage, 1977.

Gordon, Sarah Barringer. "Blasphemy and the Law of Religious Liberty in Nineteenth-Century America." *American Quarterly* 52, no. 4 (Dec. 2000): 682-720.

———. *The Mormon Question: Polygamy and Constitutional Conflict in Nineteenth Century America.* Chapel Hill: University of North Carolina Press, 2002.

———. "'Our National Hearthstone': Anti-Polygamy Fiction and the Sentimental Campaign against Moral Diversity in Antebellum America." *Yale Journal of Law* 8 (Summer 1976): 295-350.

Graff, Leo W., Jr. *The Senatorial Career of Fred T. Dubois of Idaho, 1890-1907.* New York: Garland, 1988.

Graham, Stephen R. *Cosmos in the Chaos: Philip Schaff's Interpretation of Nineteenth Century American Religion.* Grand Rapids, Mich.: Eerdmans, 1995.

Halbwachs, M. *Les Cadres Sociaux de la Mémoire.* Paris: Presses Universitaires de France, 1925.

———. *La Mémoire Collective.* Paris: Presses Universitaires de France, 1950.

———. "La Mémoire Collective Chez les Musiciens." *Revue Philosophique* 127 (1939): 136-65.

———. *La Topographie Légendaire Des Evangiles en Terre Sainte.* Paris: Presses Universitaires de France, 1941.

Halstead, Murat. Foreword to *Polygamy, or, The Mysteries and Crimes of Mormonism,* by J. H. Beadle. Philadelphia: World Bible House, 1882, 1904.

Hampshire, Annette P. *Mormonism in Conflict: The Nauvoo Years.* Studies in Religion and Society, vol. 11. New York: Edwin Mellen, 1985.

Handy, Robert T. "The American Religious Depression, 1925-1935." *Church History* 29 (Mar. 1960): 3-16.

———. *A Christian America: Protestant Hopes and Historical Realities.* Rev. 2d ed. New York: Oxford University Press, 1984.

Hansen, Klaus J. "The Metamorphosis of the Kingdom of God: Toward a Reinterpretation of Mormon History." In *The New Mormon History: Revisionist Essays on the Past,* edited by D. Michael Quinn, 221-46. Salt Lake City: Signature Books, 1992.

———. *Mormonism and the American Experience.* Chicago: University of Chicago Press, 1981.

———. *Quest for Empire: The Political Kingdom of God and the Council of Fifty in Mormon History.* Lansing: Michigan State University Press, 1967.

Hardy, B. Carmon. *Solemn Covenant: The Mormon Polygamous Passage.* Urbana: University of Illinois Press, 1992.

Harmer-Dionne, Elizabeth. "Once a Peculiar People: Cognitive Dissonance and the Suppression of Mormon Polygamy as a Case Study Negating the Belief-Action Distinction." *50 Stanford L. Rev.* 4 (Apr. 1998): 1295-1347.

Harmon, William, ed. *The Oxford Book of American Light Verse.* Oxford: Oxford University Press, 1979.

Hatch, William Whitridge. *There Is No Law . . . : A History of Mormon Civil Relations in the Southern States, 1865–1905.* New York: Vantage Press, 1968.

Hays, Samuel P. *The Response to Industrialism: 1855–1914.* Chicago: University of Chicago Press, 1957.

Heath, Harvard S. "Reed Smoot: The First Modern Mormon." Ph.D. diss., Brigham Young University, 1990.

———, ed. *In the World: The Diaries of Reed Smoot.* Salt Lake City: Signature Books, 1997.

Heinerman, Joseph. "Reed Smoot's 'Secret Code.'" *Utah Historical Quarterly* 57 (Summer 1989): 254–63.

Hendrix, Rev. Bishop E. R. "The Ideal State." In *Church Federation: Inter-Church Conference on Federation, New York, Nov. 15–21, 1905,* edited by Elias B. Sanford, 587–96. New York: Fleming H. Revell, 1906.

Hill, Marvin S. *Quest for Refuge: The Mormon Flight from American Pluralism.* Salt Lake City: Signature Books, 1989.

Hill, Marvin S., and James B. Allen, eds. *Mormonism and American Culture.* New York: Harper and Row, 1972.

Hinckley, Gordon B. Interview with Larry King, 8 Sept. 1998. CNN Transcript 98090800V22.

Hobsbawm, E., and T. Ranger, eds. *The Invention of Tradition.* Cambridge: Cambridge University Press, 1983.

Hofstadter, Richard. *The Age of Reform: From Bryan to F.D.R.* New York: Random House, 1955.

Holsinger, M. Paul. "For God and the American Home: The Attempt to Unseat Senator Reed Smoot, 1903–1907." *Pacific Northwest Quarterly* 60 (July 1969): 154–60.

Holzapfel, Richard Neitzel, and Paul H. Peterson. "New Photographs of Joseph F. Smith's Centennial Memorial Trip to Vermont, 1905." *BYU Studies* 39, no. 4 (2000): 107–14.

Hooker, Richard J., ed. *The Carolina Backcountry on the Eve of the Revolution: The Journal and Other Writings of Charles Woodmason, Anglican Itinerant.* Chapel Hill: University of North Carolina Press, 1953.

Hopkins, Charles Howard. *The Rise of the Social Gospel in American Protestantism, 1865–1915.* New Haven: Yale University Press, 1940.

Howe, Mark DeWolfe. *The Garden and the Wilderness: Religion and Government in American Constitutional History.* Chicago: University of Chicago Press, 1965.

Hughes, Richard T. "Why Restorationists Don't Fit the Evangelical Mold; Why Churches of Christ Increasingly Do." In *Re-Forming the Center: American Protestants, 1900 to the Present,* edited by Douglas Jacobsen and William Vance Trollinger Jr., 194–213. Grand Rapids, Mich.: Eerdmans, 1998.

Hunter, Howard W. "The Great Symbol of Our Membership." *Ensign* 24 (Oct. 1994): 2–5.

Hutchison, William R. "Protestantism as Establishment." In *Between the Times: The Travail of the Protestant Establishment in America, 1900–1960,* edited by William R. Hutchison, 3–18. Cambridge: Cambridge University Press, 1989.

Iversen, Joan Smyth. *The Anti-Polygamy Controversy in U.S. Women's Movements, 1880–1925: A Debate on the American Home*. Hamden, Conn.: Garland, 1997.

James, Edward T., ed. *Dictionary of American Biography*. 22 vols. New York: Charles Scribner's Sons, 1941–45.

Jenson, Andrew. *Church Chronology: A Record of Important Events Pertaining to the History of the Church of Jesus Christ of Latter-day Saints*. Salt Lake City: Deseret News, 1914.

———. *Latter-day Saint Biographical Encyclopedia: A Compilation of Biographical Sketches of Prominent Men and Women in the Church of Jesus Christ of Latter-day Saints*. 4 vols. Salt Lake City: Andrew Jenson, 1901.

Jesse, Dean C. "The Early Accounts of Joseph Smith's First Vision." *BYU Studies* 9 (Spring 1969): 275–96.

———, ed. *The Papers of Joseph Smith*. 2 vols. Salt Lake City: Deseret Book, 1989–92.

Johnson, Donald Bruce, and Kirk H. Porter. *National Party Platforms, 1840–1972*. Urbana: University of Illinois Press, 1973.

Johnson, Thomas Cary. *Mormonism*. Richmond, Va.: Whittet and Shepperson, 1905.

Jorgenson, Victor, and B. Carmon Hardy. "The Taylor-Cowley Affair and the Watershed of Mormon History." *Utah Historical Quarterly* 48 (Winter 1980): 4–36.

Journal of Discourses. 26 vols. Liverpool: F. D. Richards, 1855–86.

Kammen, Michael. *Mystic Chords of Memory: The Transformation of Tradition in American Culture*. New York: Knopf, 1991.

Kane, Paula M. *Separatism and Subculture: Boston Catholicism, 1900–1920*. Chapel Hill: University of North Carolina Press, 1994.

Kenner, S. A. *Utah as It Is: With a Comprehensive Statement of Utah as It Was*. Salt Lake City: Deseret News, 1904.

Kenney, Scott. "Joseph F. Smith." In *The Presidents of the Church*, edited by Leonard J. Arrington, 179–210. Salt Lake City: Deseret Book, 1986.

Kimball, Stanley B. "The Utah Gospel Mission, 1900–1950." *Utah Historical Quarterly* 44 (Spring 1978): 149–55.

Knowlton, David. "Belief, Metaphor, and Rhetoric: The Practice of Testimony Bearing." *Sunstone* 15 (Apr. 1991): 20–27.

Larson, Gustive O. *The Americanization of Utah for Statehood*. San Marino, Calif.: Huntington Library, 1970.

Larson, Stan, ed. *A Ministry of Meetings: The Apostolic Diaries of Rudger Clawson*. Salt Lake City: Signature Books in association with Smith Research Associates, 1993.

Lears, Jackson. *No Place for Grace: Antimodernism and the Transformation of American Culture, 1880–1920*. Chicago: University of Chicago Press, 1981.

Leone, Mark P. *Roots of Modern Mormonism*. Cambridge: Harvard University Press, 1970.

Lewis, Alfred Henry. "The Great Mormon Conspiracy." *Collier's*, 26 Mar. 1904, 10–12.

————. "Introduction: The Mormon Purpose." In *The Mormon Menace, Being the Confession of John Doyle Lee, Danite, an Official Assassin of the Mormon Church under the Late Brigham Young*, edited by Alfred Henry Lewis, vii–xxii. New York: Home Protection, 1905.

————. "The Viper on the Hearth." *Cosmopolitan Magazine*, Mar. 1911, 439–50.

Linenthal, Edward T. *Sacred Ground: Americans and Their Battlefields*. Urbana: University of Illinois Press, 1991.

Linford, Orma. "The Mormons and the Law: The Polygamy Cases." *Utah Law Review* 9 (Winter 1964/Summer 1965): 308–70, 543–91.

Link, Arthur, and Richard L. McCormick. *Progressivism*. Arlington Heights, Ill.: Harlan Davidson, 1983.

Lowe, Jay R. "Fred T. Dubois, Foe of the Mormons: A Study of the Role of Fred T. Dubois in the Senate Investigation of the Hon. Reed Smoot and the Mormon Church, 1903–1907." Master's thesis, Brigham Young University, 1960.

Lowenthal, D. *The Past Is a Foreign Country*. Cambridge: Cambridge University Press, 1985.

Ludwig, Arnold M. *The Importance of Lying*. Springfield, Ill.: Charles C. Thomas, 1965.

Lum, Dyer Daniel. *Utah and Its People: Facts and Statistics Bearing on the "Mormon Problem" by a Gentile*. New York: R. O. Ferrier, 1882.

Lyford, Rev. C. P. *The Mormon Problem: An Appeal to the American People*. New York: Phillips and Hunt, 1886.

Lyman, Edward Leo. "Mormon Leaders in Politics: The Transition to Statehood in 1896." *Journal of Mormon History* 24 (1998): 30–54.

————. *Political Deliverance: The Mormon Quest for Utah Statehood*. Urbana: University of Illinois Press, 1986.

Lyon, T. Edgar. "Doctrinal Development of the Church during the Nauvoo Sojourn, 1839–1846." *BYU Studies* 15 (Summer 1975): 435–46.

Malmquist, O. N. *The First One Hundred Years: A History of the Salt Lake Tribune, 1871–1971*. Salt Lake City: Utah State Historical Society, 1971.

Mangum, Garth, and Bruce Blumell. *The Mormons' War on Poverty: A History of LDS Welfare, 1830–1990*. Salt Lake City: University of Utah Press, 1993.

Mansbridge, Jane J. *Why We Lost the ERA*. Chicago: University of Chicago Press, 1986.

Marty, Martin E. *The Irony of It All, 1893–1919*. Modern American Religion, vol. 1. Chicago: University of Chicago Press, 1986.

————. *A Nation of Behavors*. Chicago: University of Chicago Press, 1976.

————. *The One and the Many: America's Struggle for the Common Good*. Cambridge: Harvard University Press, 1997.

————. *Religion and Republic: The American Circumstance*. Boston: Beacon Press, 1987.

Matthews, Robert J. "The New Publications of the Standard Works, 1979, 1981." *BYU Studies* 22 (Fall 1982): 387–424.

Maxwell, Neal A. "Some Thoughts on the Gospel and Behavioral Sciences." *BYU Studies* 16 (Summer 1976): 589–602.

Mazur, Eric Michael. *The Americanization of Religious Minorities: Confronting the Constitutional Order.* Baltimore: Johns Hopkins University Press, 1999.

McConkey, James, ed. *The Anatomy of Memory: An Anthology.* New York: Oxford University Press, 1996.

McConnell, Michael W. "The Origins and Historical Understanding of Free Exercise of Religion." *Harvard Law Review* 103 (1990): 1410–1517.

McKay, David O. *Gospel Ideals: Selections from the Discourses of David O. McKay, Ninth President of the Church of Jesus Christ of Latter-day Saints.* Salt Lake City: Improvement Era, 1953.

McLoughlin, William G. "A Nation Born Again." In *In the Great Tradition: In Honor of Winthrop S. Hudson: Essays on Pluralism, Voluntarism and Revivalism,* edited by Joseph D. Ban and Paul R. Dekar. Valley Forge, Pa.: Judson Press, 1982.

Mead, Sidney E. *The Lively Experiment: The Shaping of Christianity in America.* New York: Harper and Row, 1963.

―――. *The Shape of Protestantism in America.* Chicago: University of Chicago Press, 1954.

Merrill, Melvin Clarence, ed. *Utah Pioneer and Apostle Marriner Wood Merrill and His Family.* N.p.: Marriner Family, 1937.

Merrill, Milton R. "Reed Owen Smoot." In *Dictionary of American Biography,* edited by Edward T. James, supplemental vol. 3:726–28. New York: Charles Scribner's Sons, 1958.

―――. "Reed Smoot: Apostle in Politics." Ph.D. diss., Columbia University, 1950.

―――. *Reed Smoot: Apostle in Politics.* Logan: Utah State University Press, 1990.

Mol, Hans. *Identity and the Sacred: A Sketch for a New Social-Scientific Theory of Religion.* New York: Free Press, 1976.

Moore, John L., Jon P. Preimesberger, and David R. Tarr, eds. *Congressional Quarterly's Guide to U.S. Elections.* 2 vols. Washington, D.C.: CQ Press, 2001.

Moore, R. Laurence. *Religious Outsiders and the Making of Americans.* New York: Oxford University Press, 1986.

Mouritsen, Dale C. "A Symbol of New Directions: George Franklin Richards and the Mormon Church, 1861–1950." Ph.D. diss., Brigham Young University, 1982.

Mowry, George E. *The Era of Theodore Roosevelt and the Birth of Modern America.* New York: Harper and Row, 1958.

New Mormon Studies CD-Rom: A Comprehensive Resource Library. Salt Lake City: Smith Research Associates, 1998.

Nibley, Charles W. "Reminiscences of President Joseph F. Smith." *Improvement Era,* Jan. 1919, 191–203.

Nibley, Preston. "The Friendship of Charles W. Nibley and President Joseph F. Smith." *Relief Society Magazine,* June 1932, 350–53.

―――. *Presidents of the Church.* Salt Lake City: Deseret Book, 1971.

Nixon, Loretta D., and L. Douglas Smoot. *Abraham Owen Smoot: A Testament of His Life.* Provo, Utah: A. O. Smoot Family Organization, 1994.

Noll, Mark A. *A History of Christianity*. Grand Rapids, Mich.: Eerdmans, 1992.

Nora, Pierre. "Between Memory and History: Les Lieux de Mémoire." *Representations* 26 (Spring 1989): 7–25.

———. *Les Lieux de la Mémoire*. Paris, 1984.

Official Report of the Semi-Annual Conference of The Church of Jesus Christ of Latter-day Saints. Salt Lake City: Deseret News, 1897–1964; Church of Jesus Christ of Latter-day Saints, 1965–present.

Olsen, Steven L. "Celebrating Cultural Identity: Pioneer Day in Nineteenth-Century Mormonism." *BYU Studies* 36, no. 1 (1996–97): 159–77.

———. "Community Celebrations and Mormon Ideology of Place." *Sunstone* 5 (May/June 1980): 40–45.

———. "Joseph Smith and the Structure of Mormon Identity." *Dialogue: A Journal of Mormon Thought* 14 (Autumn 1981): 89–98.

Orcutt, Dana. *Burrows of Michigan and the Republican Party*. New York: Longmans, Green, 1917.

Painter, Nell. *Standing at Armageddon: The United States, 1877–1919*. New York: Norton, 1987.

Parker, Steven. "Deseret." In *Encyclopedia of Mormonism*, edited by Daniel H. Ludlow, 1:370–71. New York: Macmillan, 1992.

Parrish, Alan K. *John A. Widtsoe: A Biography*. Salt Lake City: Deseret Book, 2003.

Paulsen, David L. "The Doctrine of Divine Embodiment: Restoration, Judeo-Christian, and Philosophical Perspectives." *BYU Studies* 35, no. 4 (1995–96): 7–94.

Persons, William R. "An Analysis of Changes in the Interpretation and Utilization of Revelation in the Church of Jesus Christ of Latter Day Saints, 1830–1918." Ph.D. diss., Iliff School of Theology, Denver, Colo., 1964.

Phelps, William W. "Praise to the Man." In *Hymns of The Church of Jesus Christ of Latter-Day Saints*, no. 27. Salt Lake City: Deseret Book, 1989.

"A Priceless Golden Wedding." *Relief Society Magazine*, July 1916, 369–73.

Proceedings at the Dedication of the Joseph Smith Memorial Monument. Salt Lake City: privately published, 1906.

Quinn, D. Michael. "L.D.S. Church Authority and New Plural Marriages, 1890–1904." *Dialogue: A Journal of Mormon Thought* 18 (Spring 1995): 9–104.

———. *The Mormon Hierarchy: Extensions of Power*. Salt Lake City: Signature Books, 1997.

———. "Plural Marriage and Mormon Fundamentalism." *Dialogue: A Journal of Mormon Thought* 31 (Summer 1998): 1–68.

Reeve, Rex C., Jr., and Richard O. Cowan. "The Hill Called Cumorah." In *Regional Studies in Latter-day Saint Church History: New York*, edited by Larry C. Porter, Milton V. Backman Jr., and Susan Easton Black, 71–89. Provo, Utah: Department of Church History and Doctrine, Brigham Young University, 1992.

Rice, Claton. *Ambassador to the Saints*. Boston: Christopher Publishing House, 1965.

Richey, Russell E. "Denominations and Denominationalism: An American Morphology." In *Reimagining Denominationalism: Interpretive Essays*, edited by Robert Bruce Mullin and Russell E. Richey, 74–98. New York: Oxford University Press, 1994.

Ricocur, Paul. *From Text to Action: Essays in Hermeneutics*. Vol. 2, trans. Kathleen Blarney and John B. Thompson. Evanston, Ill.: Northwestern University Press, 1991.

———. "A Response by Paul Ricoeur." In *Hermeneutics and the Human Sciences*, edited by John B. Thompson, 32 40. Cambridge: Cambridge University Press, 1981.

———. *The Symbolism of Evil*. Boston: Beacon Press, 1967.

Roberts, Brigham H. *Comprehensive History of the Church of Jesus Christ of Latter-Day Saints*. 6 vols. Provo, Utah: Brigham Young University Press, 1965.

———. *Defense of the Faith and the Saints*. Salt Lake City: Deseret News, 1907.

Rotundo, E. Anthony. *American Manhood: Transformations in Masculinity from the Revolution to the Modern Era*. New York: Basic Books, 1993.

Russell, Issac. "Mr. Roosevelt to the Mormons." *Collier's Weekly*, 15 Apr. 1911, 28.

Sandel, Michael J. *Democracy's Discontent: America in Search of a Public Philosophy*. Cambridge: Belknap Press of Harvard University Press, 1996.

Sanford, Elias B. *Origin and History of the Federal Council of the Churches of Christ in America*. Hartford, Conn.: S. S. Scranton, 1916.

———, ed. *Church Federation: Inter-Church Conference on Federation, New York, Nov. 15-21, 1905*. New York: Fleming H. Revell, 1906.

Seager, Richard Hughes. *The World's Parliament of Religions: The East West Encounter, Chicago, 1893*. Bloomington: Indiana University Press, 1995.

Sears, L. Rex. "Punishing the Saints for Their 'Peculiar Institution': Congress on the Constitutional Dilemmas." *Utah Law Review* 2001, no. 3 (2001): 581–658.

Selected Collections from the Archives of the Church of Jesus Christ of Latter-day Saints. 2 vols. Provo, Utah: Brigham Young University Press, 2002.

Shepherd, Gordon, and Gary Shepherd. *A Kingdom Transformed: Themes in the Development of Mormonism*. Salt Lake City: University of Utah Press, 1984.

Shields, Steven L. *Divergent Paths to the Restoration: A History of the Latter Day Saint Movement*. Bountiful, Utah: Restoration Research, 1975.

Shipps, Jan. "Another Side of Early Mormonism." In *The Journals of William E. McLellin, 1831-1836*, edited by Jan Shipps and John W. Welch, 3–12. Urbana: University of Illinois Press; Provo, Utah: BYU Studies, 1994.

———. *Mormonism: The Story of a New Religious Tradition*. Urbana: University of Illinois Press, 1985.

———. "The Principle Revoked: A Closer Look at the Demise of Plural Marriage." *Journal of Mormon History* 11 (1984): 65–77.

———. "The Public Image of Sen. Reed Smoot, 1902-1932." *Utah Historical Quarterly* 45 (Fall 1977): 380–400.

———. *Sojourner in the Promised Land: Forty Years among the Mormons*. Urbana: University of Illinois Press, 2000.

Short, Dennis R. *Questions on Plural Marriage with a Selected Bibliography and 1600 References*. Salt Lake City: privately published, 1975.

Smith, Joseph, Jr. *History of the Church of Jesus Christ of Latter-day Saints.* 7 vols. 2d ed., rev. Salt Lake City: Deseret Book, 1974.

———. "Joseph Smith—History: Extracts from the History of Joseph Smith, the Prophet." In *The Pearl of Great Price*. Salt Lake City: Church of Jesus Christ of Latter-day Saints, 1981.

———. *Teachings of the Prophet Joseph Smith*. Compiled by Joseph Fielding Smith Jr. Salt Lake City: Deseret Book, 1938.

Smith, Joseph F. "Celebration of the Twenty-Fourth of July by the Sunday Schools." *Juvenile Instructor*, 15 Mar. 1905, 176.

———. "Congress and the Mormons." *Improvement Era*, Apr. 1903, 469–73.

———. "The Father and the Son." *Improvement Era*, Aug. 1916, 934–42.

———. "The Fruit Good, the Tree Bad." *Juvenile Instructor*, 1 Mar. 1906, 144–46.

———. *Two Sermons by President Joseph F. Smith*. Sermon tract. Chattanooga, Tenn.: Southern States Mission, 1906.

Smith, Joseph Fielding, Jr. *Essentials in Church History: A History of the Church from the Birth of Joseph Smith to the Present Time, with Introductory Chapters on the Antiquity of the Gospel and the "Falling Away."* Salt Lake City: Deseret Book, 1950.

———. *Life of Joseph F. Smith, Sixth President of the Church of Jesus Christ of Latter-day Saints*. 1938. Reprint, Salt Lake City: Deseret Book, 1999.

Smith, Lucy Mack. *Biographical Sketches of Joseph Smith, the Prophet, and His Progenitors for Many Generations*. Liverpool: S. W. Richards, 1853.

———. *The History of Joseph Smith by His Mother*. Edited by Preston Nibley. Salt Lake City: Bookcraft, 1958.

Smith, Maud E. "Reed Smoot: Senator from Utah." Master's thesis, Columbia University, 1933.

Smith, Rodney K. "Getting Off on the Wrong Foot and Back on Again: A Reexamination of the History of the Framing of the Religion Clauses of the First Amendment and a Critique of the Reynolds and Everson Decisions." *Wake Forest Law Review* 20 (1984): 569–643.

Stark, Rodney. "So Far, So Good: A Brief Assessment of Mormon Membership Projections." *Review of Religious Research* 38 (Dec. 1996): 175–78.

Strong, Josiah. *The New Era, or The Coming Kingdom*. New York: Baker and Taylor, 1893.

———. *Our Country: Its Possible Future and Its Present Crisis*. Rev. ed. New York: Baker and Taylor, 1891.

Szasz, Ferenc. *The Divided Mind of Protestant America, 1880–1930*. University: University of Alabama Press, 1982.

Tanner, Annie Clark. *A Mormon Mother: An Autobiography by Annie Clark Tanner*. Salt Lake City: Tanner Trust Fund, University of Utah Library, 1983.

Tarbell, Ida M. *The History of the Standard Oil Company*. New York: McClure, Phillips, 1902, 1904.

Taylor, Charles F. "Mormon Marriage and Its Canonical Consequences."
  Institutum Utriusque Juris. Theses ad Laureeam N. 138. Rome: Pontificia
  Universitas Lateranensis, 1959.

Taylor, Samuel Woolley. *Family Kingdom.* Salt Lake City: Western Epics, 1974.

Testi, Arnaldo. "The Gender of Reform Politics: Theodore Roosevelt and the
  Culture of Masculinity." *Journal of American History* 81 (Mar. 1995): 1509-33.

Thelan, David. "Memory and American History." *Journal of American History* 75
  (Mar. 1989): 1117-29.

Thomas, John C. "Apostolic Diplomacy: The 1923 European Mission of Senator
  Reed Smoot and Professor John A. Widtsoe." *Journal of Mormon History* 28
  (2002): 130-65.

Thorp, Malcolm R. "'The Mormon Peril': The Crusade against the Saints in
  Britain, 1911-1914." *Journal of Mormon History* 2 (1975): 69-88.

"The Trial of Apostle John W. Taylor." *New Mormon Studies CD-ROM:
  A Comprehensive Resource Library.* Salt Lake City: Smith Research Associates,
  1998.

Turner, Frederick Jackson. "The Significance of the Frontier in American History."
  In *Rereading Frederick Jackson Turner,* edited by John Mack Garagher, 31-60.
  New York: Henry Holt, 1994.

Twain, Mark. *Roughing It.* Hartford, Conn., 1872. New York: Oxford University
  Press, American Publishing Co., 1996.

Underwood, Grant. *The Millenarian World of Early Mormonism.* Urbana: University
  of Illinois Press, 1993.

Van Orden, Bruce A. *Building Zion: The Latter-day Saints in Europe.* Salt Lake
  City: Deseret Book, 1996.

Van Wagenen, Lola. "In Their Own Behalf: The Politicization of Mormon Women
  and the 1870 Franchise." In *Battle for the Ballot: Essays on Woman Suffrage in
  Utah, 1870-1896,* edited by Carol Cornwall Madsen, 60-74. Logan: Utah State
  University Press, 1997.

Van Wagoner, Richard S. *Mormon Polygamy: A History.* Salt Lake City: Signature
  Books, 1986.

Vernon, George Robinson. "The Public Career of Reed Smoot, 1903-1933."
  Master's thesis, University of California, 1937.

Vogel, Dan. "The Earliest Mormon Concept of God." In *Line upon Line: Essays on
  Mormon Doctrine,* edited by Gary James Bergera, 17-33. Salt Lake City:
  Signature Books, 1989.

———. *Religious Seekers and the Advent of Mormonism.* Salt Lake City: Signature
  Books, 1988.

White, Jean Bickmore, ed. *Church, State, and Politics: The Diaries of John Henry
  Smith.* Salt Lake City: Signature Books in association with Smith Research
  Associates, 1990.

Whittaker, David J. *Mormon Americana: A Guide to Sources and Collections in the
  United States.* Provo, Utah: BYU Studies, 1995.

Widtsoe, John A. *Evidences and Reconciliations.* Reprint (3 vols. in 1), edited by
  G. Homer Durham. Salt Lake City: Bookcraft, 1960.

Wiebe, Robert H. *The Search for Order, 1877-1920*. New York: Hill and Wang, 1967.

Williams, Rev. Meade C. "The Multitude of Denominations." *Princeton Theological Review* 3 (Jan. 1905): 23-31.

Wilson, John, ed. *Church and State in American History*. Boston: D. C. Heath, 1965.

Wood, Gordon S. "Evangelical America and Early Mormonism." *New York History* 61 (Oct. 1980): 359-86.

Woodford, Robert J. "The Historical Development of the Doctrine and Covenants." Ph.D. diss., Brigham Young University, Provo, Utah, 1974.

Young, Brigham. *Discourses of Brigham Young*. 3d ed., compiled by John A. Widtsoe. Salt Lake City: Deseret Book, 1941.

INDEX

Numbers in italics refer to illustrations.

Critchlow, Edward B., 13, 74, 76
Cullom, Shelby, 5

Democratic Party, 24
Denominationalism, 20; in America,
    21–22; and Mormonism, 8, 22
Depew, Chauncey M., 48; against con-
    centrated Mormon power, 50; after
    Smoot hearing, 161; and vote in
    committee, 145
Dillingham, William P., 48; and mo-
    nopolies, 149; after Smoot hearing,
    161; in support of Smoot, 155
Dolliver, Jonathan P., 48, 205 (n. 23);
    on church as monopoly, 151; after
    Smoot hearing, 161; and vote in
    committee, 145, 206 (n. 33)
Dubois, Fred T., 20, 48, 91; against
    Smoot, 146; description of, 49–50,
    143; election campaign of, 81, 206
    (n. 33); on L.D.S. Church, 22, 28;
    on polygamy, 66

Edmunds Act (1882), 28, 64, 79, 191
    (n. 28)
Edmunds-Tucker Act (1887), 28, 61,
    191 (n. 28)
Ellis, Margaret Dye, 60

First Vision, the, *119*; canonized, 121;
    doctrines in, 117–18, 121–22; and
    L.D.S. identity, 120–22; as mas-
    ter narrative, 122; original lack of
    interest in, 118, 202 (n. 29); and
    persecution, 120; replaces plural
    marriage, 118, 120–21
Foraker, Joseph B., 48, 75; after Smoot
    hearing, 161; in support of Smoot,
    153
Frazier, James B., 161

Gender politics, 162–64
General Assembly of the Presbyterian
    Church, 13

Gibbs, George, 107
Gibson, Charles Dana, 69
Gordon, Sarah Barringer, 151
Grant, Heber J., *52*; comments on
    wives, 53, 75; and court subpoena,
    53, 200 (n. 5); not chosen to be
    disciplined, 92; on Smoot, 176–77;
    support of Taylor and Cowley, 94,
    139

Halbwachs, Maurice, 114
Hale, Eugene, 48
Hamlin, Teunis S., 60
Hanna, Marcus, 35, 46, 48
Hansbrough, Henry C., 161–62
Harding, Warren G., 169, *170*
Hill Cumorah, 128
Hinckley, Gordon B., 165
Hoar, George Frisbie, 48, 49, 75; on
    monopolies, 148, 149; on religious
    inquiry, 77
Hopkins, Albert J., 48; on Consti-
    tutional concerns, 146–47; after
    Smoot hearing, 161; in support of
    Smoot, 153, 155
Howell, Joseph, 48, 99, 100

Independence, Mo., 130, 135
Ivins, Anthony, 141

Johnson, Rev. Thomas Cary, 45
Joseph F. Smith monument, *113*, *116*,
    166; conception of, 110; construc-
    tion of, 111; dedication of, 135;
    message of, 112, 114; symbolism of,
    117
"The Joseph Smith Story," 133; church
    principles in, 122; and continuity,
    125; divine communication in, 124;
    and L.D.S. identity, 127–28; and
    model of ideal seeker, 124; as Mor-
    mon origin myth, 126; narrative
    uses of, 122–23; necessity of reve-
    lation in, 125; and ordinances, 125;

and permanent authority, 125, 126–27; persecution in, 123; replaces polygamy, 166; triumph over opposition in, 125

ish Mormonism, 15; and distrust
of L.D.S. Church, 86; and efforts
to strengthen nation, 83–84; lose
ground in Smoot hearing, 81; and
nature of church authority, 76–80;
and petitions against Smoot, 13–
15; political cartoon of, 6; present
L.D.S. Church as monopoly, 149;
as primary opponents to Smoot,
2; and reaction to Smoot hearing,
160–61; strategy of, 51, 55, 140–43;
in Utah, 25–26, 50

Made in the USA
Middletown, DE
24 February 2024

50161114R00151